Sarah Woo

Webber Fun Sheets 2

Set Two - SH, CH, TH, K, G, F & V!

Cards created by Sharon G. Webber M.S., CCC-SLP

Written by Ashley Drennan, Karla Duncan, Clint Johnson, and Amy Jundi

Edited by Thomas Webber

Copyright ©2001, SUPER DUPER® PUBLICATIONS, a division of Super Duper®, Inc. All rights reserved. Permission is granted for the user to reproduce the material contained herein in limited form for classroom use only. Reproduction of this material for an entire school or school system is strictly prohibited. No part of this material may be reproduced (except as noted above), stored in a retrieval system, or transmitted in any form or by any means (mechanically, electronically, recording, web, etc.) without the prior written consent and approval of Super Duper® Publications.

www.superduperinc.com
1-800-277-8737

ISBN 978-1-58650-212-6

teeth
"TH" final

fox
"F" initial

igloo
"G" medial

starfish
"SH" final

valentine
"V" initial

beach ball
"CH" medial

kangaroo
"K" initial

#BK-291 Webber® Artic Fun Sheets 2 • ©2002 Super Duper® Publications • www.superduperinc.com • 1-800-277-8737

Introduction

Webber® Artic Fun Sheets Set 2 – SH, TH, CH, K, G, F & V—will help reinforce your students' production of target speech sounds at the word, phrase, and sentence levels. This book goes hand in hand with the *Webber® Articulation Cards Set 2* published by Super Duper® Publications.

Each of the *Webber® Artic Decks* comes with 32 matching pairs of cards, with target sounds in the initial, medial, and final positions of words. *Webber® Artic Fun Sheets* uses the same words and pictures found in the *Set 2 Cards* and displays them in a worksheet format. You can use the activity sheets in therapy or for homework.

The activity pages work best with students ages three and up. As they complete each fun activity, your students will learn to accurately produce their target sounds at the word, phrase, or sentence level. Each page also builds vocabulary skills and encourages following directions.

These pages provide a variety of amusing activities, including word searches, crossword puzzles, mazes, sentence scrambles, football games, memory games, cube rolls, matching questions to pictures, and more! You also receive a parent letter, two different tracking forms, award certificates, and an answer key. Have fun!

Table of Contents

SH Activites 1-38
Initial SH Words 2-7
Initial SH Phrases 8-10
Initial SH Sentences 11-13
Final SH Words 14-20
Final SH Phrases 21-23
Final SH Sentences 24-26
Medial SH Words 27-32
Medial SH Phrases 33-35
Medial SH Sentences 36-38

CH Activites 39-76
Initial CH Words 40-45
Initial CH Phrases 46-48
Initial CH Sentences 49-51
Final CH Words 52-57
Final CH Phrases 58-60
Final CH Sentences 61-63
Medial CH Words 64-69
Medial CH Phrases 70-72
Medial CH Sentences 73-76

TH Activities 77-114
Initial TH Words 78-83
Initial TH Phrases 84-86
Initial TH Sentences 87-89
Final TH Words 90-95
Final TH Phrases 96-98
Final TH Sentences 99-101
Medial TH Words 102-108
Medial TH Phrases 109-111
Medial TH Sentences 112-114

K Activities 115-152
Initial K Words 116-121
Initial K Phrases 122-124
Initial K Sentences 125-127
Final K Words 128-133
Final K Phrases 134-136
Final K Sentences 137-139
Medial K Words 140-145
Medial K Phrases 146-148
Medial K Sentences 149-152

Table of Contents

G Activities **153-190**
    Initial G Words 154-159
    Initial G Phrases 160-163
    Initial G Sentences 164-165
    Final G Words 166-171
    Final G Phrases 172-174
    Final G Sentences 175-177
    Medial G Words 178-183
    Medial G Phrases 184-186
    Medial G Sentences 187-190

F Activities **191-228**
    Initial F Words 192-197
    Initial F Phrases 198-200
    Initial F Sentences 201-203
    Final F Words 204-209
    Final F Phrases 210-212
    Final F Sentences 213-215
    Medial F Words 216-221
    Medial F Phrases 222-224
    Medial F Sentences 225-228

V Activities **229-268**
    Initial V Words 230-235
    Initial V Phrases 236-238
    Initial V Sentences 239-241
    Final V Words 242-248
    Final V Phrases 249-251
    Final V Sentences 252-254
    Medial V Words 255-261
    Medial V Phrases 262-264
    Medial V Sentences 265-268

Awards **269-276**

Open–Ended Games **277-278**

Answers **279-280**

Parent/Helper Letter

Date: _____

Dear Parent/Helper:

    Your child is currently working on _____ in Speech and Language Class.

    The attached worksheet(s) will help your child practice and reinforce skills reviewed in the classroom.

☐ Please complete these exercises with your child and return them signed _____.

☐ Please complete these exercises with your child. You do not need to return them to me.

☐ _____
_____
_____

Thank you for your support.

_____   _____
               Name   Parent/Helper's Signature

Tracking Sheet

_____ _____ _____
Name   SLP   Date

Date _____

_____Sound
Initial/Medial/Final/Blends

_____
Word/Phrase/Sentence Level

Correct Responses/Total Percentage

☐☐☐☐☐☐☐☐☐☐ = ___%

Date _____

_____Sound
Initial/Medial/Final/Blends

_____
Word/Phrase/Sentence Level

Correct Responses/Total Percentage

☐☐☐☐☐☐☐☐☐☐ = ___%

Date _____

_____Sound
Initial/Medial/Final/Blends

_____
Word/Phrase/Sentence Level

Correct Responses/Total Percentage

☐☐☐☐☐☐☐☐☐☐ = ___%

Date _____

_____Sound
Initial/Medial/Final/Blends

_____
Word/Phrase/Sentence Level

Correct Responses/Total Percentage

☐☐☐☐☐☐☐☐☐☐ = ___%

Progress Chart

Student Name _____

Date	Sound	I/M/F	W/P/S	✔ or -	%

SH Sound

Paper Chain

Directions: Read/say aloud each picture–word below. Cut out the word strips. Turn them face down. Pick up a strip, read/say the word aloud, and then, staple/glue it to make a chain link. Remember to use your good SH sound as you make your chain.

- shark
- shaggy dog
- shampoo
- sheep
- shovel
- shoe
- shoulders
- shirt
- shaving

Homework Partner Date Speech-Language Pathologist

Initial SH Words

3 Games in 1

Directions: Say aloud the picture–words below, using your good SH sound. Then, play one of the following games:

☐ Lotto – Caller reads out a word and student repeats the word and covers it with a token/chip.

☐ Tic–Tac–Toe – Each time you write an **X** or **O**, say the word you mark over.

☐ Memory – Cut out all the cards and place face down. Try to find matching pairs. Say aloud each word you find. Keep all matches.

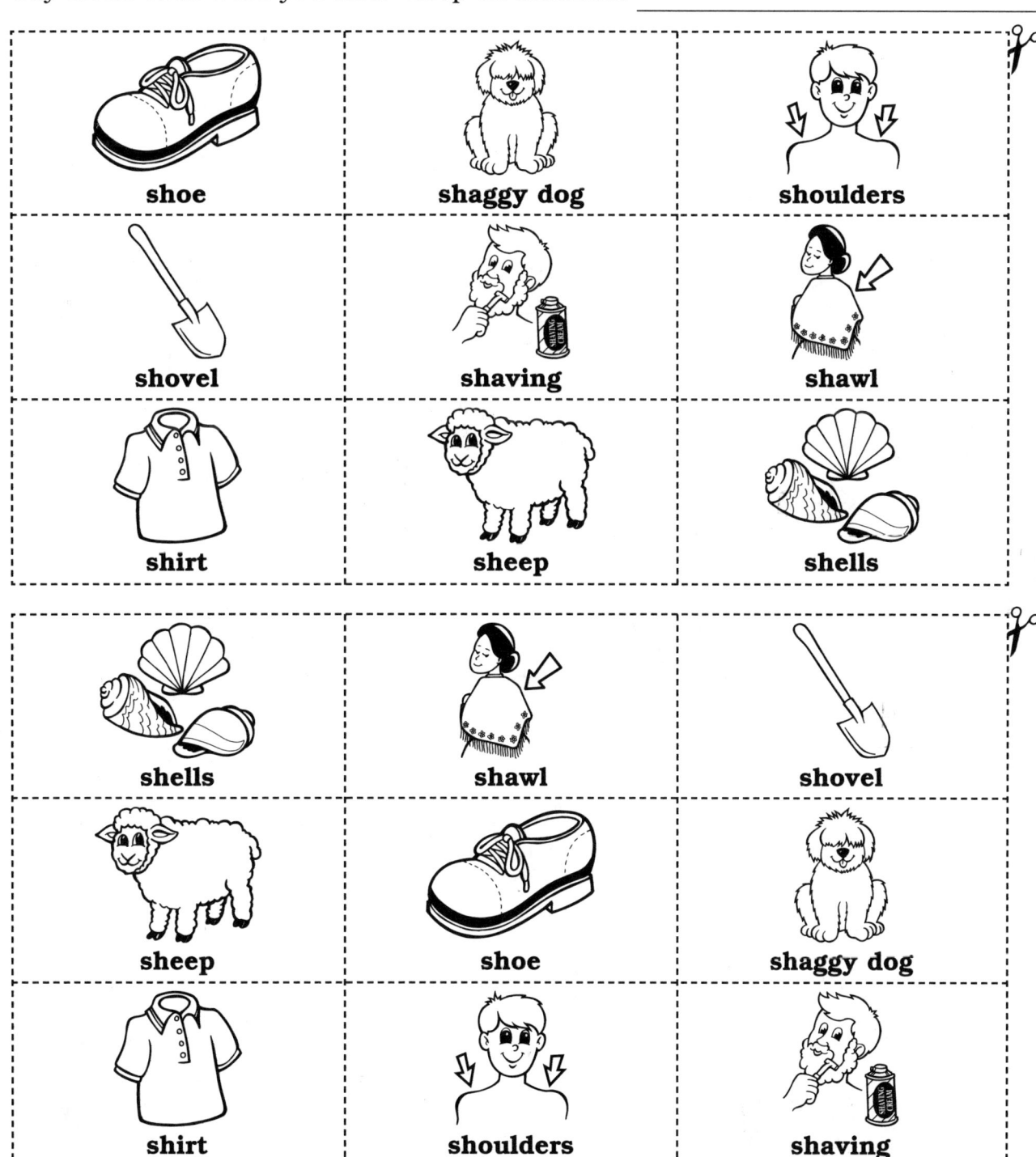

shoe	shaggy dog	shoulders
shovel	shaving	shawl
shirt	sheep	shells
shells	shawl	shovel
sheep	shoe	shaggy dog
shirt	shoulders	shaving

_____ _____ _____
Homework Partner   Date   Speech-Language Pathologist

Initial SH Words

#BK-291 Webber® Artic Fun Sheets 2 • ©2002 Super Duper® Publications • www.superduperinc.com • 1-800-277-8737

3

Counting Sheep

Directions: Count the number of sheep that have the target pictures below. Write the number on the line provided. Say the target word that many times. Remember to use your best SH sound.

1. **shoulders** _____
2. **shirt** _____
3. **shells** _____
4. **shovel** _____
5. **shawl** _____
6. **shampoo** _____

Answer Key: 1.2, 2.1, 3.3, 4.2, 5.2, 6.1

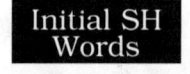

Homework Partner   Date   Speech-Language Pathologist

Initial SH Words

Old Shirt

Directions: Copy this page twice and cut out the cards below. Deal all cards evenly to each student. To play, first student takes one card from another student, keeps it, and says it aloud. If the card matches a card in first player's hand, first player makes a match. Play continues in turn. Most matches wins! Use your good SH sound.

shoe	shaggy dog	shoulders
sheriff	shovel	shaving
shark	shampoo	sheep
shirt	shells	shawl

Homework Partner   Date   Speech-Language Pathologist

Initial SH Words

Give Me Another Name

Directions: Read/say the words in the Word Bank aloud. Find the correct answers in the Word Bank and write the answer in the blanks. Then, read/say the word aloud. Use your best SH sound.

Word Bank

shark   sheriff   sheep   shampoo

shaggy dog   shovel   shoe   shoulders

1. long-haired animal _____

2. a sea animal _____

3. hair soap _____

4. police officer _____

5. lamb _____

6. body part _____

7. yard tool _____

8. footwear _____

_____ _____ _____
Homework Partner   Date   Speech-Language Pathologist

Initial SH Words

Hide-and-Seek

Directions: Read/say aloud the picture–words. If you prefer, glue the pictures on a file folder/cardboard. Cut out the pictures and badge. Place the pictures face up. Have your partner hide the badge under a picture. Name the picture where you think the badge is hidden. (Shampoo?) First player to find the badge wins! Use your good SH sound.

shoe	shaggy dog	shawl
shells	shaving	shark
shirt	shampoo	sheriff

SHERIFF

Homework Partner | Date | Speech-Language Pathologist

Initial SH Words

SH Phrase It

Directions: Assemble the cube as follows: Glue onto construction paper for added durability. Cut along the dotted lines. Fold on solid lines and glue as indicated. To play: Roll both cubes. Read/say the words and pictures together aloud to make up a phrase (blue shoe). Use your good SH sound.

Cube 1 (pictures): shoe, shark, shoulders, shirt, sheriff, shovel

Cube 2 (words): wide, happy, clean, large, heavy, blue

Initial SH Phrases

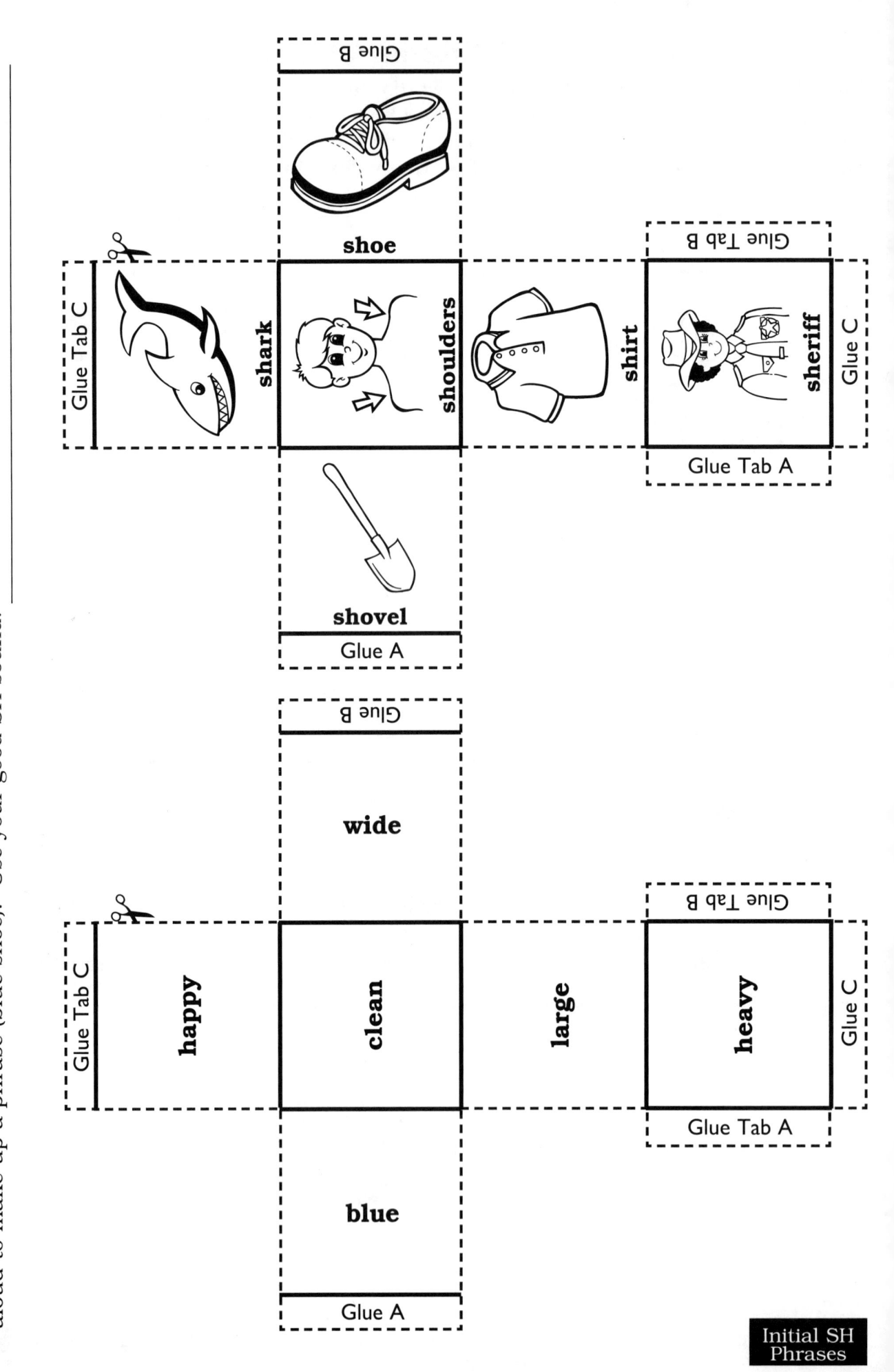

It Goes Together

Directions: Read/say aloud the picture–words on the right. Then, draw a line from the word on the left to a picture–word that goes with it. Then, read/say each phrase aloud (beach and shells). Remember to use your good SH sound!

1. knees   A.   **sheriff**

2. sock   B.   **shirt**

3. outlaw   C.   **shoulders**

4. pants   D.   **shoe**

5. hoe   E.   **shovel**

6. whale   F.   **shark**

Answers: 1.C 2.D 3.A 4.B 5.E 6.F

Homework Partner   Date   Speech-Language Pathologist

Initial SH Phrases

X and O

Directions: Cut out each **X** and **O** below. Have each player/partner choose **X** or **O**. The first player reads/says a picture–phrase aloud and places an **X** or **O** on the square. Play continues in turn. The first person to get three in a row wins.

big shirt	heavy shovel	round shoulders
mean shark	one shoe	good sheriff
pretty shells	shaving cream	my shampoo

X X X X X

O O O O O

Homework Partner   Date   Speech-Language Pathologist

Initial SH Phrases

Category Sort

Directions: Read/say aloud the picture–words below. Then, answer the questions in the form of a sentence using words from the Word Bank. (What can you wear? I can wear a shirt.) Write the answers in the blank spaces. Some questions may have more than one answer. Read/say your answer sentences aloud, using your good SH sound.

Word Bank

shoe	shaggy dog	shark
shells	shaving	shirt
sheep	shampoo	shawl

1. What can you wear? _____

2. What has four legs? _____

3. What do you find in the sea? _____

4. What do you do in the morning? _____

5. What has teeth? _____

6. What has fur? _____

Homework Partner   Date   Speech-Language Pathologist

Initial SH Sentences

Order Up!

Directions: Pretend you are ordering at a restaurant. Look at the menu and read/say a complete sentence for each item you order. (I'll have the shark dinner, please.) Use your best SH sound.

Appetizers

- shoe salad
- shawl soup
- shaving chicken wings

Entrees

- shaggy dog sandwich
- shark dinner
- sheep burger
- shells & cheese

Desserts

- shoulders pie
- sheriff cake
- shampoo cookies
- shovel sundae
- shirt dessert

Homework Partner — Date — Speech-Language Pathologist

Initial SH Sentences

Get a Clue

Directions: Read each clue sentence aloud. Then, guess the answer from the Word Bank below. Say your answers in complete sentences. (It has a handle and you dig with it. It's a shovel.) Use your good SH sound.

1. It has a sole, laces, and you wear it on your foot.

2. It has a handle and you dig with it.

3. It is an animal that lives in the water and has sharp teeth.

4. It is a person who protects the community and wears a badge.

5. It is a piece of clothing with a collar, buttons, and sleeves.

6. It is an animal with a lot of fur that barks and wags its tail.

7. It is a bath item that helps you clean your hair.

8. It is an item that people find on the beach in the sand and collect.

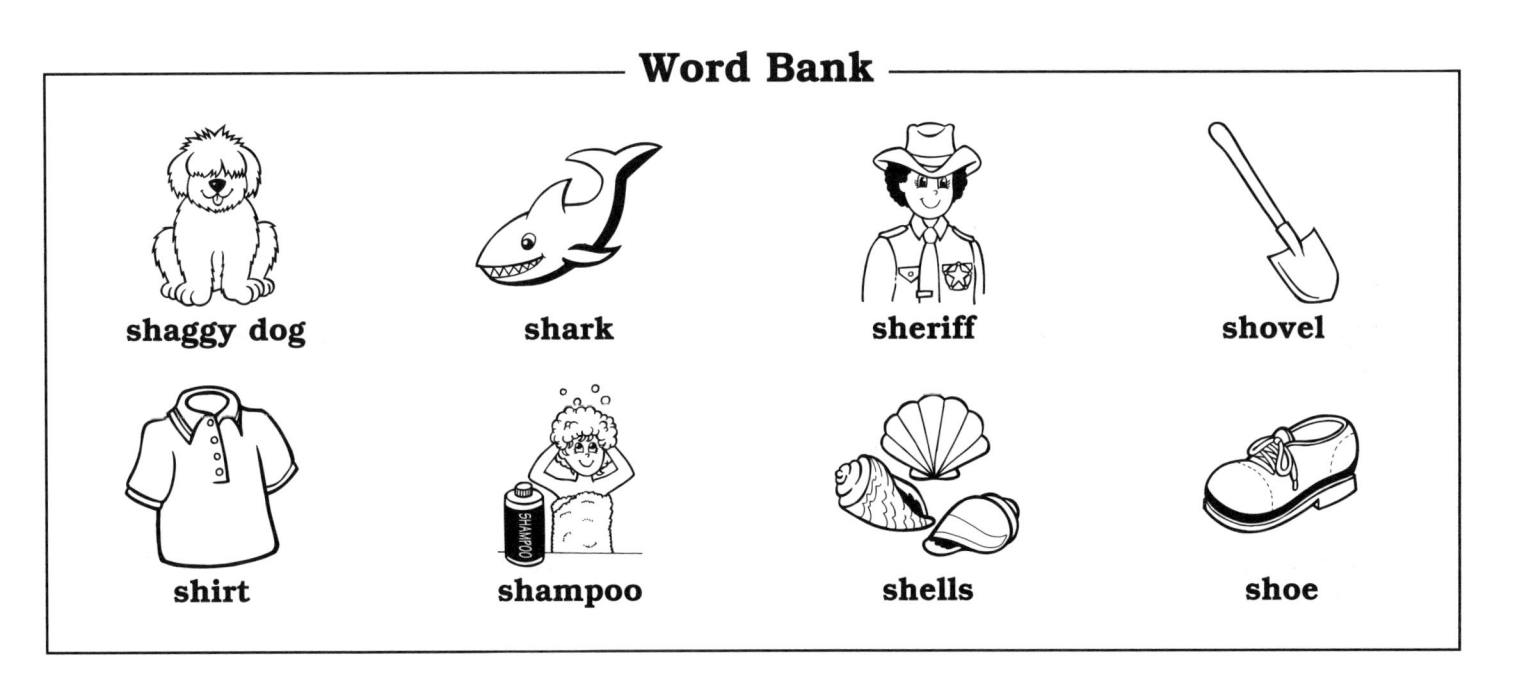

Word Bank

| shaggy dog | shark | sheriff | shovel |
| shirt | shampoo | shells | shoe |

Homework Partner   Date   Speech-Language Pathologist

Initial SH Sentences

Pick a Squash

Directions: Read the questions below. Then, pick a squash with the correct answer. Color the squash any color you choose. Say the words aloud. Use your good SH sound.

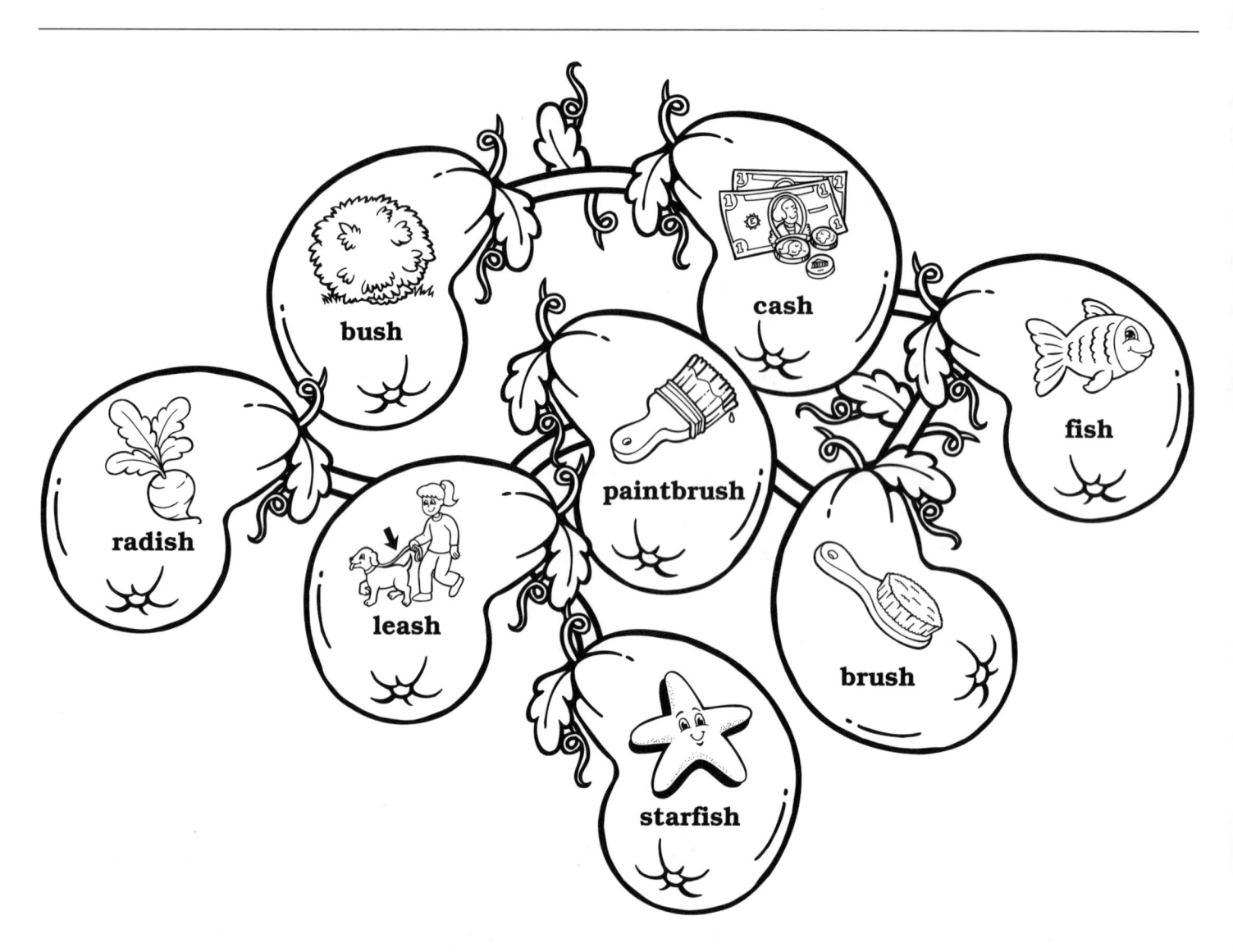

- bush
- cash
- fish
- radish
- paintbrush
- leash
- brush
- starfish

1. What do you put on a dog?

2. What is a red vegetable?

3. What is another name for money?

4. What swims?

5. What is found in the sea?

6. What do you use on your hair?

7. What is a painting tool?

8. What is another name for a green plant?

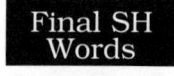

Homework Partner   Date   Speech-Language Pathologist

Final SH Words

Starfish to Starfish

Directions: Cut out the starfish, and place them face down. Turn two fish over, and read/ say aloud the picture–words on them as you look to see if they match. Keep all matches. Student with the most matches wins. Use your good SH sound. _____

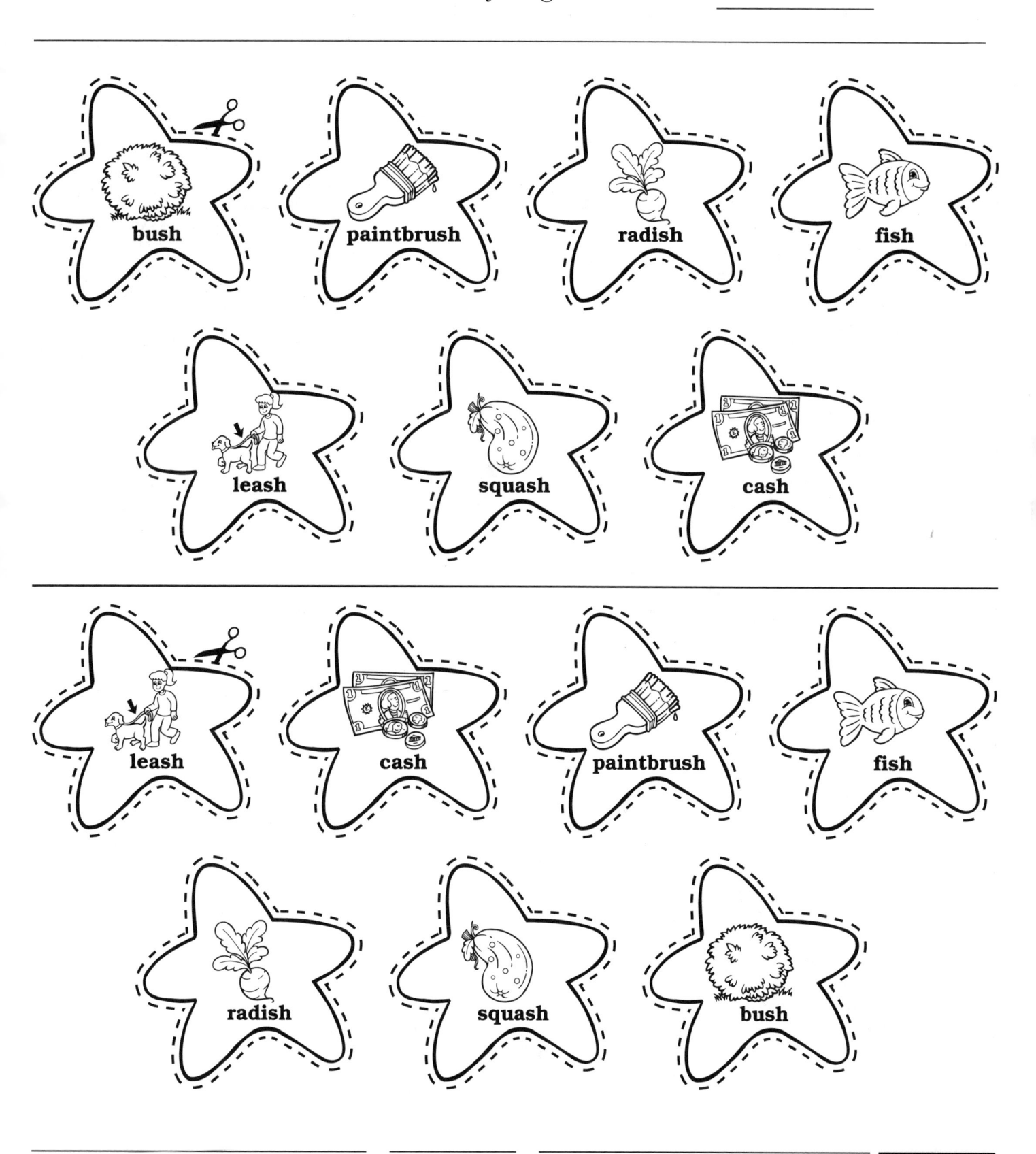

bush   paintbrush   radish   fish

leash   squash   cash

leash   cash   paintbrush   fish

radish   squash   bush

Homework Partner   Date   Speech-Language Pathologist

Final SH Words

Fire and Ice

Directions: Have your partner pick a picture on this page, but tell him/her not to tell you what it is. Then, try to figure out which picture your partner chose by asking questions. (Does it swim?) If the picture he/she chose is close to the target word, your partner should say, "You are hot." If it is far away from the target, he/she should say, "You are cold." Keep trying until you guess your partner's picture. Then, switch places. Use your good SH sound.

fish	radish	cash
paintbrush	**bush**	**leash**
starfish	**brush**	**squash**

Homework Partner   Date   Speech-Language Pathologist

Final SH Words

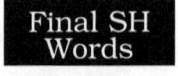

Secret Word

Directions: Read/say aloud each picture–word below. Write the answers from the Word Bank in the blank spaces. The letters in the square will spell out a secret word. Use the Bonus Clue to help you. Say aloud the secret word, using your good SH sound.

Word Bank

fish   radish   toothbrush   leash

cash   brush   squash   bush

1. I am a yellow vegetable. ▢ ___ ___ ___ ___ ___ ___

2. I clean your teeth. ▢ ___ ___ ___ ___ ___ ___ ___ ___ ___

3. I am also called money. ___ ___ ▢ ___

4. You use this to fix your hair. ___ ▢ ___ ___ ___

5. I live in the water and have fins. ___ ▢ ___ ___

6. I am a red vegetable that grows in the ground. ___ ___ ___ ___ ▢ ___ ___

7. Dogs wear these on their collars. ___ ___ ___ ▢ ___

8. I am a plant, but not a tree. ___ ___ ▢ ___

Bonus Clue

I am a sea animal.

Secret Word

▢ ▢ ▢ ▢ ▢ ▢ ▢ ▢
1　2　3　4　5　6　7　8

Answer Key on Page 279

Homework Partner   Date   Speech-Language Pathologist

Final SH Words

How Many Parts?

Directions: Cut out the cards and place in a pile. Students sit in a circle. The first student picks a card and reads/says the word aloud to determine the number of syllables. The student walks around the group, tapping the number of students that match the syllable number (radish: two taps). The last student he taps gets to select a card. Play continues in turn. The student with the most cards wins. Use your good SH sound.

fish	radish	toothbrush
leash	cash	brush
starfish	bush	squash

Homework Partner   Date   Speech-Language Pathologist

Final SH Words

Word Math

Directions: In Section I, read/say the words aloud. Then, write the number of letters in each word in the blank space. In Section II, use these numbers to solve each math problem. Say the answer in a sentence aloud (fish + cash = 8). Use your good SH sound.

Section I. How many letters?

A. toothbrush _____
B. radish _____
C. starfish _____
D. leash _____
E. brush _____

F. squash _____
G. fish _____
H. cash _____
I. bush _____
J. paintbrush _____

Answers: A. 10, B. 6, C. 8, D. 5, E. 5, F. 6, G. 4, H. 4, I. 4, J. 10

Section II. Solve the problems.

1. A + C = _____
2. B − D = _____
3. F + H = _____
4. G + E = _____

5. C − E = _____
6. B + G = _____
7. D − H = _____
8. A + I = _____

Answers: 1. 18, 2. 1, 3. 10, 4. 9, 5. 3, 6. 10, 7. 1, 8. 14

Homework Partner   Date   Speech-Language Pathologist   Final SH Words

Riddle Detective

Directions: Read/say aloud the picture–words. Then, read the riddles below. Choose the correct answers from the Word Bank. Write the answers in the spaces. Read/say your answers aloud using your good SH sound.

Word Bank

fish   squash   leash   paintbrush

brush   cash   toothbrush   radish

---

1. I live in the water.
   I have fins.
   You try to catch me,
   But you never win.

   I am a _____.

2. I keep a dog safe,
   So he can't run away.
   I go around his neck.
   I come in many colors.

   I am a _____.

3. I am a vegetable,
   that lives on a vine.
   You can eat me or
   Use me for decorating.

   I am a _____.

4. I clean your teeth,
   Morning and night.
   Put toothpaste on me and
   I make your teeth bright.

   I am a _____.

5. I am called money.
   I buy things for you.
   I go in your wallet,
   Or jingle in your pocket.

   I am _____.

6. I can paint a house,
   And a picture, too.
   Artists paint with me,
   When fingers just won't do.

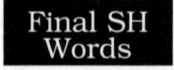

   I am a _____.

Answers: 1. fish, 2. leash, 3. squash, 4. toothbrush, 5. cash, 6. paintbrush

Homework Partner   Date   Speech-Language Pathologist   **Final SH Words**

Color It In!

Directions: Read/say the picture–words below. Then, color each crayon. Use a different color for each one. Then say a phrase aloud about each crayon, using the color on that crayon (a blue fish). Use your good SH sound.

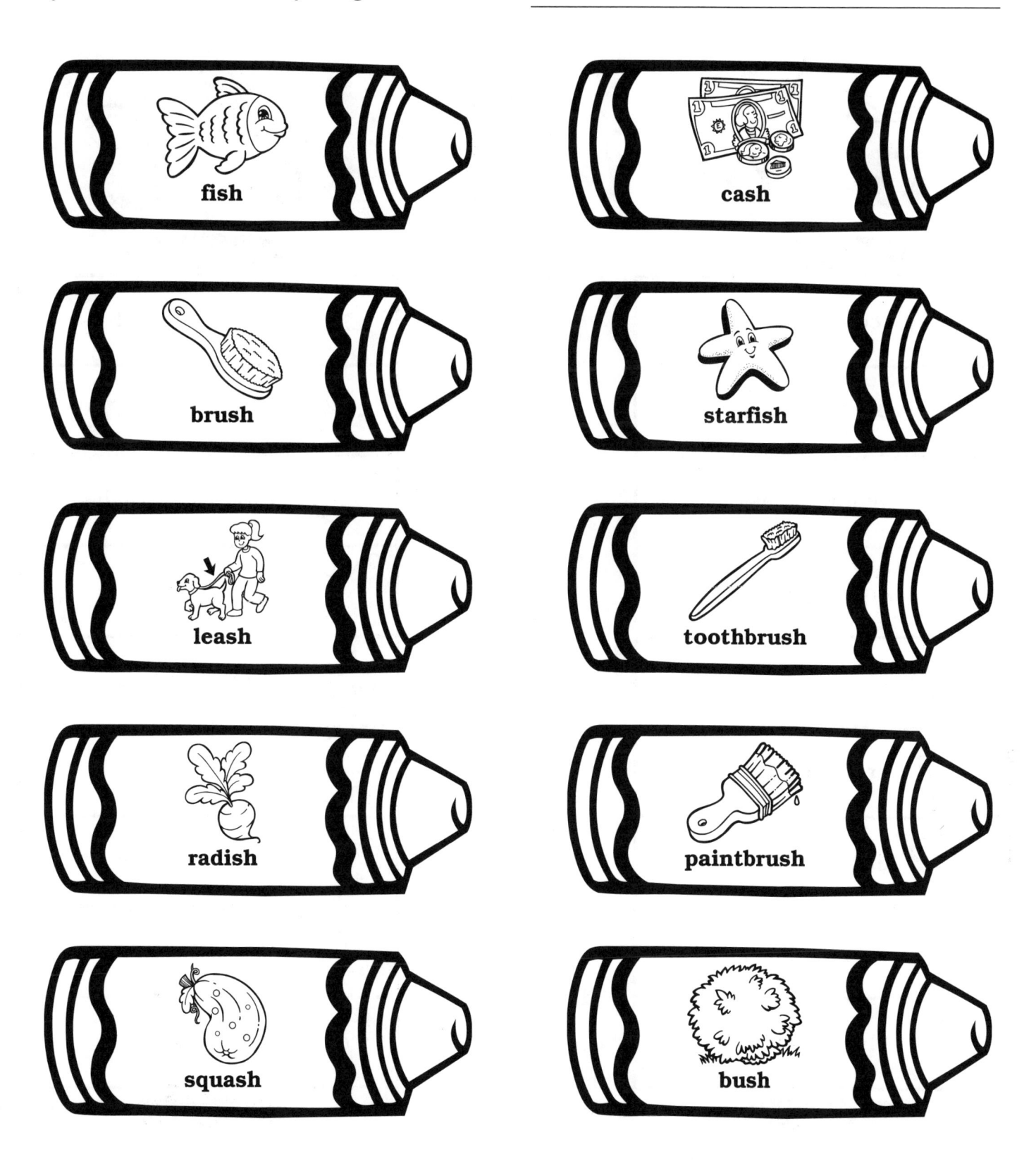

- fish
- cash
- brush
- starfish
- leash
- toothbrush
- radish
- paintbrush
- squash
- bush

Homework Partner   Date   Speech-Language Pathologist

Final SH Phrases

Phrase Racing

Directions: Cut out the cars. Give one to the student and one to a race partner. Begin at the starting line. Use a coin to determine the number of spaces to advance (heads=2, tails=1). Read/say aloud each phrase as you land on it. First one to the Finish wins! Play again. Use your best SH sound.

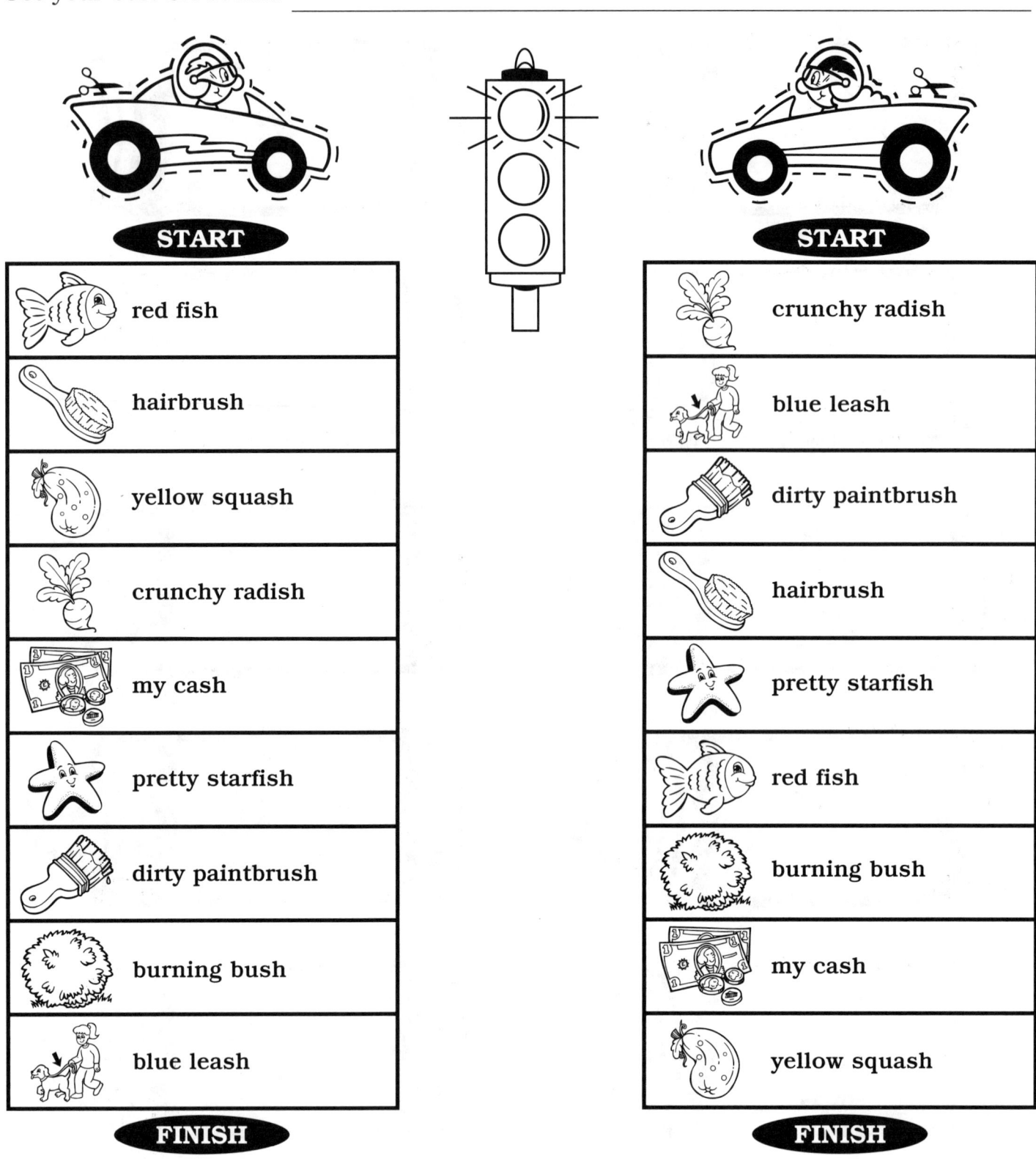

START

	red fish
	hairbrush
	yellow squash
	crunchy radish
	my cash
	pretty starfish
	dirty paintbrush
	burning bush
	blue leash

FINISH

START

	crunchy radish
	blue leash
	dirty paintbrush
	hairbrush
	pretty starfish
	red fish
	burning bush
	my cash
	yellow squash

FINISH

Homework Partner   Date   Speech-Language Pathologist

Final SH Phrases

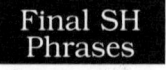

22

Cross the Line

Directions: Read/say aloud each picture–word. Then, draw a line from an adjective to an SH noun. Make up phrases to say aloud using your best SH sound (yellow fish). They can be silly or serious.

Adjectives	SH Nouns
tasty…	fish
yellow…	paintbrush
sweet…	radish
dirty…	cash
long…	leash
big…	starfish
lost…	squash

Homework Partner   Date   Speech-Language Pathologist

Final SH Phrases

At the Market

Directions: Read/say aloud each picture–word below. Then, roll a die. Make a sentence including the number from the die and the picture–word. (I want to buy one fish.) Use your good SH sound.

| fish | squash | radish | starfish |

| paintbrush | leash | brush | toothbrush |

At the market, I want to buy _____ _____.

Homework Partner   Date   Speech-Language Pathologist

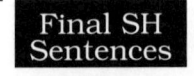

Final SH Sentences

Dip the Paintbrush

Directions: Draw a line from the paintbrush to a paint can to make a sentence. Read/say the complete sentence aloud, using your good SH sound.

I want to catch...

Clean your teeth...

Sally loves to eat...

David walks the dog...

Every morning you must...

Please pay with...

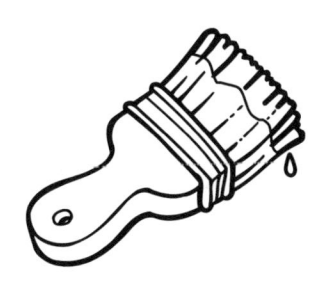

At the sea...

...squash casserole.

...with a **leash**.

...check or **cash**.

...**brush** your hair.

...we collect **starfish**.

...a little **fish**.

...with a **toothbrush**.

Homework Partner   Date   Speech-Language Pathologist

Final SH Sentences

Scrambled Sentences

Directions: Try to unscramble each sentence. Write it on the line below the egg. Then read/say the sentence aloud using your best SH sound.

1. _____.

   (got, Paula, for, her, birthday, cash)

2. _____.

   (ball, bush, The, rolled, under, the)

3. _____.

   (for, a, The, radish, rabbit, ate, breakfast)

4. _____.

   (Remember, bring, to, your, brush)

5. _____.

   (dog's, is, closet, in, hanging, The, leash, the)

6. _____.

   (a, bought, store, paintbrush, the, at, Dad)

7. _____.

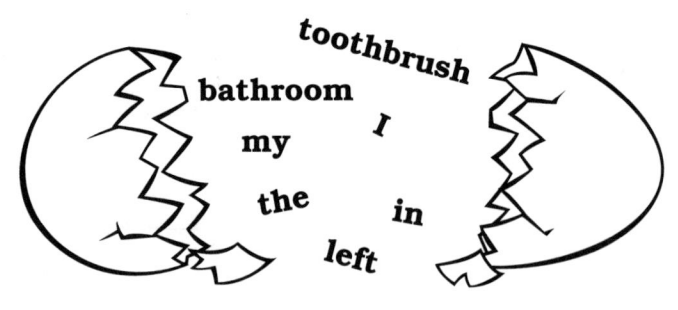

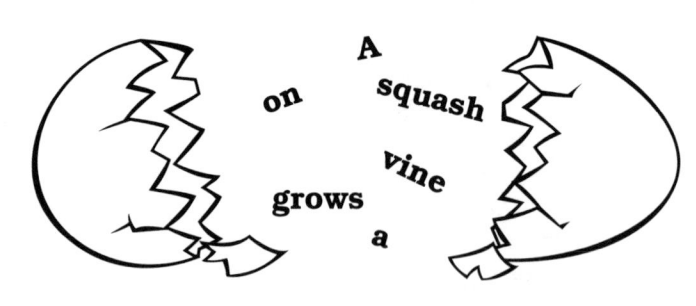

   (toothbrush, bathroom, I, my, the, in, left)

8. _____.

   (A, on, squash, vine, grows, a)

Answer Key on Page 279

Homework Partner   Date   Speech-Language Pathologist

Final SH Sentences

Cream of Mushroom Soup

Directions: Cut out the mushrooms below. The student reads/says aloud the picture-word on each mushroom and counts the syllables. Then, the student repeats the word as many times as the number of syllables in the word (dishes: two syllables = dishes, dishes). Glue the mushrooms in the bowl. Use your good SH sound.

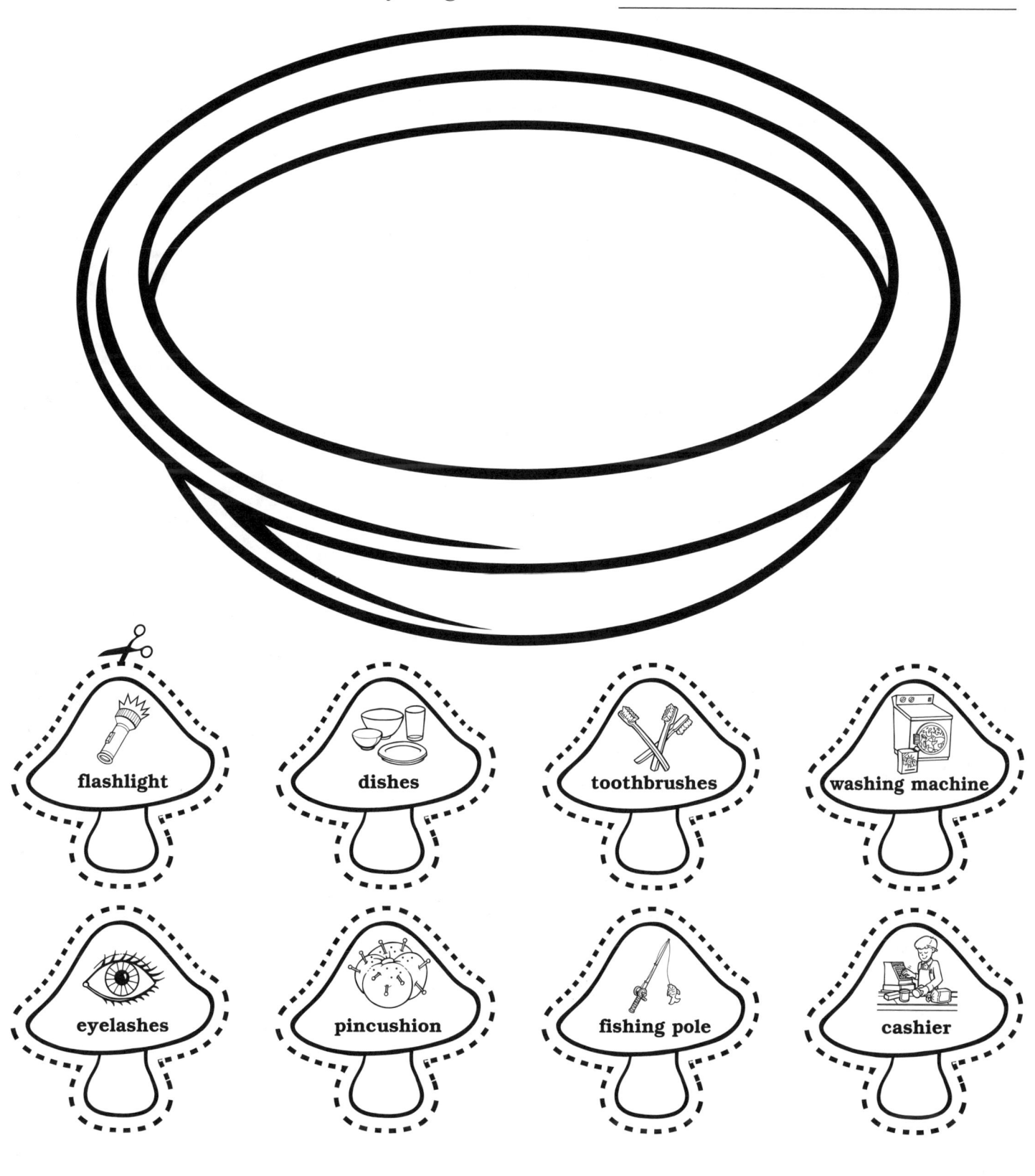

- flashlight
- dishes
- toothbrushes
- washing machine
- eyelashes
- pincushion
- fishing pole
- cashier

Homework Partner   Date   Speech-Language Pathologist

Medial SH Words

Stack the Dishes

Directions: Read/say aloud the words below. Then, cut out the dishes, and place them face down. Flip over a dish and read/say the word aloud. As you play, stack the dishes on top of each other.

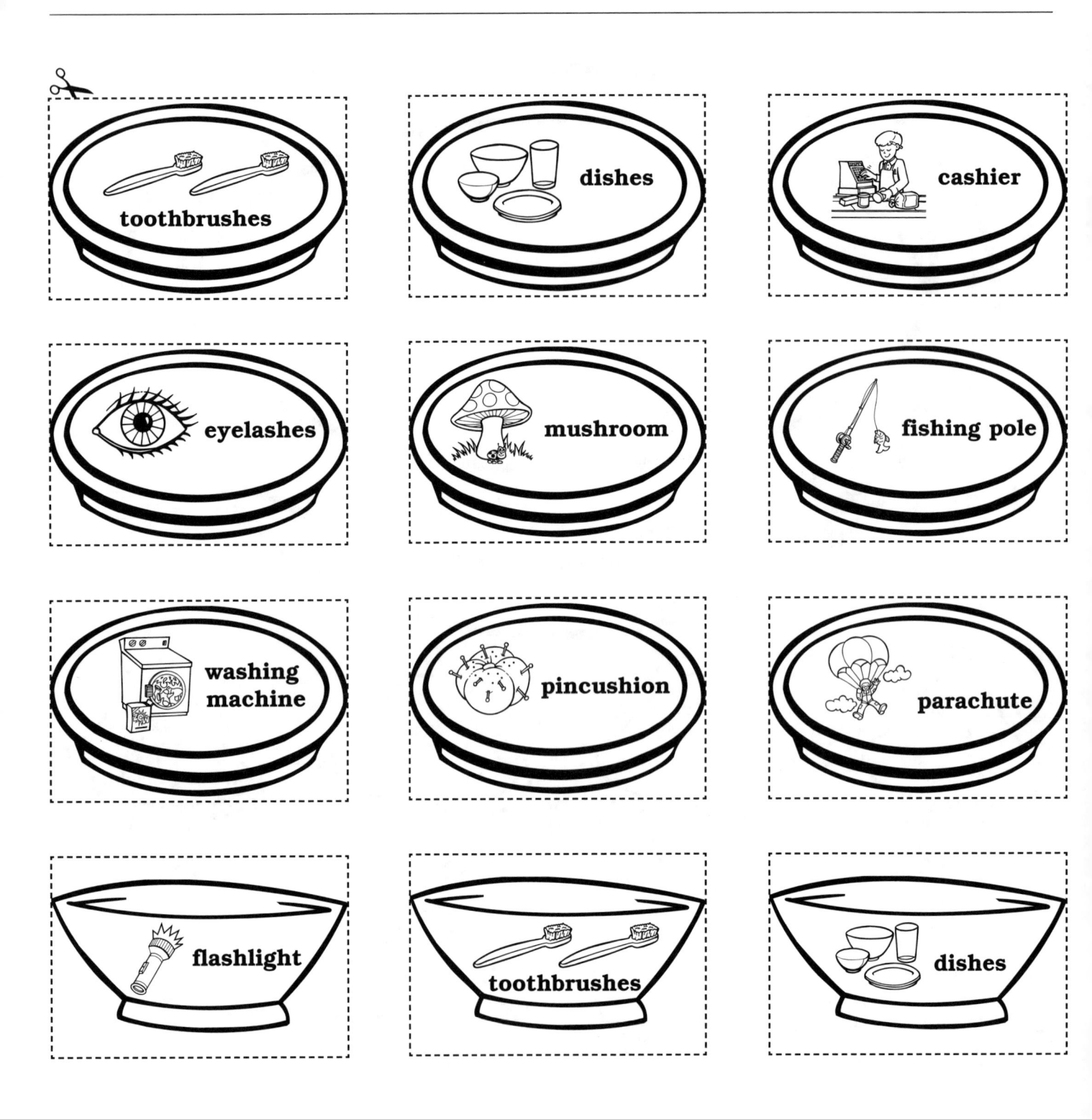

toothbrushes	dishes	cashier
eyelashes	mushroom	fishing pole
washing machine	pincushion	parachute
flashlight	toothbrushes	dishes

Homework Partner   Date   Speech-Language Pathologist

Medial SH Words

Fishing Adventure

Directions: Toss a coin or roll a die on the pond. Read/say the word aloud on the fish that the coin or die lands on. Color or write your name on that fish. Student with most colored or labeled fish wins. Remember to use your good SH sound.

- washing machine
- cashier
- mushroom
- dishes
- flashlight
- parachute
- pincushion
- toothbrushes
- eyelashes

Homework Partner Date Speech-Language Pathologist

Medial SH Words

3 Games in 1

Directions: Say aloud the picture–words below, using your good SH sound. Then, play one of the following games:

- ☐ Lotto – Caller reads a word and student repeats the word and covers it with a token/chip.
- ☐ Tic–Tac–Toe – Each time you write an **X** or **O**, say the word you mark over.
- ☐ Memory – Cut out all the cards and place face down. Try to find matching pairs. Say aloud each word you find. Keep all matches.

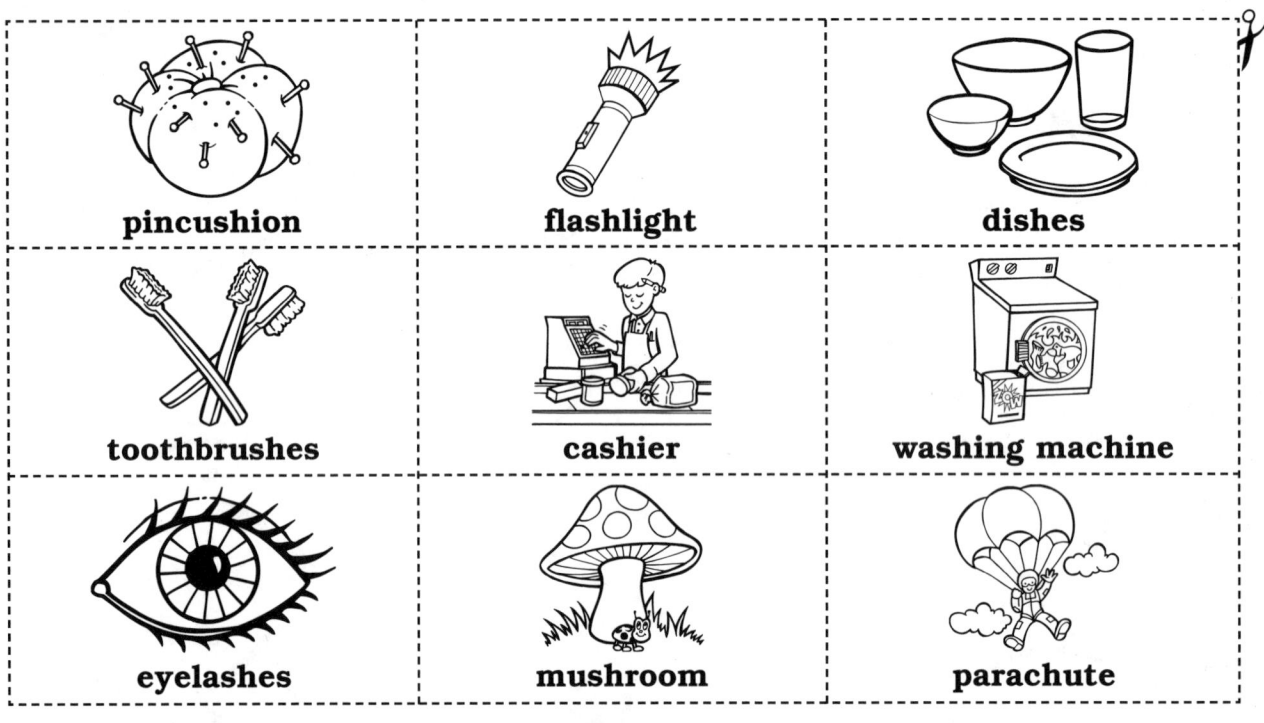

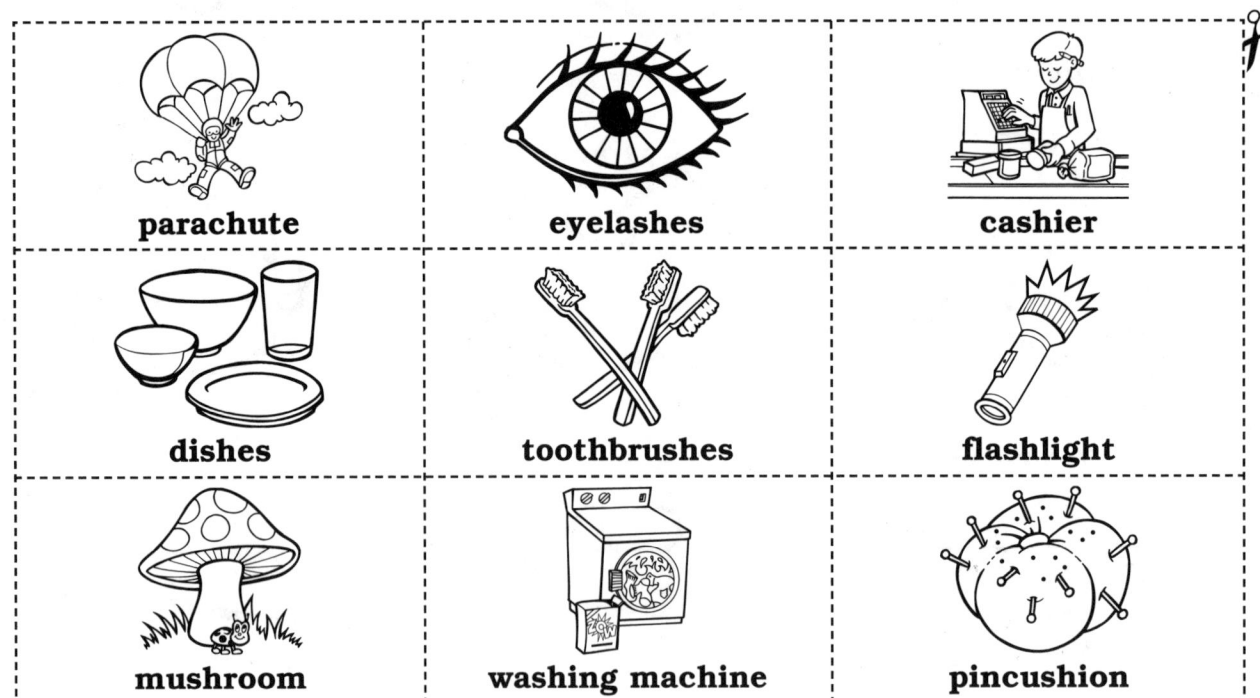

pincushion	flashlight	dishes
toothbrushes	cashier	washing machine
eyelashes	mushroom	parachute
parachute	eyelashes	cashier
dishes	toothbrushes	flashlight
mushroom	washing machine	pincushion

Homework Partner   Date   Speech-Language Pathologist

Medial SH Words

Pass It Around!

Directions: Copy and cut out picture–word cards below. Give 2-4 cards to each student, depending on the number playing. Student chooses a card in his/her hand and reads/says the word aloud. He/she then passes it around the group to the same number of students as syllables in the word (dishes passed two times). Whoever it stops at keeps the card. The student with most cards at the end wins. Remember to use your good SH sound.

washing machine	dishes	pincushion
cashier	parachute	mushroom
flashlight	fishing pole	toothbrushes

_____   _____   _____
Homework Partner   Date   Speech-Language Pathologist

Medial SH Words

Which Is?

Directions: Read/say the following questions aloud. Then, answer the question, using your best SH sound.

1. Which is longer - a **flashlight** or a **fishing pole**?

2. Which is harder - **dishes** or a **pincushion**?

3. Which is bigger - a **mushroom** or a **washing machine**?

4. Which is softer - **eyelashes** or **toothbrushes**?

5. Which is heavier - a **flashlight** or a **washing machine**?

6. Which is lighter - **eyelashes** or **dishes**?

Answers: 1. fishing pole, 2. dishes, 3. washing machine, 4. eyelashes, 5. washing machine, 6. eyelashes

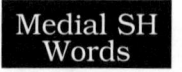

Homework Partner   Date   Speech-Language Pathologist

Medial SH Words

Push the Pincushion

Directions: Cut out the picture–phrases below and place them face down in a pile. Draw a card. Then, read/say the phrases aloud and draw the number of pins on the large pincushion that are on the card. Remember to use your good SH sound.

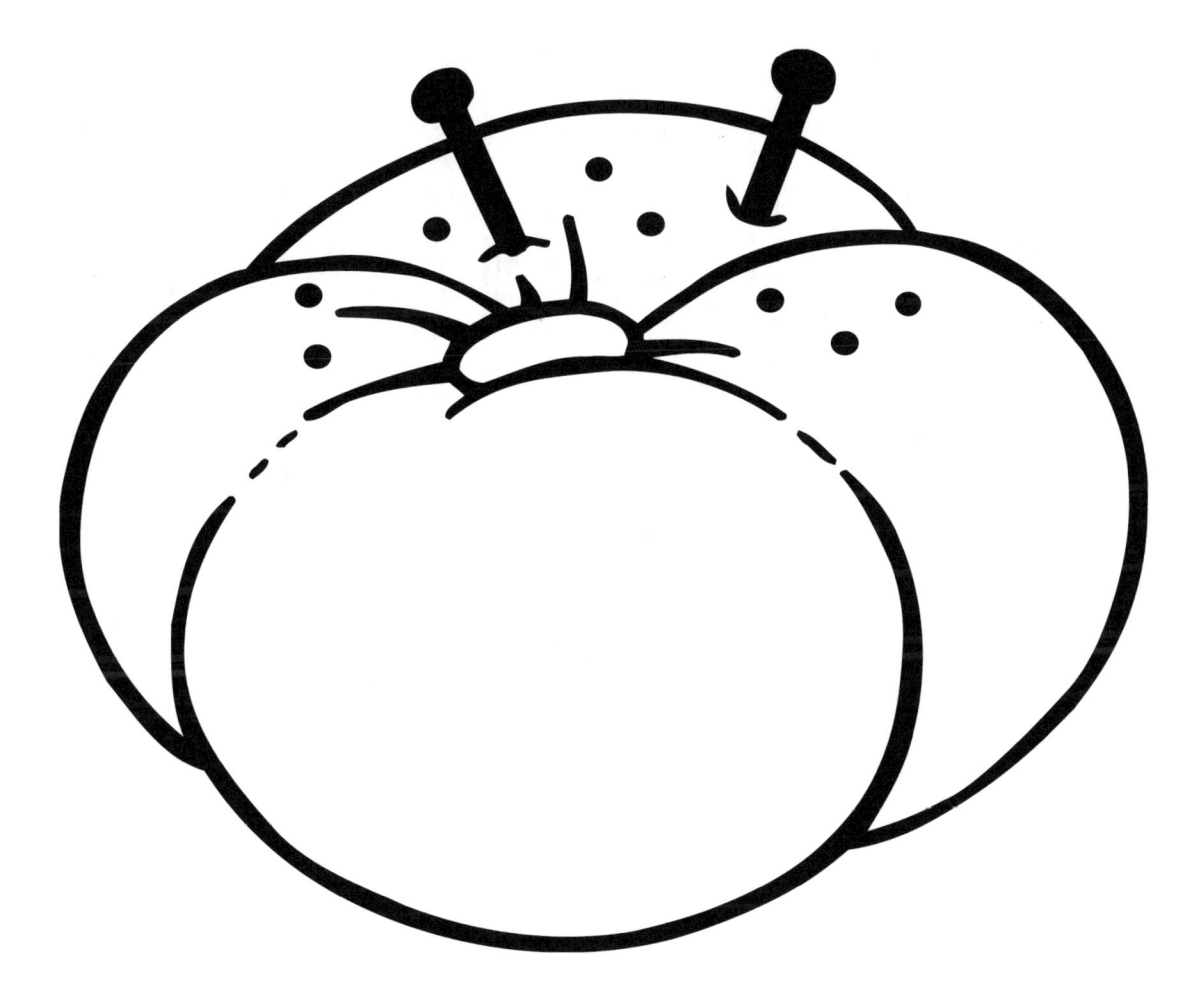

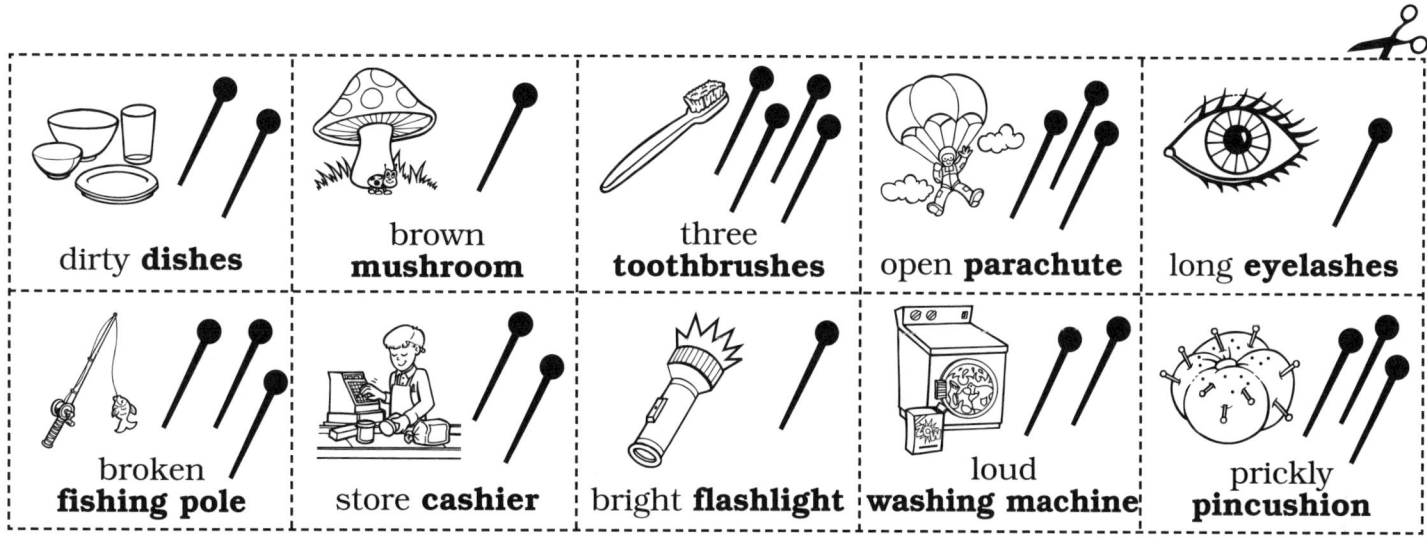

dirty **dishes**	brown **mushroom**	three **toothbrushes**	open **parachute**	long **eyelashes**
broken **fishing pole**	store **cashier**	bright **flashlight**	loud **washing machine**	prickly **pincushion**

Homework Partner   Date   Speech-Language Pathologist

Medial SH Phrases

SH Phrase It

Directions: Assemble the cube as follows: Glue onto construction paper for added durability. Cut along the dotted lines. Fold on solid lines and glue as indicated. To play: roll both cubes. Read/say the words and pictures together aloud to make up a phrase (broken flashlight). Use your good SH sound.

Cube 1 (pictures):
- Glue B / mushroom
- Glue Tab C / fishing pole
- washing machine
- dishes
- Glue Tab B / pincushion / Glue C / Glue Tab A
- Glue A / flashlight

Cube 2 (words):
- Glue B / long
- Glue Tab C / dirty
- bright
- beautiful
- Glue Tab B / open / Glue C / Glue Tab A
- Glue A / broken

Medial SH Phrases

34 #BK-291 Webber® Artic Fun Sheets 2 • ©2002 Super Duper® Publications • www.superduperinc.com • 1-800-277-8737

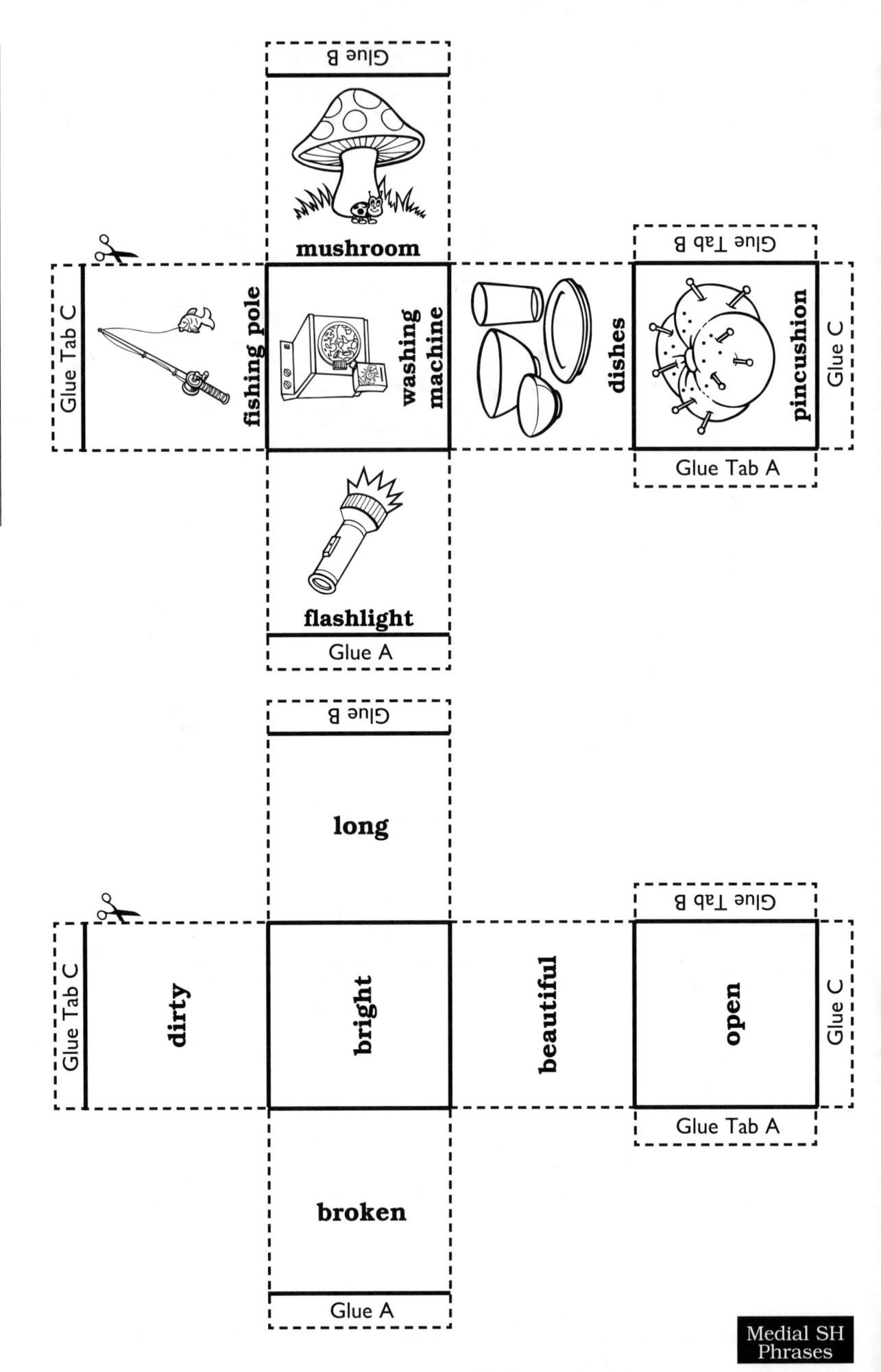

Number It Up!

Directions: Read/say aloud the picture–words. Number the words in the Word Bank below from 1-8 in any order you desire. Then, put the words on the line below that match the corresponding numbers (wild mushroom). Read/say the phrases aloud using your good SH sound.

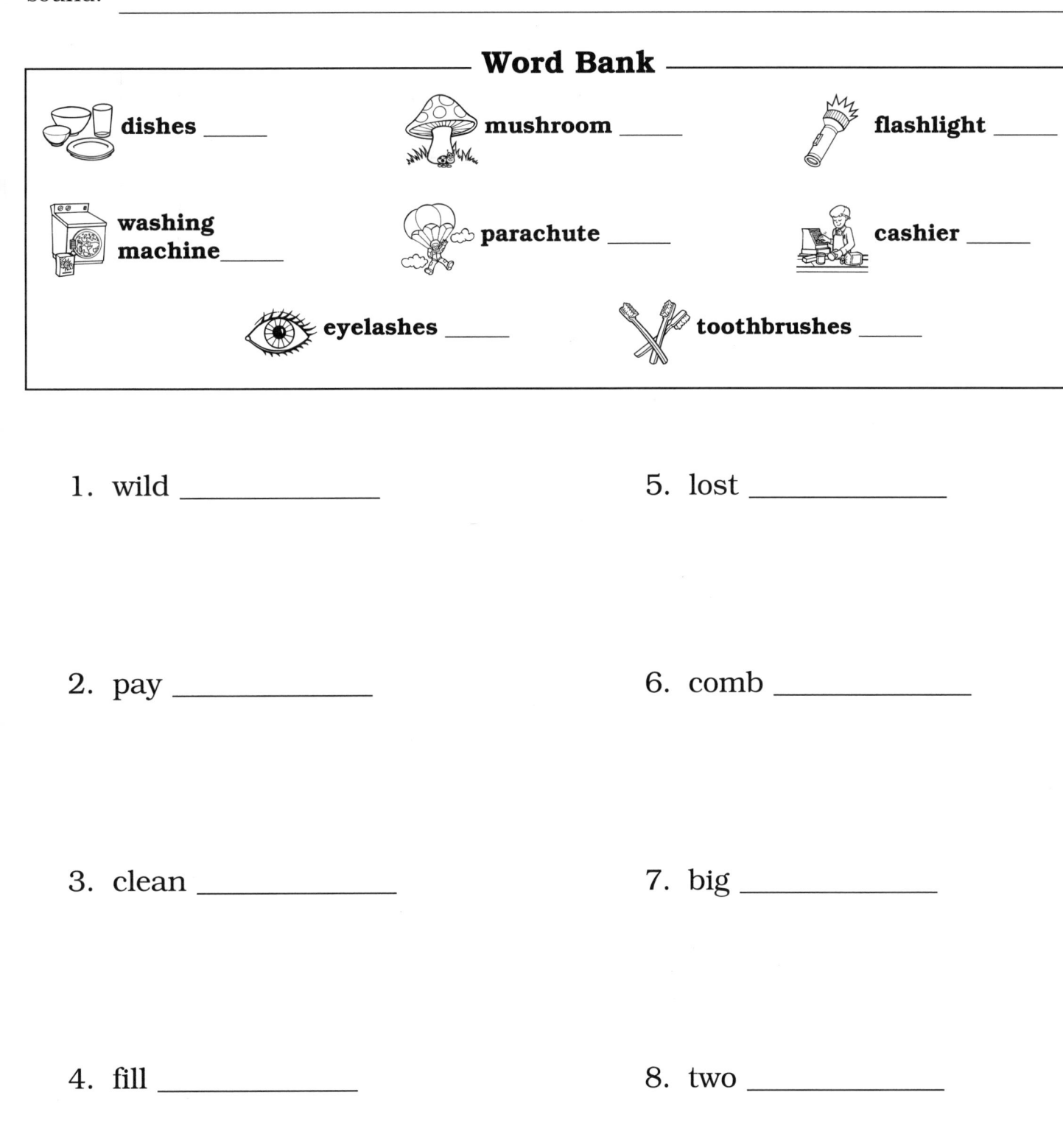

Word Bank

dishes _____   mushroom _____   flashlight _____

washing machine _____   parachute _____   cashier _____

eyelashes _____   toothbrushes _____

1. wild _____

2. pay _____

3. clean _____

4. fill _____

5. lost _____

6. comb _____

7. big _____

8. two _____

Homework Partner Date Speech-Language Pathologist

Medial SH Phrases

Yes or No?

Directions: Read the questions. Then, put an **X** in the correct boxes. Say your answers aloud in sentence form. (Yes, mushrooms grow on the ground.) Remember to use your good SH sound.

	Yes	No
1. Do mushrooms grow on the ground?	☐	☐
2. Can a pincushion talk?	☐	☐
3. Can you curl eyelashes?	☐	☐
4. Do you play a washing machine?	☐	☐
5. Do you pay a cashier?	☐	☐
6. Do you use a flashlight in the daytime?	☐	☐
7. Can you eat on dishes?	☐	☐
8. Do you wear a parachute when jumping from a plane?	☐	☐
9. Do you use toothbrushes to clean your hair?	☐	☐

Answers: 1. yes 2. no 3. yes 4. no 5. yes 6. no 7. yes 8. yes 9. no

Homework Partner   Date   Speech-Language Pathologist

Medial SH Sentences

What Do You Think?

Directions: Read the sentences and circle the correct answers. Then, read/say each correct sentence aloud. Remember to use your good SH sound.

1. Dishes **can/can't** break.

2. A mushroom **does/doesn't** grow.

3. You **do/don't** give jellybeans to a cashier.

4. You **can/can't** cook in a washing machine.

5. You **do/don't** catch dogs with a fishing pole.

6. Everyone's eyes **do/don't** have eyelashes.

7. A pincushion **does/doesn't** hold food.

8. You **do/don't** use a flashlight to write.

9. You **can/can't** eat a parachute.

10. You **can/can't** use two toothbrushes at once.

Homework Partner   Date   Speech-Language Pathologist

Medial SH Sentences

Parachute Parade

Directions: Have student read/say the sentences aloud. Then, cut out the tokens. Students flip a coin to advance (heads=2, tails=1). First student to reach the finish line wins. Remember to use your good SH sound. _____

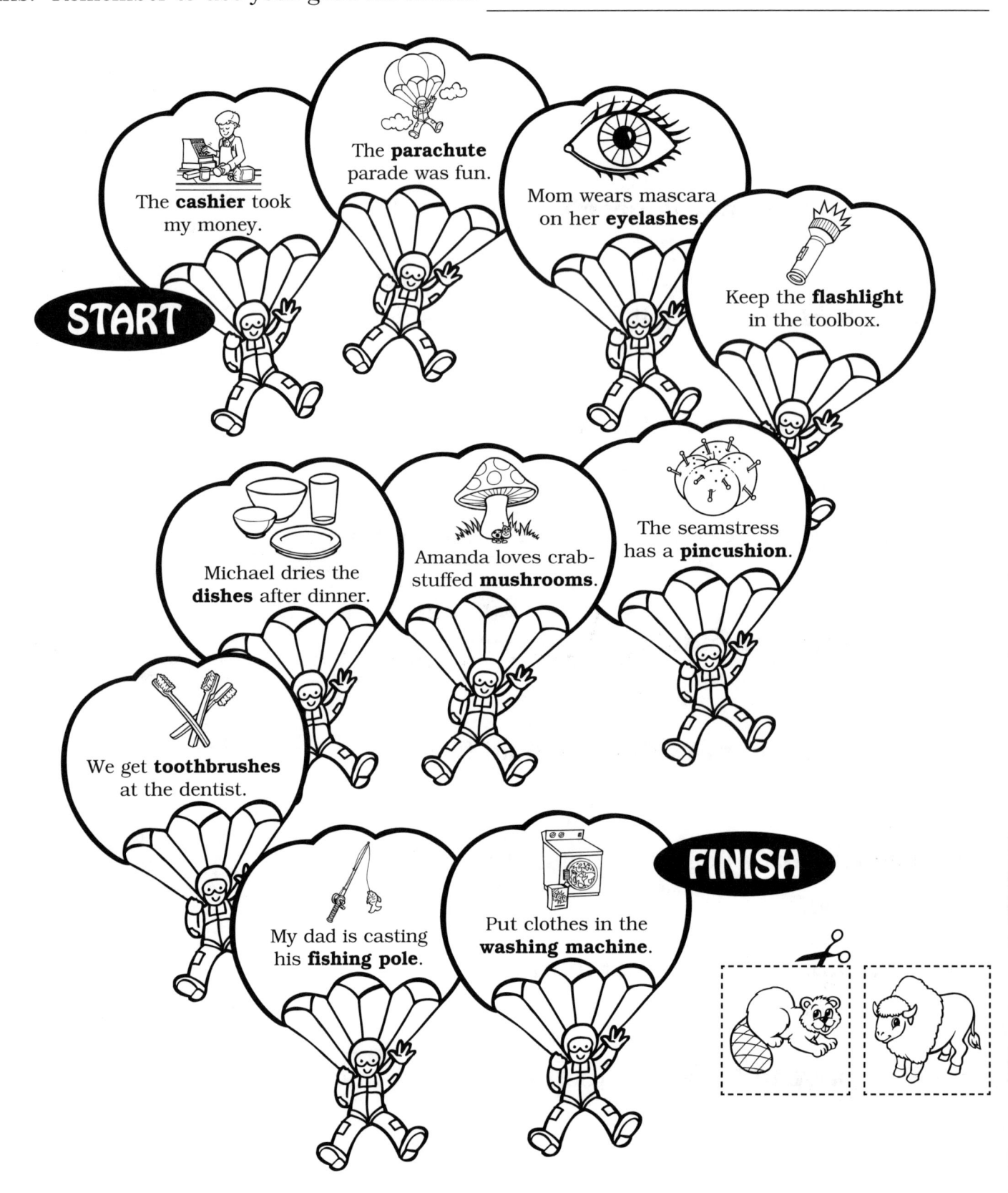

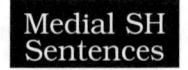

START

- The **cashier** took my money.
- The **parachute** parade was fun.
- Mom wears mascara on her **eyelashes**.
- Keep the **flashlight** in the toolbox.
- Michael dries the **dishes** after dinner.
- Amanda loves crab-stuffed **mushrooms**.
- The seamstress has a **pincushion**.
- We get **toothbrushes** at the dentist.
- My dad is casting his **fishing pole**.
- Put clothes in the **washing machine**.

FINISH

Homework Partner   Date   Speech-Language Pathologist

Medial SH Sentences

CH Sound

#BK-291 Webber® Artic Fun Sheets 2 • ©2002 Super Duper® Publications • www.superduperinc.com • 1-800-277-8737

X and O

Directions: Cut out each **X** and **O** below. Have each player/partner choose **X** or **O**. The first player reads/says a picture–word aloud and places an **X** or **O** on the square. Play continues in turn. The first person to get three in a row wins.

cheese	chair	children
chipmunk	chow mein	chain
chicken	chimney	cherries

X X X X X

O O O O O

Homework Partner   Date   Speech-Language Pathologist

Initial CH Words

40

Paper Chain

Directions: Read/say aloud each picture–word below. Cut out the word strips. Turn them face down. Pick up a strip, read/say the word aloud, and then, staple/glue it to make a chain link. Remember to use your good CH sound as you make your chain.

- chair
- cherries
- cheese
- chain
- chow mein
- chimney
- chicken
- chick
- chocolate milk

Homework Partner Date Speech-Language Pathologist

Initial CH Words

Unscramble the Words

Directions: Read/say the picture–words on the page. Then, unscramble the words on the left and write the answers in the blanks. Read/say your answers aloud. Say the words again using your good CH sound.

1. **ckich** ___ ___ ___ ___ ___

2. **pikmnuch** ___ ___ ___ ___ ___ ___ ___ ___

   chow mein

3. **nihc** ___ ___ ___ ___

   chimney

4. **ahicr** ___ ___ ___ ___ ___

   chair

5. **mynehci** ___ ___ ___ ___ ___ ___ ___

6. **whco enim** ___ ___ ___ ___ ___ ___ ___ ___

   chain

7. **rrecihse** ___ ___ ___ ___ ___ ___ ___ ___

8. **nkhecic** ___ ___ ___ ___ ___ ___ ___

   chicken

9. **anihc** ___ ___ ___ ___ ___

chipmunk   chin   cherries   chick

Answers: 1. chick, 2. chipmunk, 3. chin, 4. chair, 5. chimney, 6. chow mein, 7. cherries, 8. chicken, 9. chain

Homework Partner   Date   Speech-Language Pathologist

Initial CH Words

Pick a Chick

Directions: Cut out the chicks and the picture–word cards. Place one card under each chick. Roll a die or spin a spinner. Pick the chick for the number you spun/rolled and read/say the picture–word under the chick aloud. If said correctly, keep the card. Replace cards until all the picture–words have been used. Remember to use your good CH sound.

| 1 | 2 | 3 |
| 4 | 5 | 6 |

| chimney | chain | chocolate milk | chair | cherries |
| cheese | chow mein | chipmunk | chin | chicken |

Homework Partner Date Speech-Language Pathologist

Initial CH Words

Secret Word

Directions: Read/say aloud each picture–word below. Then, read each sentence. Find the answers to the sentences in the Word Bank. Fill in the answers in the blank spaces. The letters in the square will spell out a secret word. Use the Bonus Clue to help you. Say aloud the secret word, using your good CH sound. _____

Word Bank

chimney	children	chow mein	chocolate milk
chicken	chin	cherries	chain

1. Plural for child. □ ___ ___ ___ ___ ___ ___ ___

2. An animal that lays eggs. ___ □ ___ ___ ___ ___ ___ ___

3. Metal loops linked together. ___ ___ □ ___ ___

4. These fruits have pits. ___ ___ ___ □ ___ ___ ___ ___

5. Smoke comes out of this. ___ ___ ___ □ ___ ___ ___

6. A beard grows on this body part. ___ ___ ___ ___

7. Chinese food entree. ___ ___ ___ ___ ___ ___ ___ ___

Bonus Clue

This is a type of bracelet.

Secret Word

□ □ □ □ □
1 2 3 4 5

Check it Out!

Directions: Read/say aloud the picture-words. Choose a word from the Word Bank and write it in the correct alphabetical space, or say the word aloud that goes in the correct space. Read/say the CH word again, using your best CH sound.

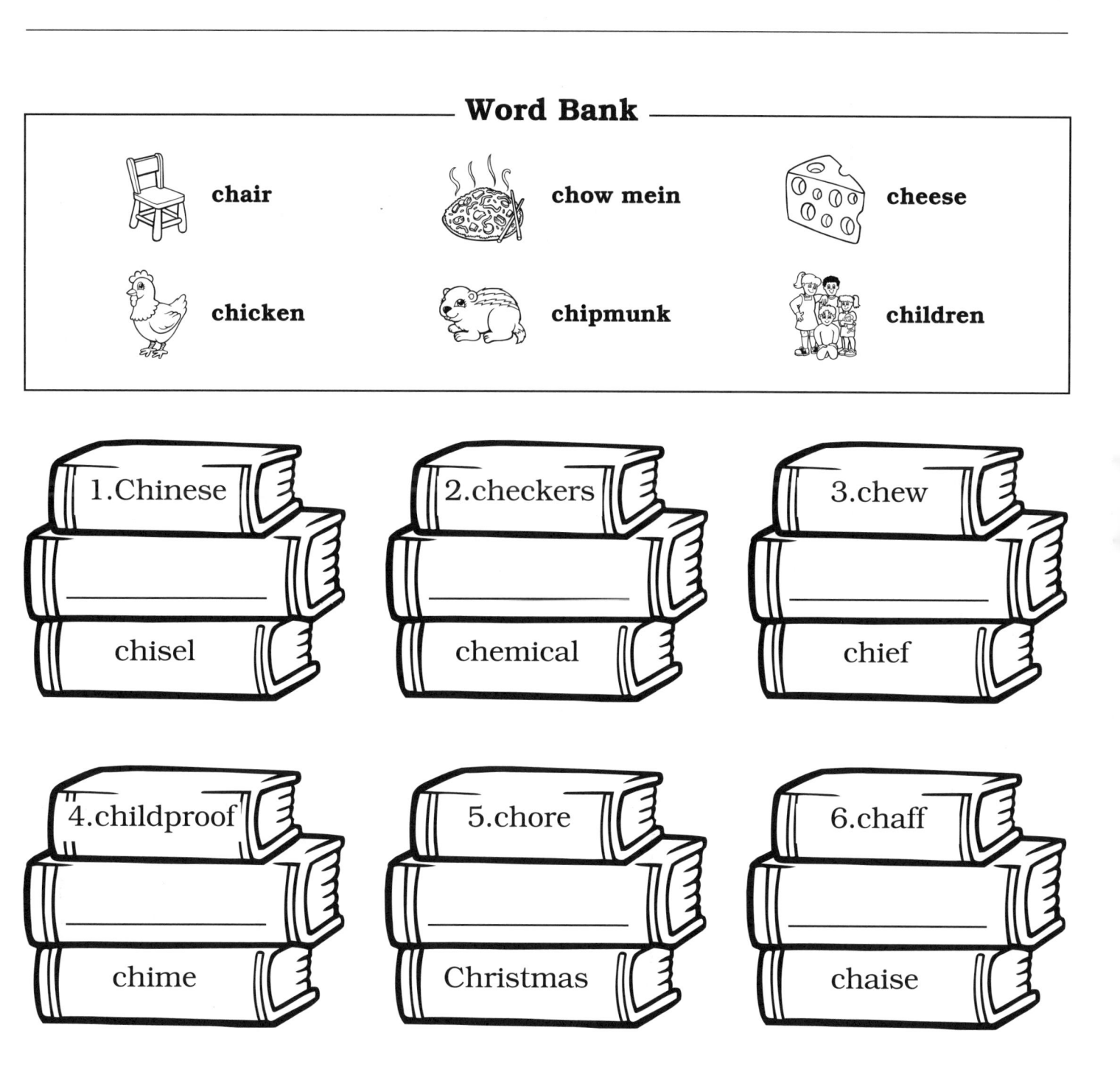

Word Bank

- chair
- chow mein
- cheese
- chicken
- chipmunk
- children

1. Chinese
_____
chisel

2. checkers
_____
chemical

3. chew
_____
chief

4. childproof
_____
chime

5. chore
_____
Christmas

6. chaff
_____
chaise

Answers: 1. chipmunk, 2. cheese, 3. chicken, 4. children, 5. chow mein, 6. chair

Homework Partner   Date   Speech-Language Pathologist

Initial CH Words

CH Phrase It

Directions: Assemble the cube as follows: Glue onto construction paper for added durability. Cut along the dotted lines. Fold on solid lines and glue as indicated. To play: roll both cubes. Read/say the word and picture together aloud to make up a phrase (hot chow mein). Use your good CH sound.

Cube 1 faces: chipmunk, chow mein, chin, chair, chain, cheese

Cube 2 faces: hot, metal, soft, hairy, quick, white

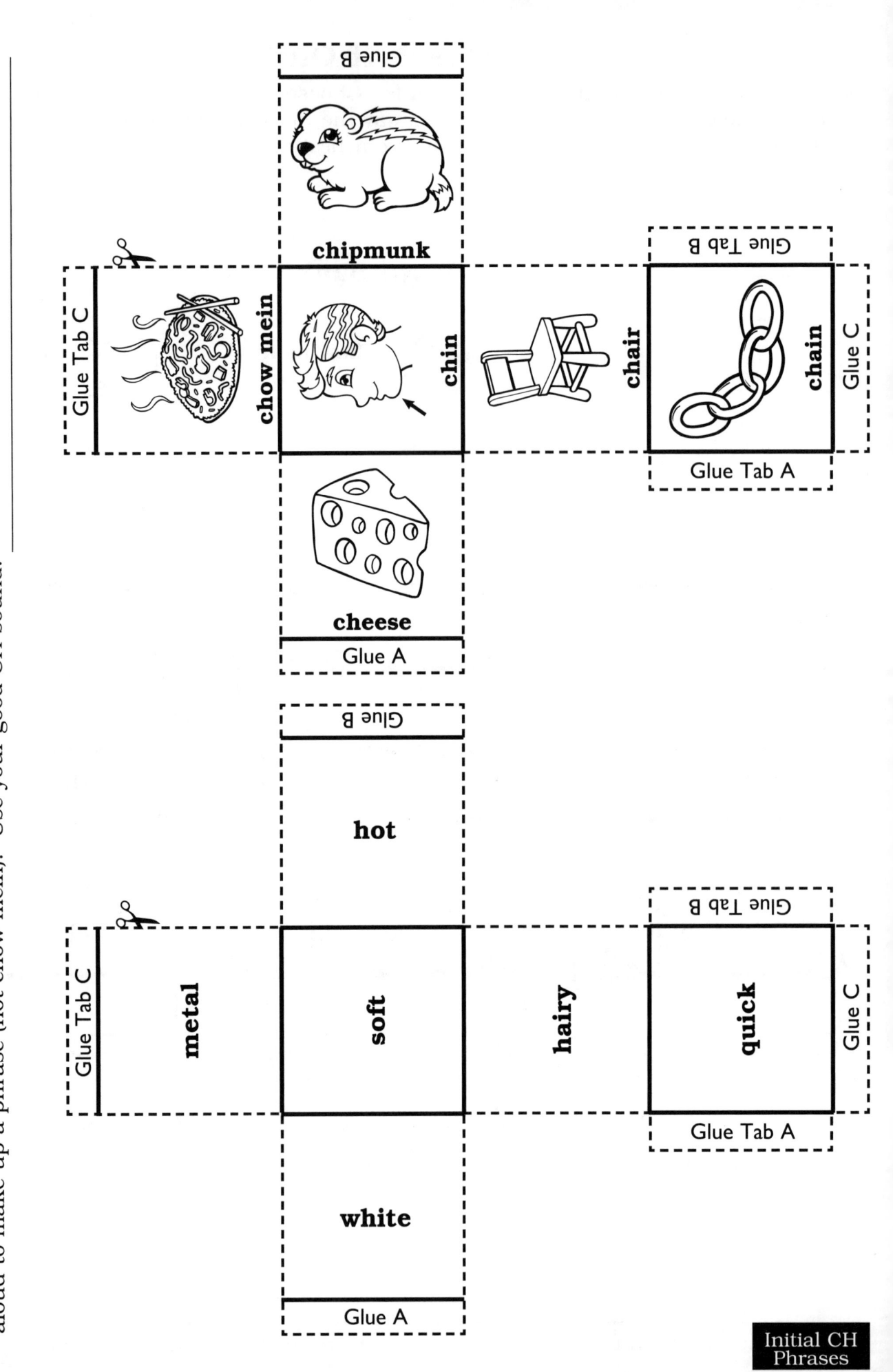

Initial CH Phrases

Phrase Racing

Directions: Cut out the cars. Give one to the student and one to a race partner. Begin at the starting line. Use a coin to determine the number of spaces to advance (heads=2, tails=1). Read/say aloud each phrase as you land on it. First one to the Finish wins! Play again.

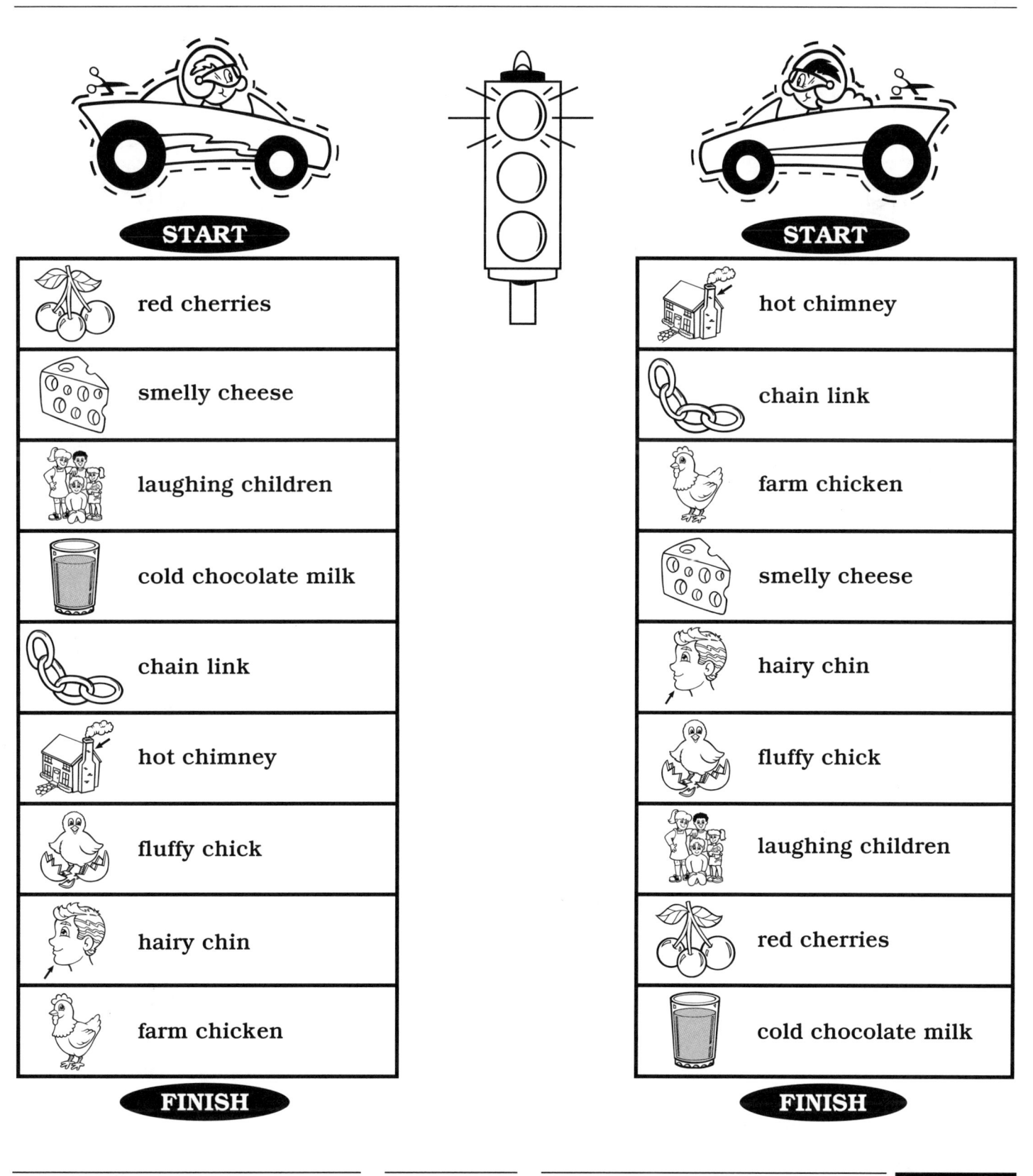

START (left)

	red cherries
	smelly cheese
	laughing children
	cold chocolate milk
	chain link
	hot chimney
	fluffy chick
	hairy chin
	farm chicken

FINISH

START (right)

	hot chimney
	chain link
	farm chicken
	smelly cheese
	hairy chin
	fluffy chick
	laughing children
	red cherries
	cold chocolate milk

FINISH

Homework Partner   Date   Speech-Language Pathologist

Initial CH Phrases

Who Said That?

Directions: Read/say each CH picture–word aloud. Read the statements in the middle. Then, ask, **"Who said that?"** Answer with the phrase, "A _____." Then, draw a line from the sentence to the correct picture. Remember to use your good CH sound.

chair

"Life is like a bowl of these."

cheese

"Santa jumps down me."

chipmunk

"I am made from milk."

chin

"I look like a small squirrel."

cherries

"My mother is a hen."

"Goldilocks broke me."

chimney

"I am a part of your face."

children

"We like to play."

chick

Homework Partner | Date | Speech-Language Pathologist

Initial CH Phrases

Story Loop

Directions: Read/say aloud each picture–word. Make up a story using all of the pictures in the circle. You can start anywhere in the circle and go in either direction, but you must always end where you started to complete the loop. Say your story aloud, using your good CH sound.

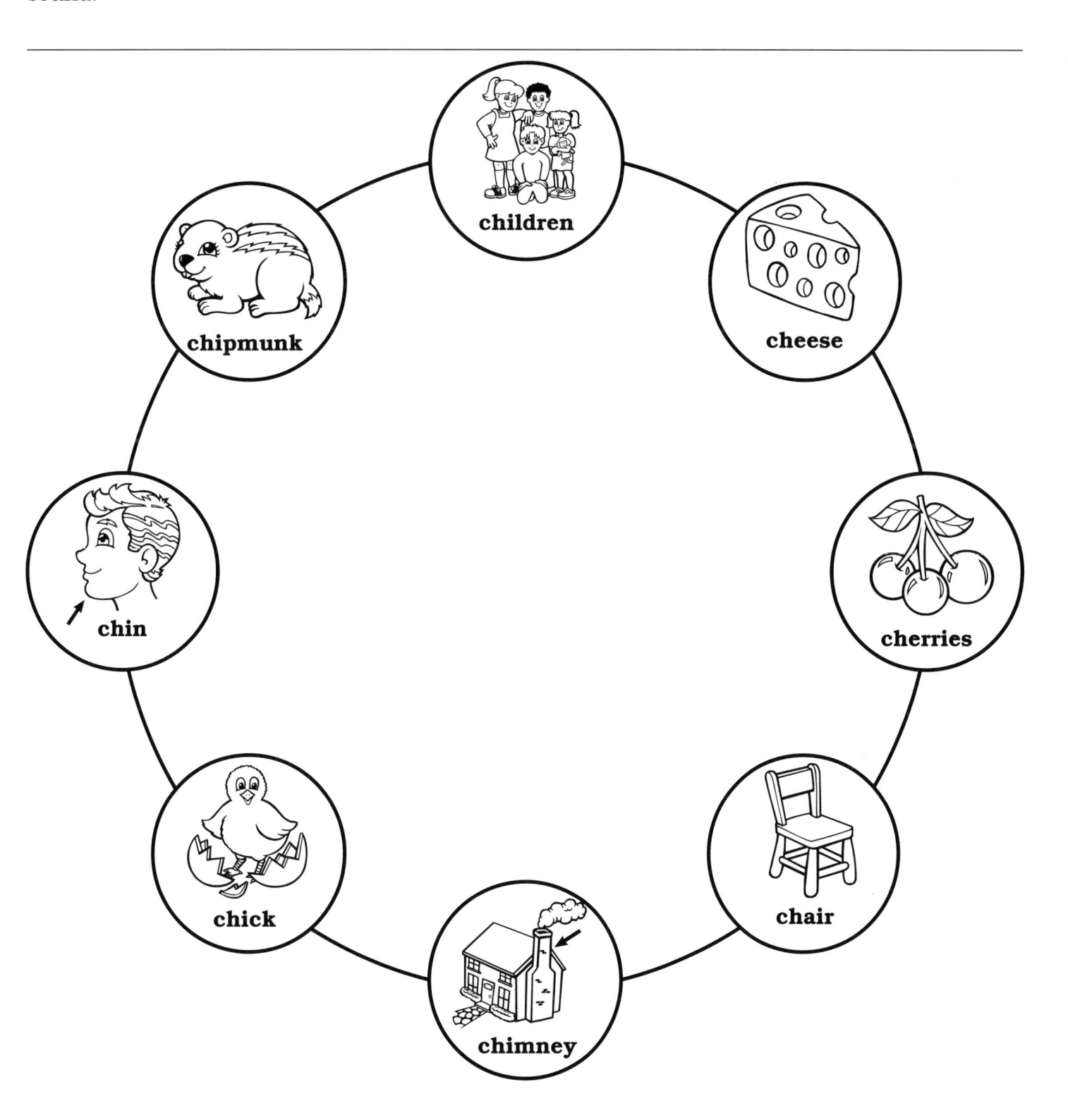

- children
- cheese
- cherries
- chair
- chimney
- chick
- chin
- chipmunk

Homework Partner   Date   Speech-Language Pathologist

Initial CH Sentences

Grid a Sentence

Directions: Pick one word from the side of the grid, and one word from the top, and say or write a sentence using both words. (The chimney is strong.) Use your good CH sound.

	strong	happy	sweet
chimney			
chicken			
chair			
children			
chain			
cheese			

Homework Partner   Date   Speech-Language Pathologist

Initial CH Sentences

Analogies

Directions: Read/say aloud the picture-words below. Then, read each analogy and choose an answer from the Word Bank. Read/say the entire analogy aloud using your good CH sound.

Word Bank

chair   children   chocolate milk   chain

chow mein   cherries   cheese   chimney

1. Squash are to vegetables as _____ are to fruit.

2. Lettuce is to salad as noodles are to _____ .

3. Lemon is to lemonade as cocoa is to _____ .

4. Men and women are to adults as boys and girls are to _____ .

5. String is to thread as rope is to _____ .

6. Exhaust is to muffler as smoke is to _____ .

7. Stool is to counter as _____ is to table.

Answers: 1. cherries 2. chow mein 3. chocolate milk 4. children 5. chain 6. chimney 7. chair

Homework Partner   Date   Speech-Language Pathologist

Initial CH Sentences

3 Games in 1

Directions: Say aloud the picture-words below, using your good CH sound. Then, play one of the following games:

☐ Lotto – Caller reads a word and student repeats the word and covers it with a token/chip.

☐ Tic–Tac–Toe – Each time you write an **X** or **O**, say the word you mark over.

☐ Memory – Cut out all the cards and place face down. Try to find matching pairs. Say aloud each word you find. Keep all matches.

wrench	lunch	crutch
coach	peach	bench
sandwich	ostrich	watch
watch	sandwich	lunch
ostrich	bench	peach
wrench	coach	crutch

Homework Partner   Date   Speech-Language Pathologist   Final CH Words

Finger Hopscotch

Directions: Read/say aloud the picture–words below. Then, slide a penny across the hopscotch board. Hop your finger to the square it lands on. Read/say the name of the picture–word again, practicing your good CH sound. Play again until you have landed on all the words.

bench

hopscotch | witch

coach

sandwich | lunch

ostrich

peach | crutch

watch

START

Homework Partner Date Speech-Language Pathologist

Final CH Words

First to the Top!

Directions: Cut out the number cards and pawns. Place number cards face down. Flip a coin to determine how many spaces to move on the stairs (heads=2, tails=1). Then, turn over a number card. Read/say the picture–word on the step the number of times indicated on the card. If correct, score one point. If incorrect, score no points. The student with the most points at the end wins. Remember to use your good CH sound.

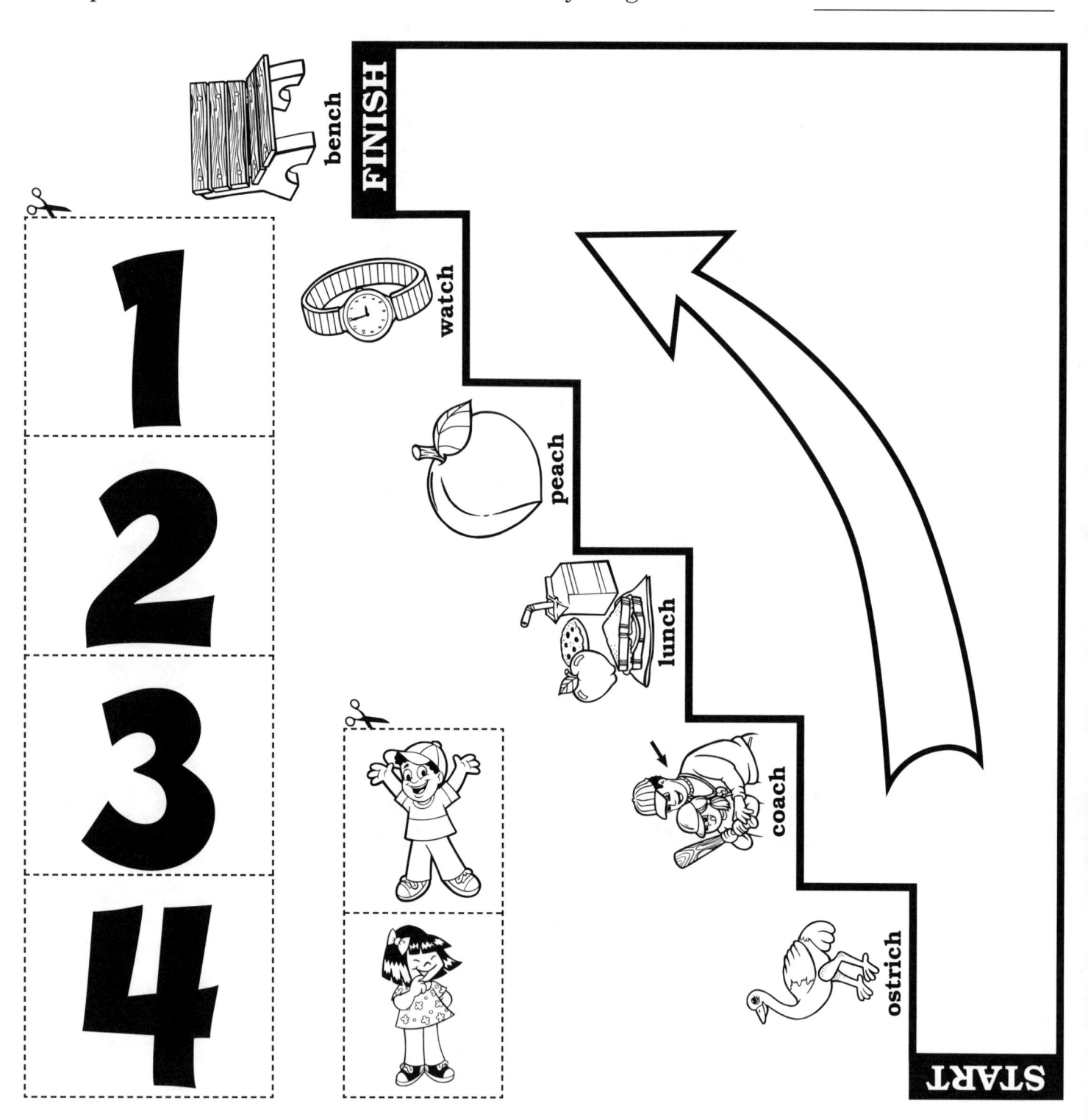

FINISH — bench
watch
peach
lunch
coach
ostrich
START

1
2
3
4

Homework Partner　　Date　　Speech-Language Pathologist

Final CH Words

Watch It!

Directions: Cut out the watch face and hand. Glue this page to construction paper for added durability. Use a brad to connect the hand to the watch. Spin the hand. Read/say the picture–word the hand lands on aloud. Player scores the number of points next to the picture–word. The student with the most points at the end wins. Use your good CH sound.

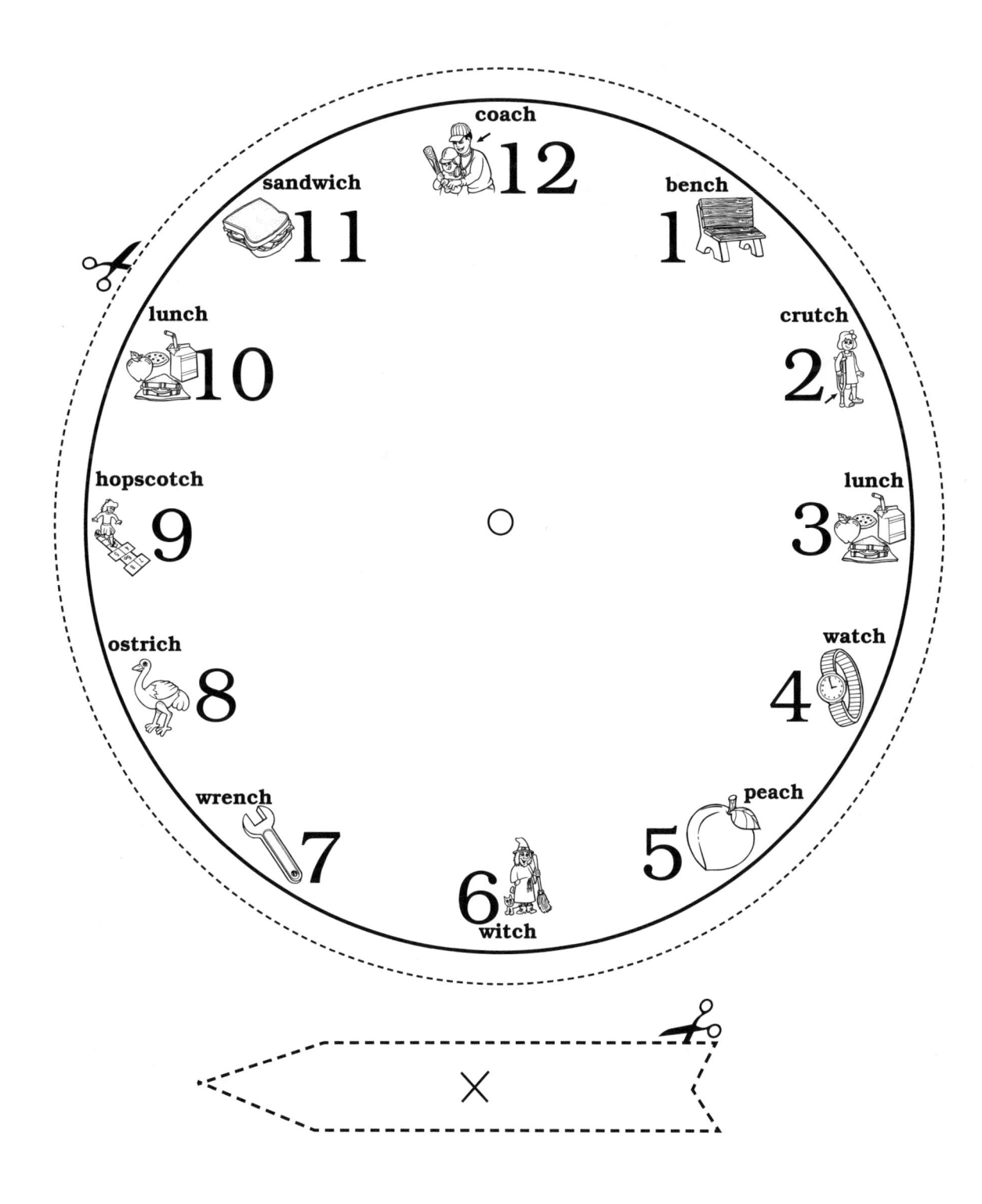

- 12 coach
- 1 bench
- 2 crutch
- 3 lunch
- 4 watch
- 5 peach
- 6 witch
- 7 wrench
- 8 ostrich
- 9 hopscotch
- 10 lunch
- 11 sandwich

Homework Partner • Date • Speech-Language Pathologist

Final CH Words

What's for Lunch?

Directions: Cut out the food below. Cut the slit in the lunchbox. Choose a picture–word to read/say aloud and put it into the lunchbox. Remember to use your good CH sound.

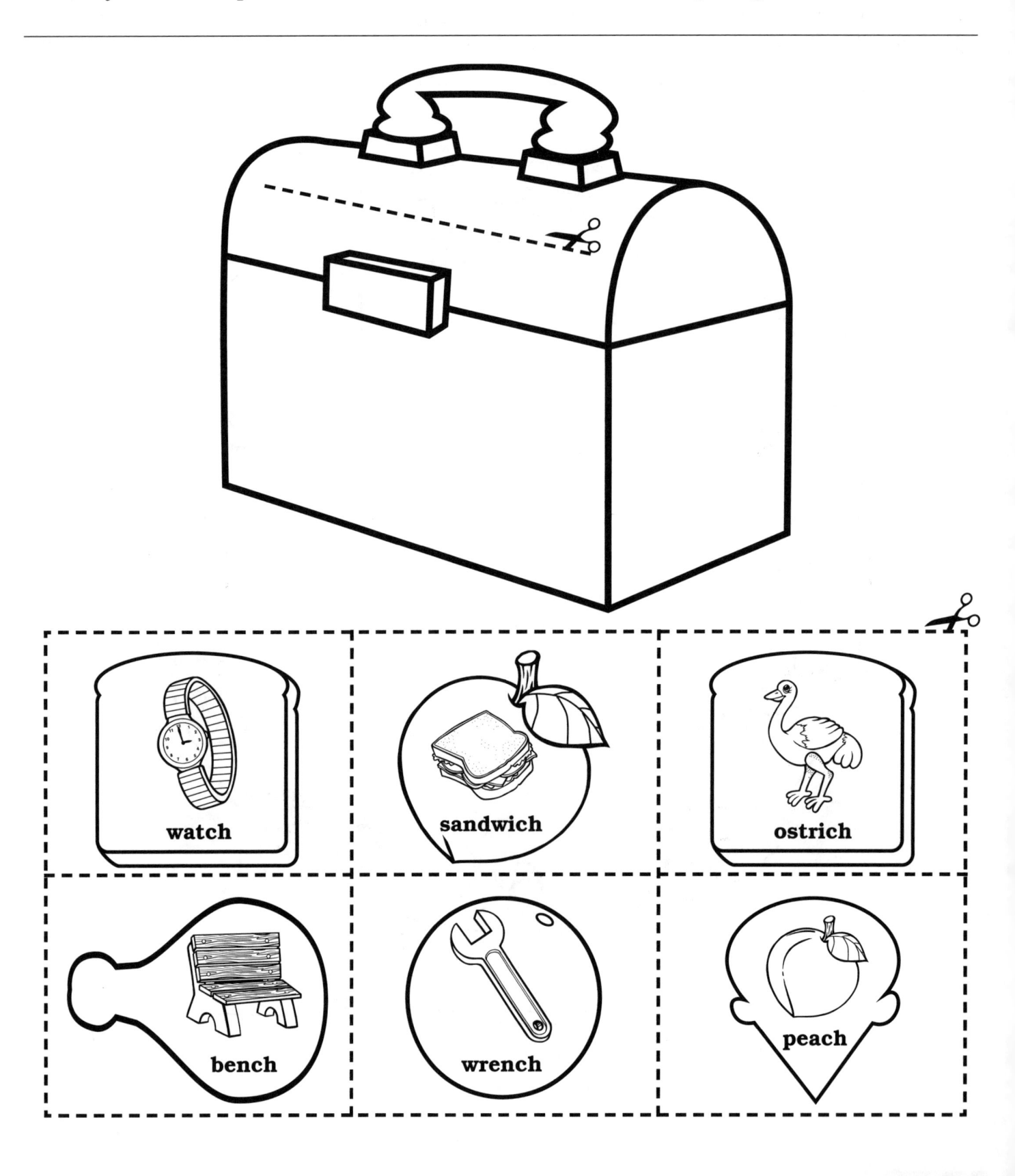

watch

sandwich

ostrich

bench

wrench

peach

_____   _____   _____
Homework Partner   Date   Speech-Language Pathologist

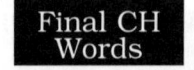

Final CH Words

Newspaper Search

Directions: Read/say aloud each picture–word below. Then, search for and circle the same pictures and/or words in the newspaper. Read/say aloud each one you find. Use your good CH sound.

Word Bank

ostrich   lunch   peach

coach   crutch   bench

The Daily Peach

Coach of the Year!

Gigantic Ostrich Escapes from Zoo!

School Lunch Menu

Girl Climbs Mountain Using One Crutch!

Park Bench Missing

Peach is Voted Favorite Fruit

Homework Partner   Date   Speech-Language Pathologist

Final CH Words

#BK-291 Webber® Artic Fun Sheets 2 • ©2002 Super Duper® Publications • www.superduperinc.com • 1-800-277-8737

Pick a Peach

Directions: Read/say each picture–word below. Then, cut out all the peach pictures below. Say aloud the phrase "_____ in a tree" using each peach word (<u>new watch</u> in a tree). Use your good CH sound. Glue/tape or place the pictures onto the tree.

- new watch
- park bench
- fast ostrich
- yummy sandwich
- scary witch
- lunch hour
- baseball coach
- hopscotch square
- big wrench
- one crutch

Homework Partner Date Speech-Language Pathologist

Final CH Phrases

Hide-and-Seek

Directions: Read/say aloud the picture–words. If you prefer, glue the pictures on a file folder/cardboard. Cut out the pictures and ostrich. Place the pictures face up. Have your partner hide the ostrich under a picture. Name the picture where you think the ostrich is hidden (this peach). Use your good CH sound!

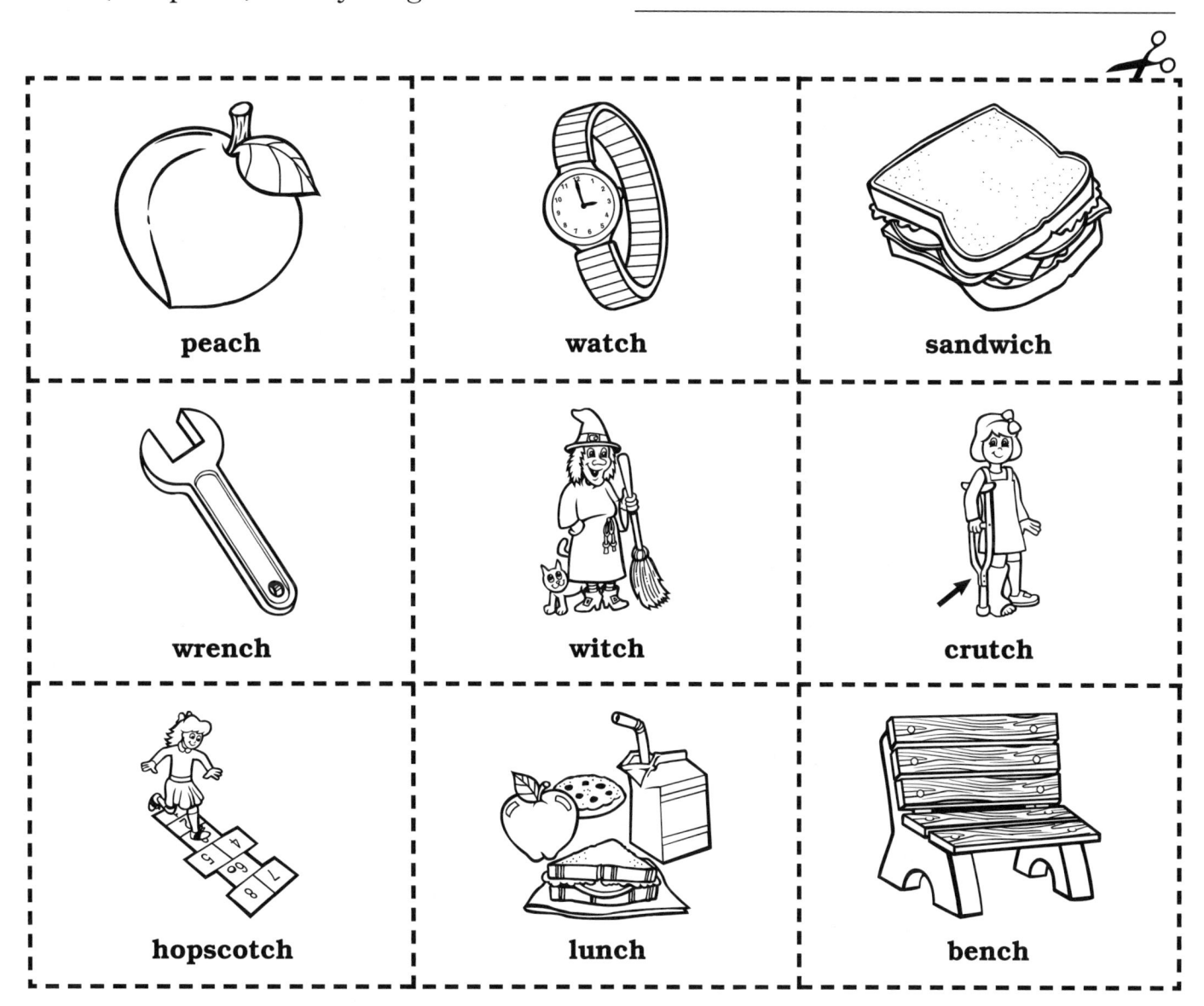

peach	watch	sandwich
wrench	witch	crutch
hopscotch	lunch	bench

Homework Partner   Date   Speech-Language Pathologist

Final CH Phrases

Mine or Yours?

Directions: Read/say each picture–word below. Cut out the pictures. At each turn, flip a coin. Heads means the student keeps the pictures and says, "My _____" (My peach). Tails means that the student gives the picture to his partner and says, "Your _____" (Your peach). Player with the most pictures at the end wins.

wrench	**lunch**
crutch	**peach**
witch	**hopscotch**
bench	**watch**
coach	**ostrich**

Homework Partner   Date   Speech-Language Pathologist

Final CH Phrases

Which One?

Directions: Read the questions. Then, circle the correct answer to the questions. Read/say each answer aloud using a complete sentence. (An ostrich lays eggs.) Use your good CH sound.

1. Which one lays eggs?

   ostrich   **peach**

2. Which one tells time?

   sandwich   **watch**

3. Which one is a fruit?

   bench   **peach**

4. Which one do you sit on?

   bench   **hopscotch**

5. Which one is a tool?

   coach   **wrench**

6. Which one is a game?

   hopscotch   **witch**

7. Which one is a meal?

   lunch   **ostrich**

8. Which one runs a team?

   crutch   **coach**

Homework Partner   Date   Speech-Language Pathologist

Final CH Sentences

Pick One

Directions: Cut out the cards below. Shuffle and place face down, keeping piles A, B, and C separate. Pick one card from each pile to make a silly sentence. (A sandwich grew.) Read/say each sentence aloud, using your good CH sound.

A	B	C
A	watch	dropped.
His	sandwich	grew.
One	ostrich	broke.
My	peach	ticks.
Your	crutch	flew.

Homework Partner   Date   Speech-Language Pathologist

Final CH Sentences

Get to the Coach

Directions: Flip a coin to advance – one space for tails, two spaces for heads. Read/say each sentence as you move around the bases. First student to get home to the coach wins.

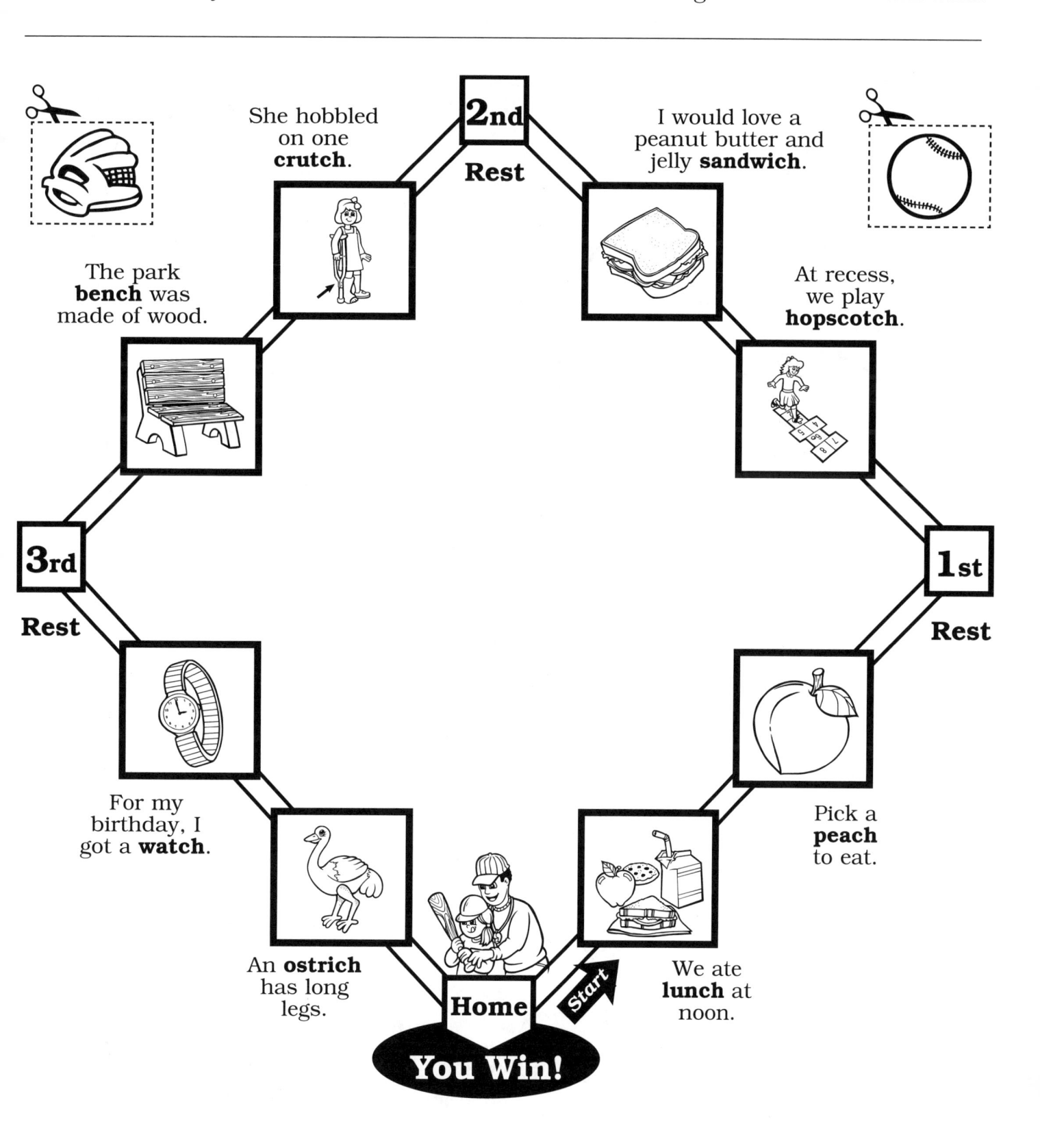

2nd Rest

1st Rest

3rd Rest

Home – You Win!

Start

She hobbled on one **crutch**.

I would love a peanut butter and jelly **sandwich**.

The park **bench** was made of wood.

At recess, we play **hopscotch**.

For my birthday, I got a **watch**.

Pick a **peach** to eat.

An **ostrich** has long legs.

We ate **lunch** at noon.

Homework Partner   Date   Speech-Language Pathologist

Final CH Sentences

Beachball Bonanza

Directions: Cut out the beachballs and place them face down. As you turn over a card, read/say aloud the word on the card. Turn over another card to try to find a match. Most matches wins. Remember to use your good CH sound.

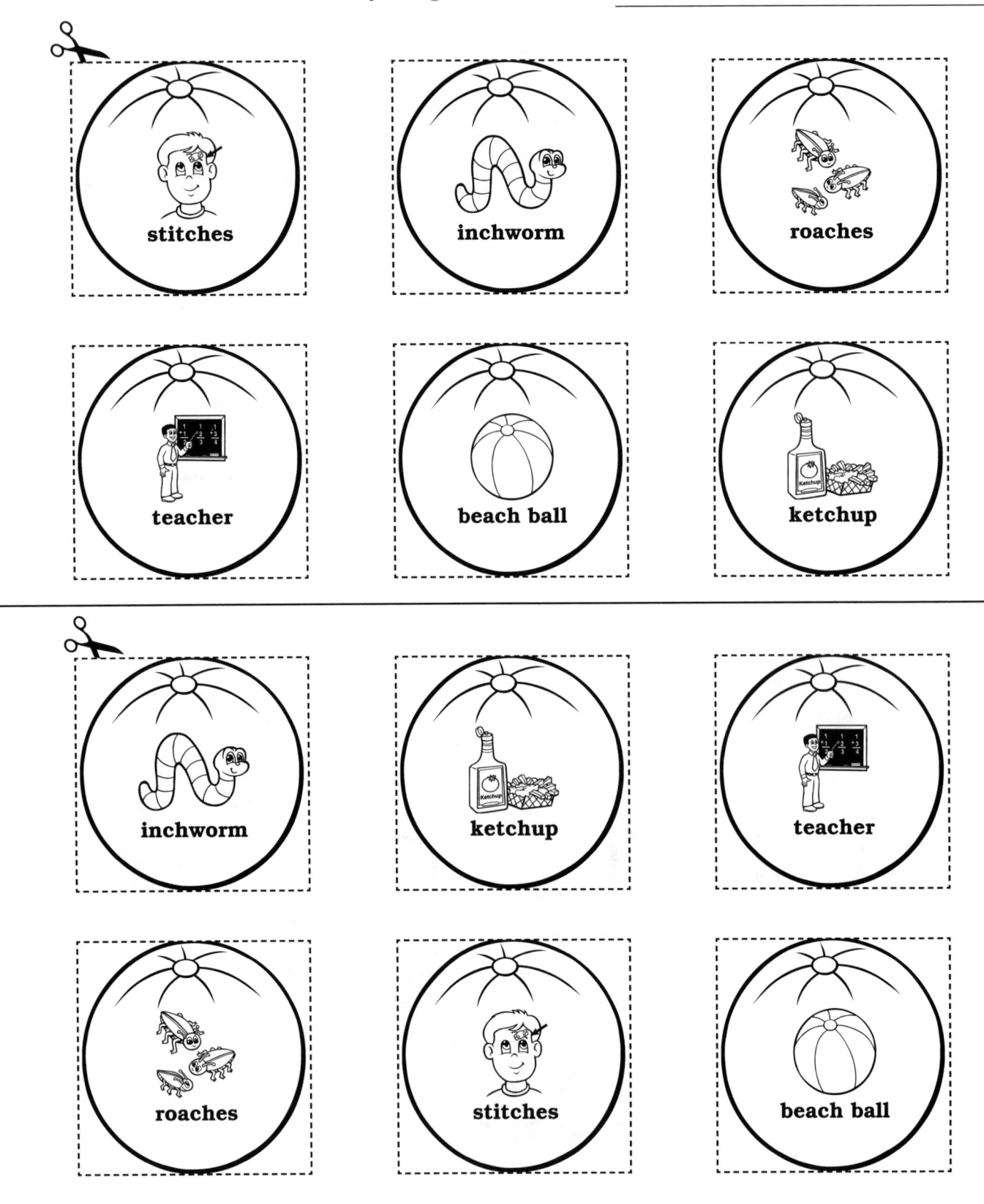

stitches	inchworm	roaches
teacher	beach ball	ketchup
inchworm	ketchup	teacher
roaches	stitches	beach ball

Homework Partner   Date   Speech-Language Pathologist

Medial CH Words

64 #BK-291 Webber® Artic Fun Sheets 2 • ©2002 Super Duper® Publications • www.superduperinc.com • 1-800-277-8737

Which Witch?

Directions: Read/say aloud each picture–word on the witches on the left. Then, find the broom on the right with the same CH word in it. Draw a line to connect the witch to the word, and read/say both words twice (ketchup, ketchup). Remember to use your good CH sound.

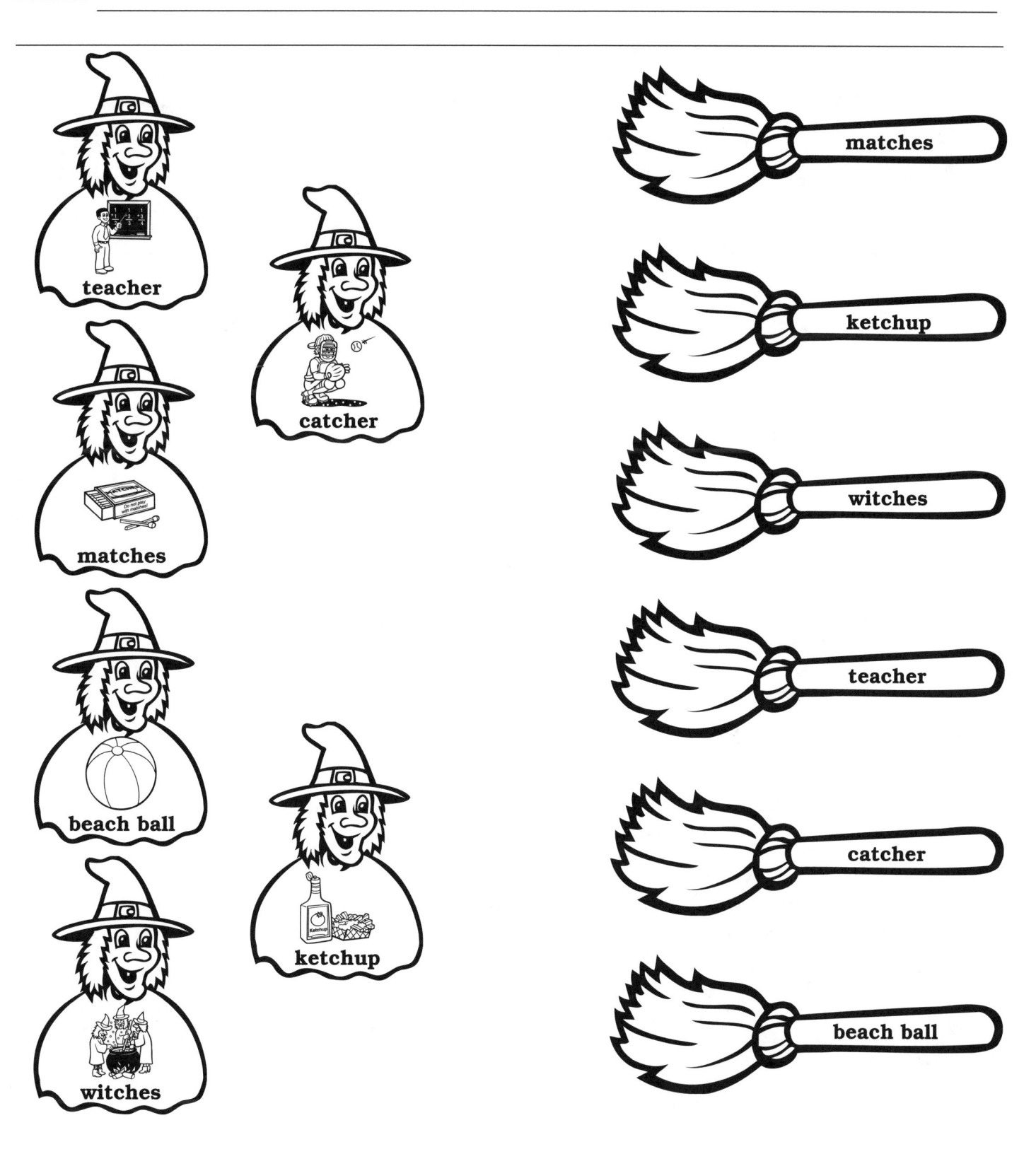

Witches (left): teacher, catcher, matches, beach ball, ketchup, witches

Brooms (right): matches, ketchup, witches, teacher, catcher, beach ball

Homework Partner   Date   Speech-Language Pathologist

Medial CH Words

CH Baseball

Directions: "Hit" each ball below with your bat. As you hit a ball, say the CH word on it.

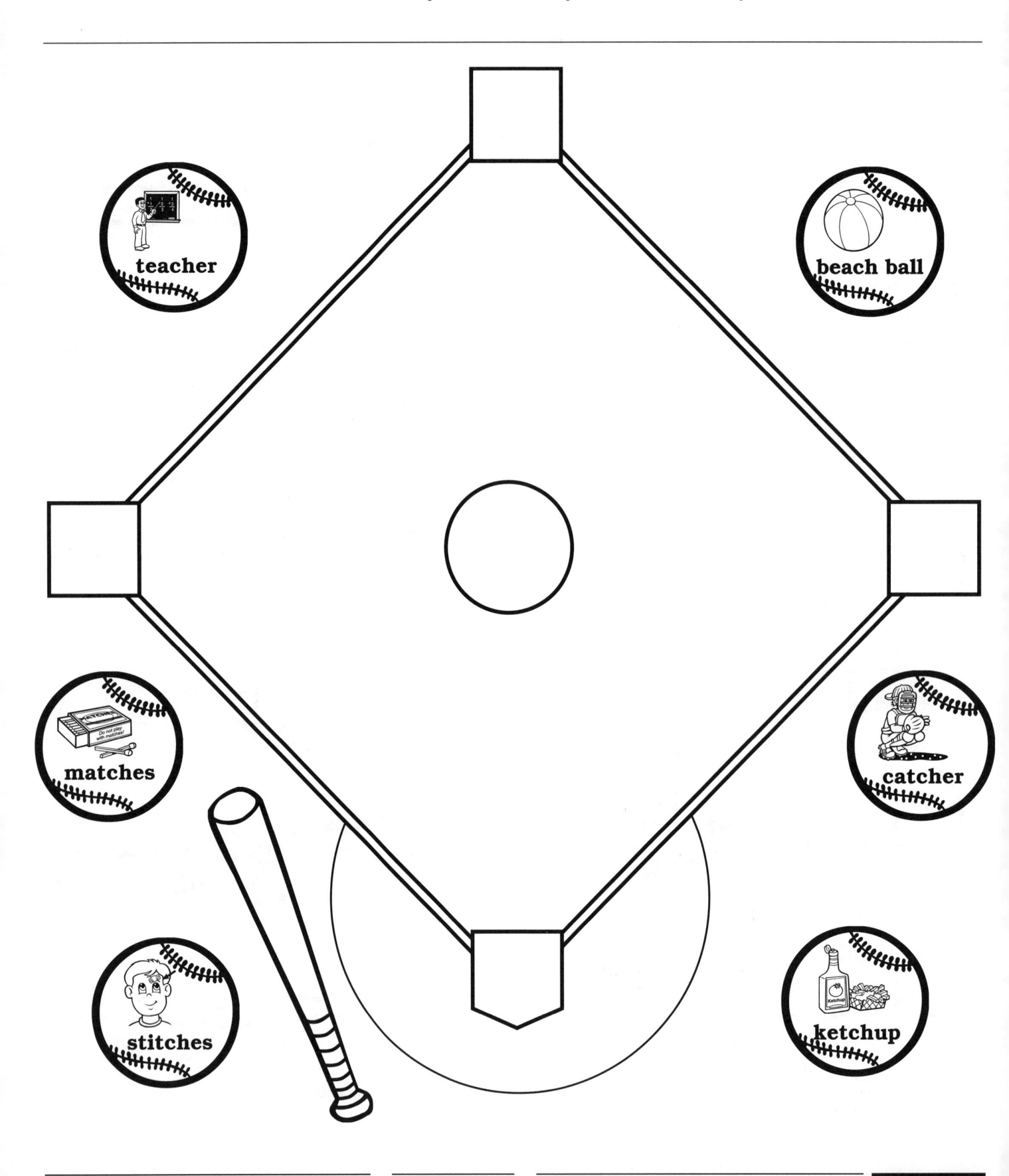

- teacher
- beach ball
- matches
- catcher
- stitches
- ketchup

Homework Partner   Date   Speech-Language Pathologist

Medial CH Words

Spin the Ketchup Bottle

Directions: Cut out the ketchup bottle and cards below. If you prefer, glue the bottle to construction paper for added durability. Spin the bottle, draw a card, and read the clue aloud. The student with the bottle pointing at them must guess the target word. Remember to use your good CH sound.

You see these at Halloween. **witches**	This person works at school in a classroom. **teacher**	These help to light a campfire. **matches**
This player kneels behind home plate. **catcher**	We set traps for these bugs. **roaches**	This toy is fun to play with at the beach. **beach ball**
You get these from the doctor after cutting yourself. **stitches**	This is made of tomatoes and comes in a bottle. **ketchup**	This creature is like a caterpillar. **inchworm**

Homework Partner   Date   Speech-Language Pathologist

Medial CH Words

Get a Clue

Directions: Read each clue sentence aloud. Then, guess the answer from the Word Bank below. Read/say each word aloud, using your good CH sound.

1. You eat this on hamburgers.

2. You light a fire with these.

3. You play with this at the beach.

4. The player on the baseball team who wears a mask.

5. They ride brooms at Halloween.

6. Bugs that crawl on the floor.

7. The thing that helps a wound heal.

8. The creature that helps you catch fish.

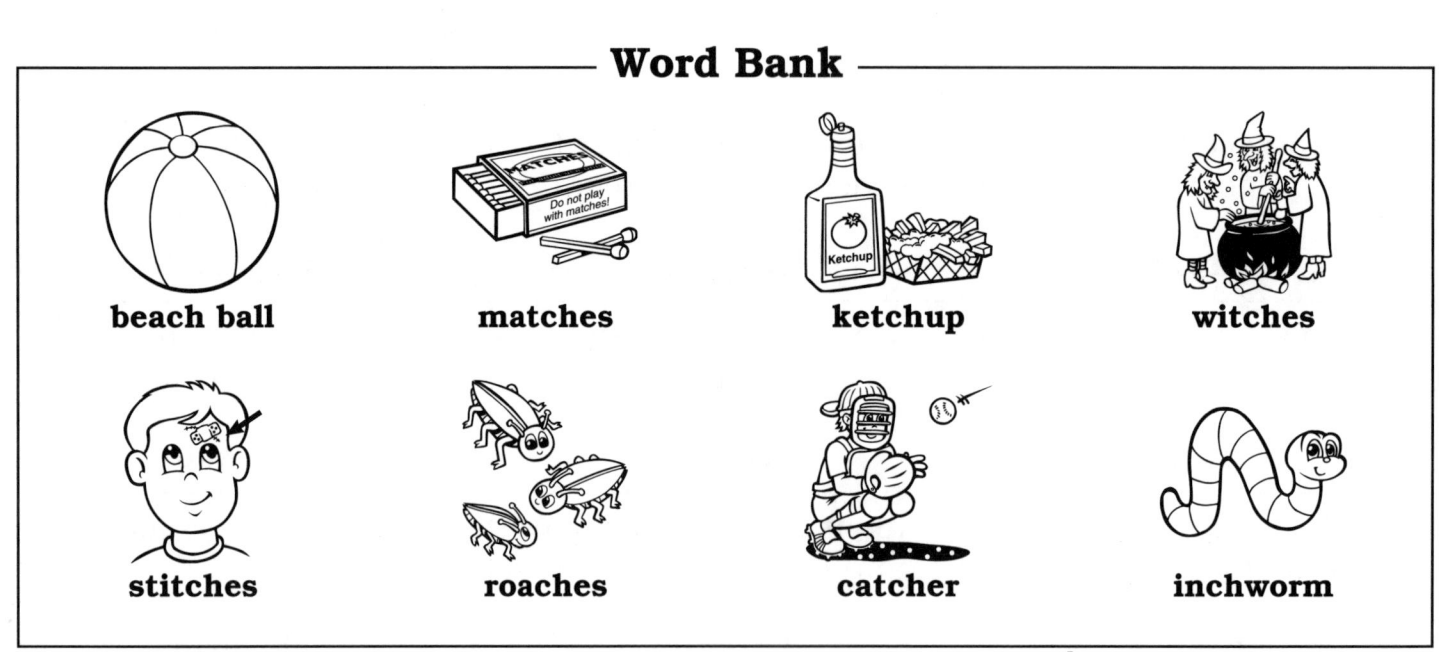

Word Bank

| beach ball | matches | ketchup | witches |
| stitches | roaches | catcher | inchworm |

Answers: 1. ketchup, 2. matches, 3. beach ball, 4. catcher, 5. witches, 6. roaches, 7. stitches, 8. inchworm

Homework Partner   Date   Speech-Language Pathologist

Medial CH Words

Say It Fast!

Directions: Read/say the words on the left quickly and determine which picture–word on the right it matches. Then, read/say the words aloud.

1. Which is?    **teacher**

2. Teach her    **matches**

3. Catch up    **stitches**

4. Stitch his    **witches**

5. Catch her    **catcher**

6. Match his    **ketchup**

Homework Partner   Date   Speech-Language Pathologist

Medial CH Words

Find the Witch's Broom

Directions: Read/say aloud the picture–words below. Then, cut out the markers. Flip a coin (heads=1, tails=2) to determine how many spaces to move. As you move, use each word in a phrase aloud, using your good CH sound. First player to reach the finish wins. _____

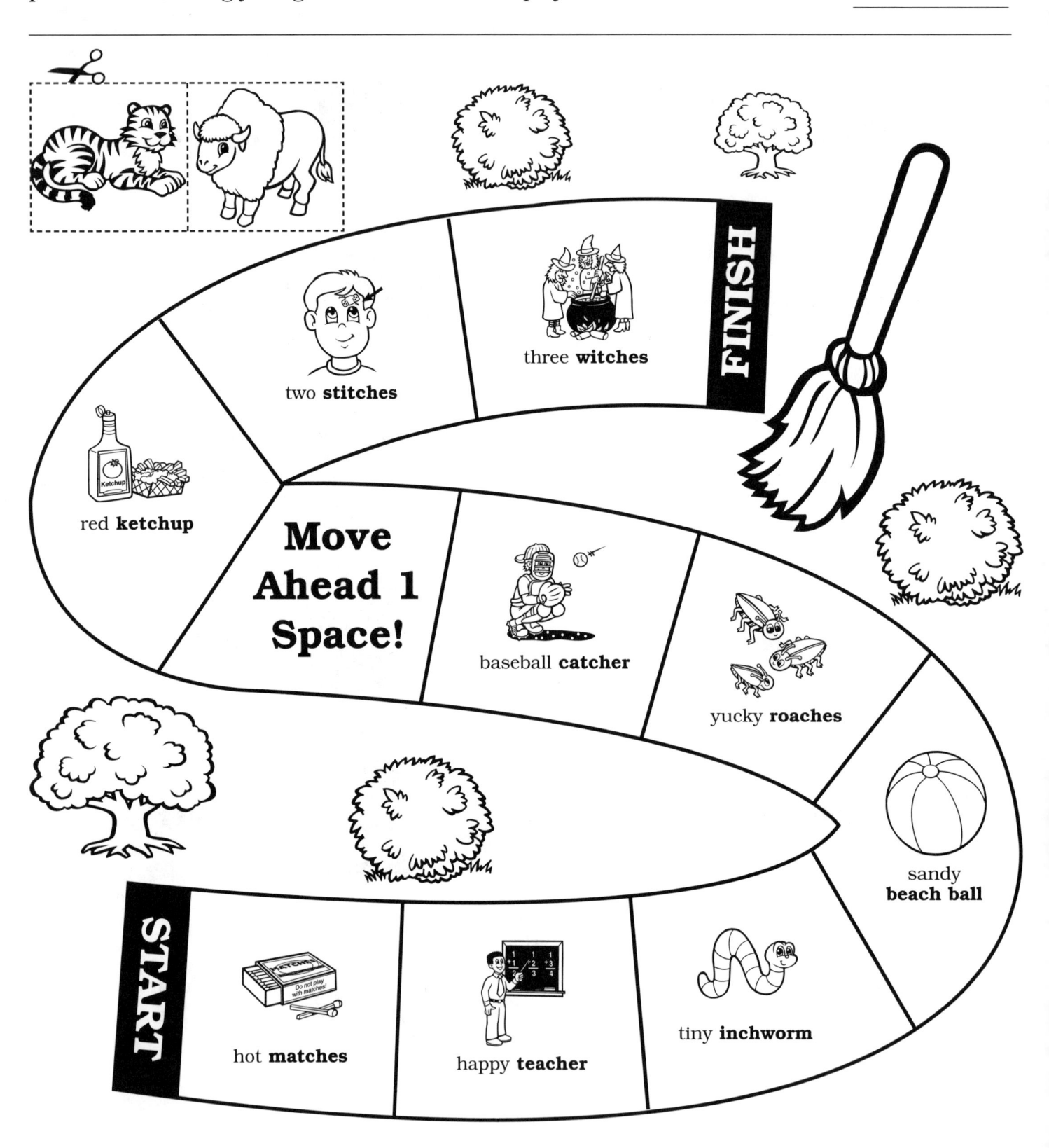

three **witches**

two **stitches**

red **ketchup**

Move Ahead 1 Space!

baseball **catcher**

yucky **roaches**

sandy **beach ball**

tiny **inchworm**

happy **teacher**

hot **matches**

FINISH

START

Homework Partner   Date   Speech-Language Pathologist

Medial CH Phrases

X and O

Directions: Cut out each **X** and **O** below. Have each player/partner choose **X** or **O**. The first player reads/says a picture–phrase aloud and places an **X** or **O** on the square. Play continues in turn. The first person to get three in a row wins. _____

catcher's mitt	two stitches	happy teacher
my beach ball	scary witches	yummy ketchup
yucky roaches	green inchworm	hot matches

X X X X X

O O O O O

_____ _____ _____ **Medial CH Phrases**
Homework Partner   Date   Speech-Language Pathologist

Descripto Match

Directions: Read/say aloud the picture–words on the right. Then, draw a line from the describing word on the left to a picture–word it describes. There may be more than one describing word for each picture. Then, read/say each phrase aloud (bouncy beach ball). Remember to use your good CH sound!

1. slimy

inchworm

2. bouncy

3. happy

teacher

4. yummy

matches

5. fast

beach ball

6. hot

7. red

ketchup

8. yucky

catcher

9. short

10. cool

roaches

Homework Partner Date Speech-Language Pathologist

Medial CH Phrases

Number It Up!

Directions: Read/say aloud the picture–words. Number the words in the Word Bank below from 1-8. Then, put the words on the line below that match the corresponding numbers. Read/say the sentences aloud using your good CH sound.

_____

---- **Word Bank** ----

catcher ____   roaches ____   beach ball ____   matches ____

stitches ____   teacher ____   ketchup ____   inchworm ____

---

1. Don't spill the _____.

2. The _____ hit the ball.

3. Talk with the _____.

4. The _____ is/are the best.

5. The doctor removed the _____.

6. Get the _____.

7. Please catch the _____.

8. I found the _____.

Homework Partner   Date   Speech-Language Pathologist

Medial CH Sentences

#BK-291 Webber® Artic Fun Sheets 2 • ©2002 Super Duper® Publications • www.superduperinc.com • 1-800-277-8737

73

Add It Up!

Directions: Copy and cut out the picture–word cards below. Place the cards face down in a pile. Choose a card and roll a die. Then, make up a sentence with the same number of words as the number on the die. Remember to use your good CH sound.

witches	roaches	teacher
inchworm	matches	stitches
ketchup	beach ball	catcher

Homework Partner Date Speech-Language Pathologist

Medial CH Sentences

True/False

Directions: Read the sentences below. Decide which ending makes the sentence true or false. Then, put a **T** for true and **F** for false on the line next to the correct answer. Read/say each true sentence aloud, using your good CH sound.

1. **Ketchup**...
   _____A. is yummy on hamburgers.
   _____B. can be blue.

2. **Matches**...
   _____A. should only be used by adults.
   _____B. can be used underwater.

3. A **beach ball**...
   _____A. is found at the zoo.
   _____B. is a very large ball.

4. A **teacher**...
   _____A. is someone who fixes cars.
   _____B. helps you learn.

5. **Witches**...
   _____A. like cats and fly on brooms.
   _____B. work at the post office.

True Answers: 1. A, 2. A, 3. B, 4. B, 5. A

Homework Partner   Date   Speech-Language Pathologist

Medial CH Sentences

Spin a Sentence

Directions: Read/say aloud the picture–words below. If you prefer, glue this page to construction paper for added durability. Cut out the arrow/dial. Use a brad to connect the dial to the circle. Spin the spinner. When you land on a sentence, complete the sentence by choosing the correct picture. Read/say the sentence aloud, using your good CH sound.

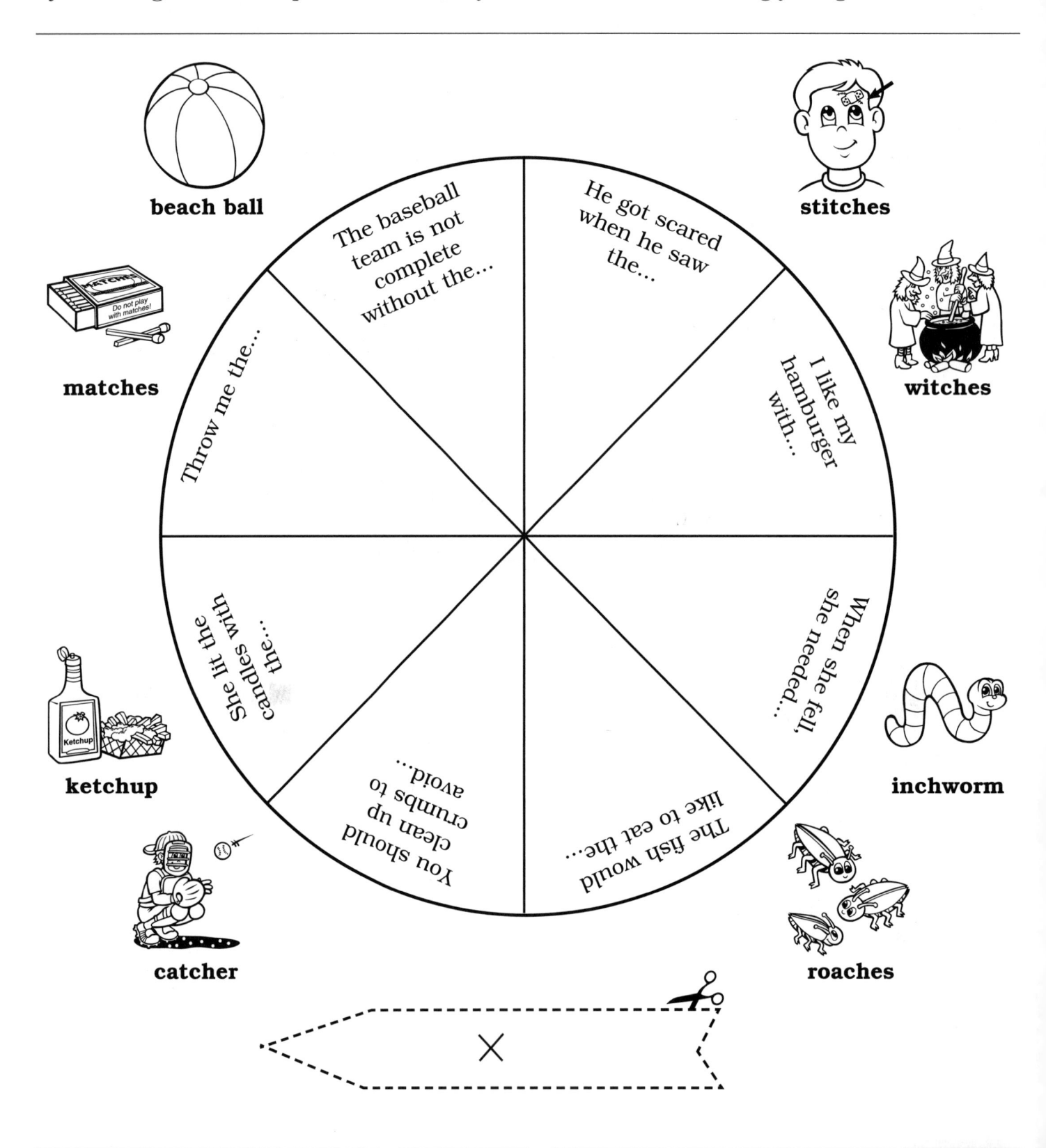

beach ball

matches

ketchup

catcher

stitches

witches

inchworm

roaches

Spinner sentences:
- The baseball team is not complete without the...
- He got scared when he saw the...
- I like my hamburger with...
- When she fell, she needed...
- The fish would like to eat the...
- You should clean up crumbs to avoid...
- She lit the candles with the...
- Throw me the...

Homework Partner   Date   Speech-Language Pathologist

Medial CH Sentences

TH Sound

Put On a Thimble

Directions: Read/say aloud the picture–words below. Cut out the thimbles. As you say each word correctly, place a thimble on a finger or thumb. Once all the fingers and thumbs have thimbles, read/say aloud each of the words again, using your good TH sound.

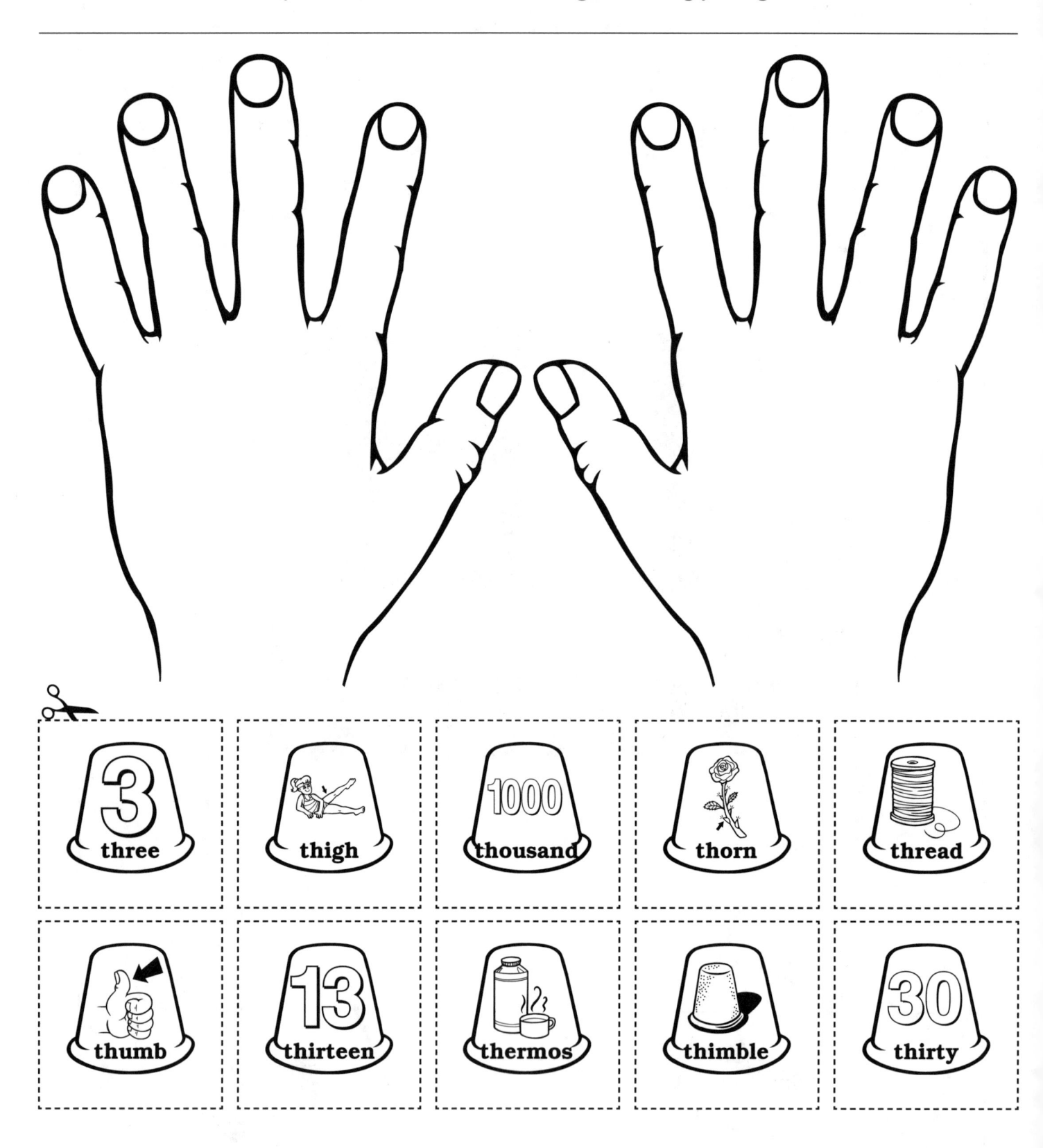

three	thigh	thousand	thorn	thread
thumb	thirteen	thermos	thimble	thirty

Homework Partner　　Date　　Speech-Language Pathologist

Initial TH Words

Temperature Rising

Directions: Read/say aloud the picture–words below. Then, cut out the markers. Flip a coin (heads=1, tails=2) to determine how many spaces to move. As you move, read/say each word aloud, using your good TH sound. First player to reach the finish wins.

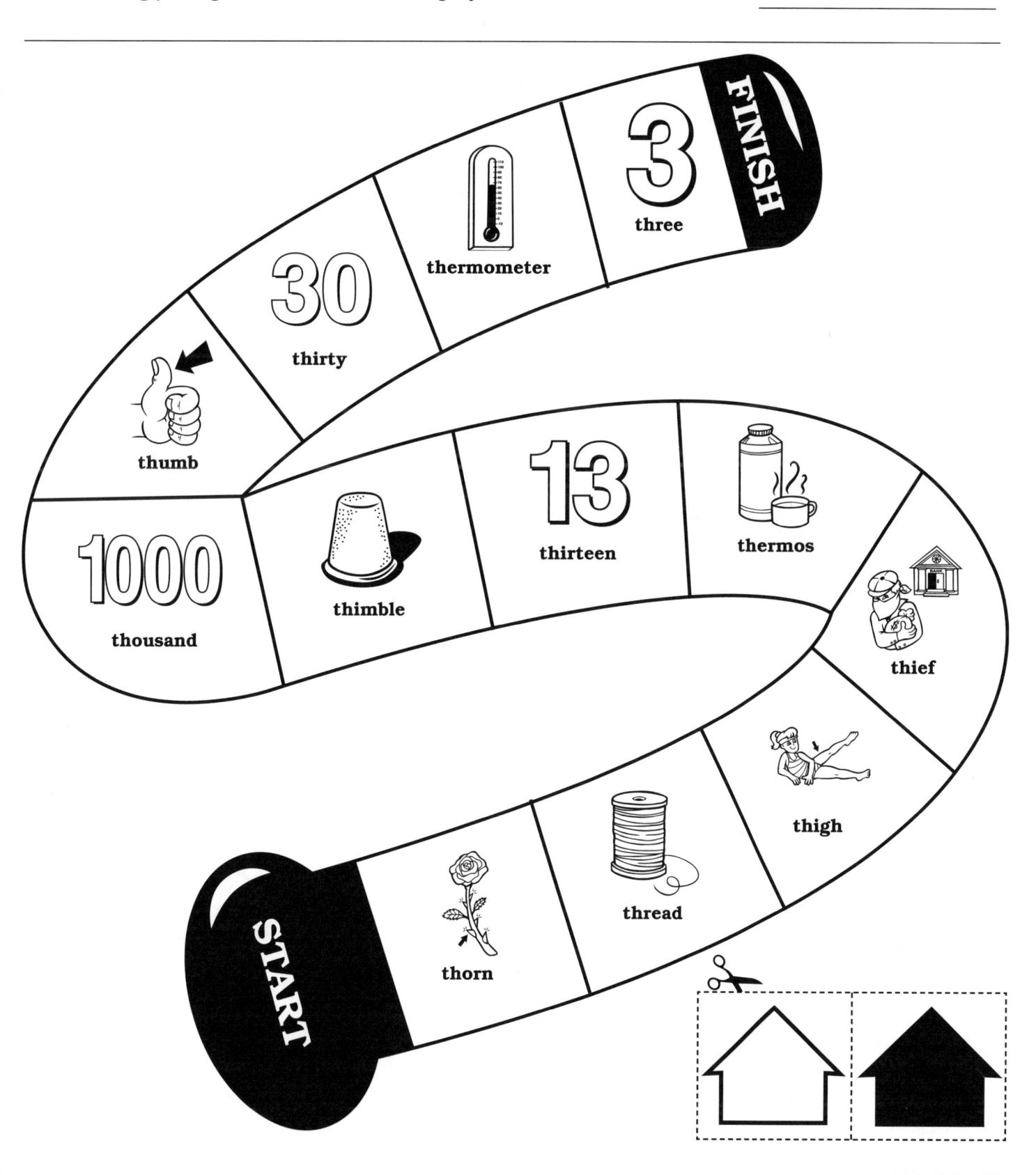

FINISH — three — thermometer — thirty — thumb — thousand — thimble — thirteen — thermos — thief — thigh — thread — thorn — **START**

Homework Partner   Date   Speech-Language Pathologist

Initial TH Words

Three Little Birds

Directions: Cut out each of the feathers below. As you glue/paste or place three tail feathers on each bird, read/say aloud the picture–word on each feather. Remember to use your good TH sound.

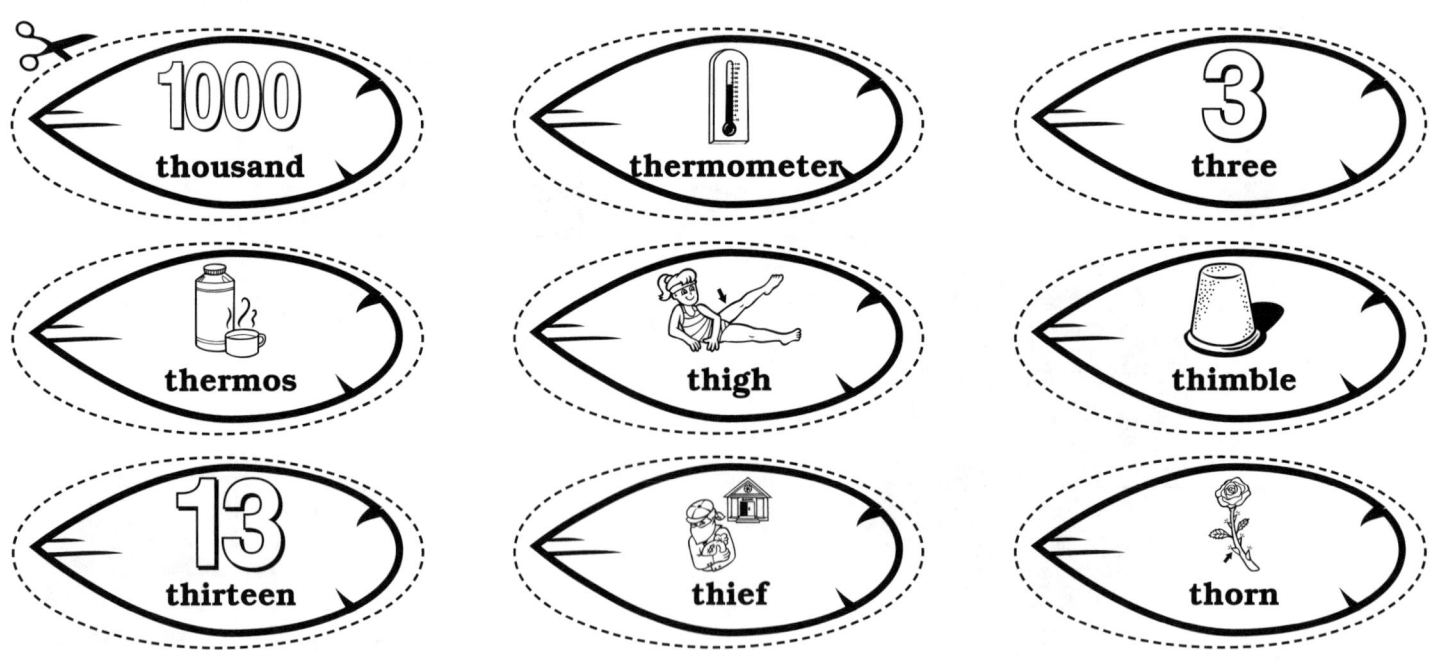

thousand	thermometer	three
thermos	thigh	thimble
thirteen	thief	thorn

Homework Partner   Date   Speech-Language Pathologist

Initial TH Words

Thumbs Up!

Directions: Copy and cut out all the pictures below. Have student read/say word on thumb. If correct, keep cards in the thumbs up position. If incorrect, change to thumbs down. Student gets one chance to fix thumbs down. Student with the most thumbs up is the winner.

three	thimble	thigh
thousand	thread	thirteen
thumb	thief	thermos

Homework Partner   Date   Speech-Language Pathologist

Initial TH Words

Blend It!

Directions: Say the TH sound on the left. Then, slowly blend into the word ending on the right (th...ree). Roll a die to determine how many times to read/say the word aloud. Use your best TH sound as you say all the words.

th

| .....ermometer |
| .....ermos |
| .....irteen |
| .....ree |
| .....umb |
| .....read |
| .....igh |
| .....ief |
| .....imble |
| .....orn |
| .....ousand |
| .....irty |

Homework Partner   Date   Speech-Language Pathologist

Initial TH Words

Which One?

Directions: Read the questions. Then, circle the correct answer to the questions. Read/say each answer aloud using your best TH sound.

1. Which one comes after twelve?

    thread   **thirteen**

2. Which one is found on a rose?

    thorn   **thermos**

3. Which one do you use with a needle?

    thermometer   **thread**

4. Which one is someone who steals?

    thief   **thigh**

5. Which one holds hot or cold drinks?

    thermos   **thimble**

6. Which one tells the temperature?

    thumb   **thermometer**

7. Which one is part of your leg?

    thigh   **thief**

8. Which one is on your hand?

    thirteen   **thumb**

Answers: 1. thirteen, 2. thorn, 3. thread, 4. thief, 5. thermos, 6. thermometer, 7. thigh, 8. thumb

Homework Partner   Date   Speech-Language Pathologist   Initial TH Words

Yo-De-Lay-De-Hoo Game

Directions: Read/say aloud the picture–words below. Then, cut out the markers. Flip a coin (heads=1, tails=2) to determine how many spaces to move. As you move, read/say each phrase aloud, using your good TH sound. First player to reach the finish wins.

FINISH

- sneaky thief
- three mice
- my thumbnail
- silver thimble
- thousand dollars
- Climb Up 1 Space!
- glass thermometer
- rose thorn
- thirteen boys
- blue thread
- coffee thermos
- thirty years
- my thigh

START

Homework Partner Date Speech-Language Pathologist

Initial TH Phrases

84 #BK-291 Webber® Artic Fun Sheets 2 • ©2002 Super Duper® Publications • www.superduperinc.com • 1-800-277-8737

Too Hot!

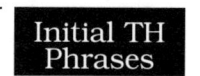

Directions: Cut out the cards below. Shuffle and place them face down. Draw a card and read/say the picture–word. Then, say the word in a phrase using one of the words on the left of the thermometer (my + thread). Every time you say a phrase, color in 10° on the thermometer. Reach 120°, you're **too hot!**

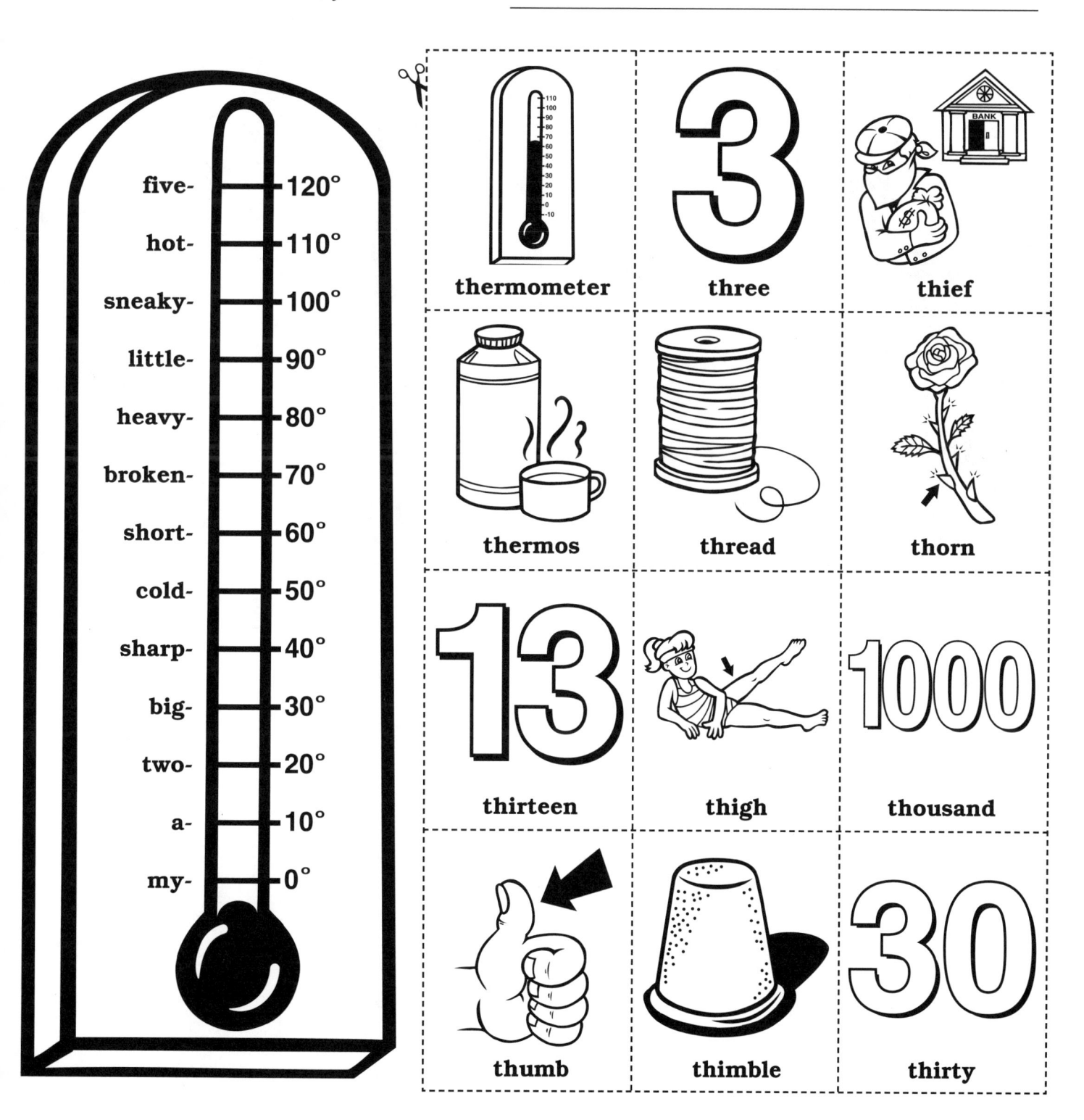

Thermometer labels:
- five- 120°
- hot- 110°
- sneaky- 100°
- little- 90°
- heavy- 80°
- broken- 70°
- short- 60°
- cold- 50°
- sharp- 40°
- big- 30°
- two- 20°
- a- 10°
- my- 0°

Cards:
thermometer	three	thief
thermos	thread	thorn
thirteen	thigh	thousand
thumb	thimble	thirty

Homework Partner · Date · Speech-Language Pathologist

Initial TH Phrases

Cut Out a Phrase

Directions: Cut out the cards below and separate into A and B piles. Have the students draw a card from each pile and make a phrase with the words. Read/say the phrase aloud, using a good TH sound (a fat thief).

A	A	A	A
thimble	thorn	thread	thigh
A thief	**A** thermos	**A** thermometer	**A** thumb
B hard	**B** long	**B** tiny	**B** cold
B heavy	**B** fat	**B** sticky	**B** sneaky

Homework Partner   Date   Speech-Language Pathologist

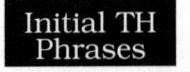

Initial TH Phrases

Thread a Needle

Directions: Draw a line or use thread to connect the sentences that make sense. Connect the sentences through the eye of the needle. Read/say the sentences aloud, using your good TH sound.

1. It says it is 90°

2. The police

3. She poured the soup

4. She bruised

5. Grandmother put

A. her **thigh**.

B. caught a **thief**.

C. on the **thermometer**.

D. into the **thermos**.

E. the **thimble** on her finger.

Answers: 1. C, 2. B, 3. D, 4. A, 5. E

Homework Partner   Date   Speech-Language Pathologist

Initial TH Sentences

#BK-291 Webber® Artic Fun Sheets 2 • ©2002 Super Duper® Publications • www.superduperinc.com • 1-800-277-8737

87

Yes or No?

Directions: Read the questions. Then, put an X in the correct boxes. Say your answers aloud in sentence form. (Yes, two comes after three.) Remember to use your best TH sound.

	Yes	No
1. Is a thigh part of the arm?	☐	☐
2. Does thirty come before thirty-four?	☐	☐
3. Do you put a thimble on your toes?	☐	☐
4. Does a thief take someone's money?	☐	☐
5. Does a thermometer tell time?	☐	☐
6. Can a thorn prick you?	☐	☐
7. Does the American flag have thirteen stripes?	☐	☐
8. Does a hand have four fingers and a thumb?	☐	☐
9. Does two come after three?	☐	☐

Homework Partner   Date   Speech-Language Pathologist

Initial TH Sentences

One, Two, Three, Roll a Silly Sentence

Directions: Each student gets three turns to roll the die. Each turn represents a phrase to be used in a silly sentence. For example, a student who rolls a two, five, and one will make a sentence with the phrases: "The little girl lost some thread and slept all day." Read/say each sentence aloud using your good TH sound.

	Roll One	Roll Two	Roll Three
1.	Thirty cows	ate grass	and slept all day.
2.	A little girl	saw a thief	on a roof.
3.	A beautiful rose	grew	into a thimble.
4.	An ugly duckling	found one thousand dollars	and swam downstream.
5.	A red shirt	lost some thread	under a bed.
6.	My aching thumb	bought a book	and drank milk.

Homework Partner   Date   Speech-Language Pathologist

Initial TH Sentences

How Many Times?

Directions: Read/say aloud the picture–words. Cut out the picture–word cards and turn them face down. Turn over a card and roll a die. Read/say the word as many times as shown on the die. Remember to use your good TH sound.

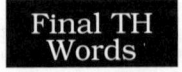

earth	moth	mouth
cloth	telephone booth	wreath
birdbath	sloth	tooth

Homework Partner   Date   Speech-Language Pathologist

Final TH Words

Decorate a Wreath

Directions: Cut out the picture–words below. As you read/say each picture–word aloud, glue the pictures onto the wreath. Use your good TH sound.

| tooth | birdbath | sloth | cloth | telephone booth |

| earth | mouth | moth | wreath | teeth |

Homework Partner   Date   Speech-Language Pathologist   **Final TH Words**

Mouth Maze

Directions: Read/say aloud the picture–words below. Then, cut out the markers. Flip a coin (heads=1, tails=2) to determine how many spaces to move. As you move, read/say each word aloud, using your good TH sound. First player to reach the finish wins.

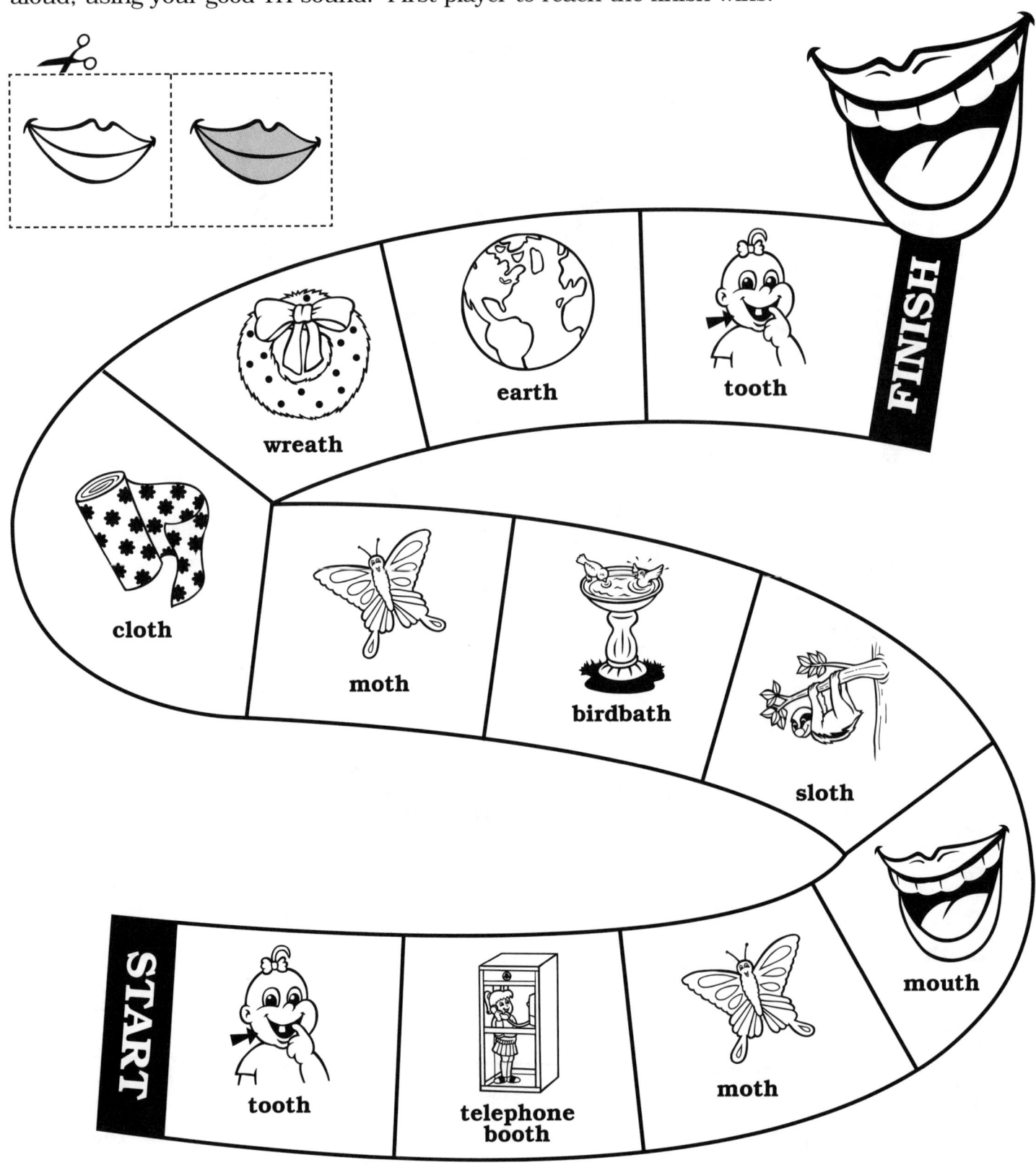

START — tooth — telephone booth — moth — mouth — sloth — birdbath — moth — cloth — wreath — earth — tooth — **FINISH**

Homework Partner   Date   Speech-Language Pathologist

Final TH Words

Where on Earth?

Directions: Cut out the continents below. Read/say the picture–word on the continent, using your good TH sound. Then, glue/tape or place it on the earth.

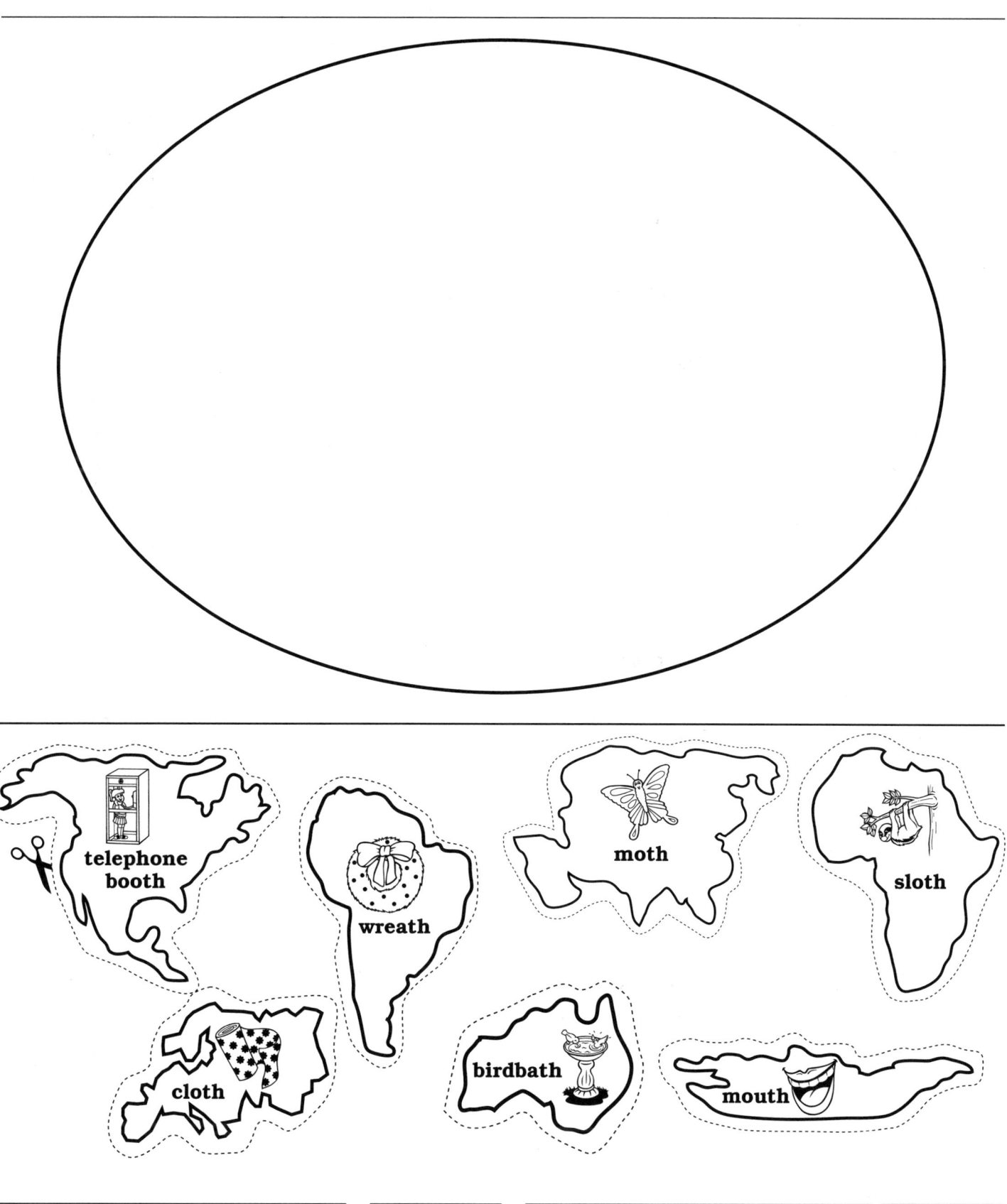

- telephone booth
- wreath
- moth
- sloth
- cloth
- birdbath
- mouth

Homework Partner   Date   Speech-Language Pathologist

Final TH Words

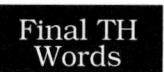

Mirror Image

Directions: Hold this page up to a mirror and read/say the words aloud that appear. Then, write the words correctly on the lines. Use the pictures on the page to help you. Say the words again, using your good TH sound.

tooth _____

cloth _____

birdbath _____

wreath _____

sloth _____

earth _____

mouth _____

telephone booth _____

teeth _____

moth _____

_____ _____ _____ Final TH Words
Homework Partner   Date   Speech-Language Pathologist

Unscramble the Words

Directions: Read/say aloud the picture–words on the right. Use them to help you unscramble the words on the left and write the answers in the blanks. Read/say your answers aloud. Use your good TH sound.

1. **ohmt** _____

2. **ahtbbidr** _____

3. **ostlh** _____

4. **thtee** _____

5. **utmoh** _____

6. **leethpeno oboht** _____

7. **rwahet** _____

8. **olthc** _____

9. **areth** _____

moth

telephone booth

sloth

birdbath

teeth

mouth

wreath

cloth

earth

Answers: 1. moth, 2. birdbath, 3. sloth, 4. teeth, 5. mouth, 6. telephone booth, 7. wreath, 8. cloth, 9. earth

_____ _____ _____
Homework Partner   Date   Speech-Language Pathologist

Final TH Words

Color Phrase

Directions: Color each picture a different color. Then, make up a phrase combining the color with the object in the picture (a blue sloth). Say each phrase aloud, using your good TH sound.

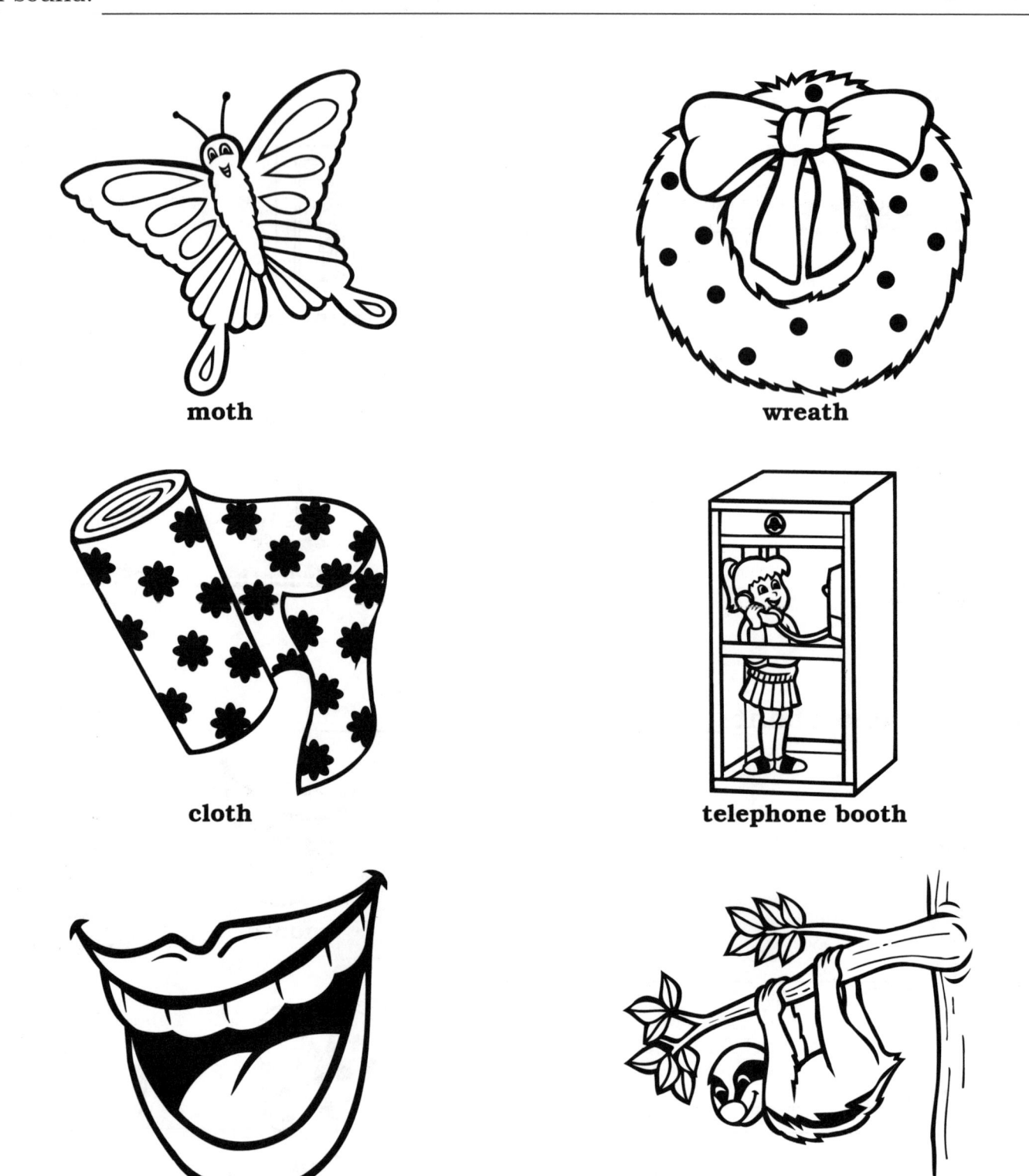

moth

wreath

cloth

telephone booth

mouth

sloth

Homework Partner   Date   Speech-Language Pathologist

Final TH Phrases

Yo-De-Lay-De-Hoo Game

Directions: Read/say aloud the picture–words below. Then, cut out the markers. Flip a coin (heads=1, tails=2) to determine how many spaces to move. As you move, read/say each phrase aloud, using your good TH sound. First player to reach the finish wins. _____

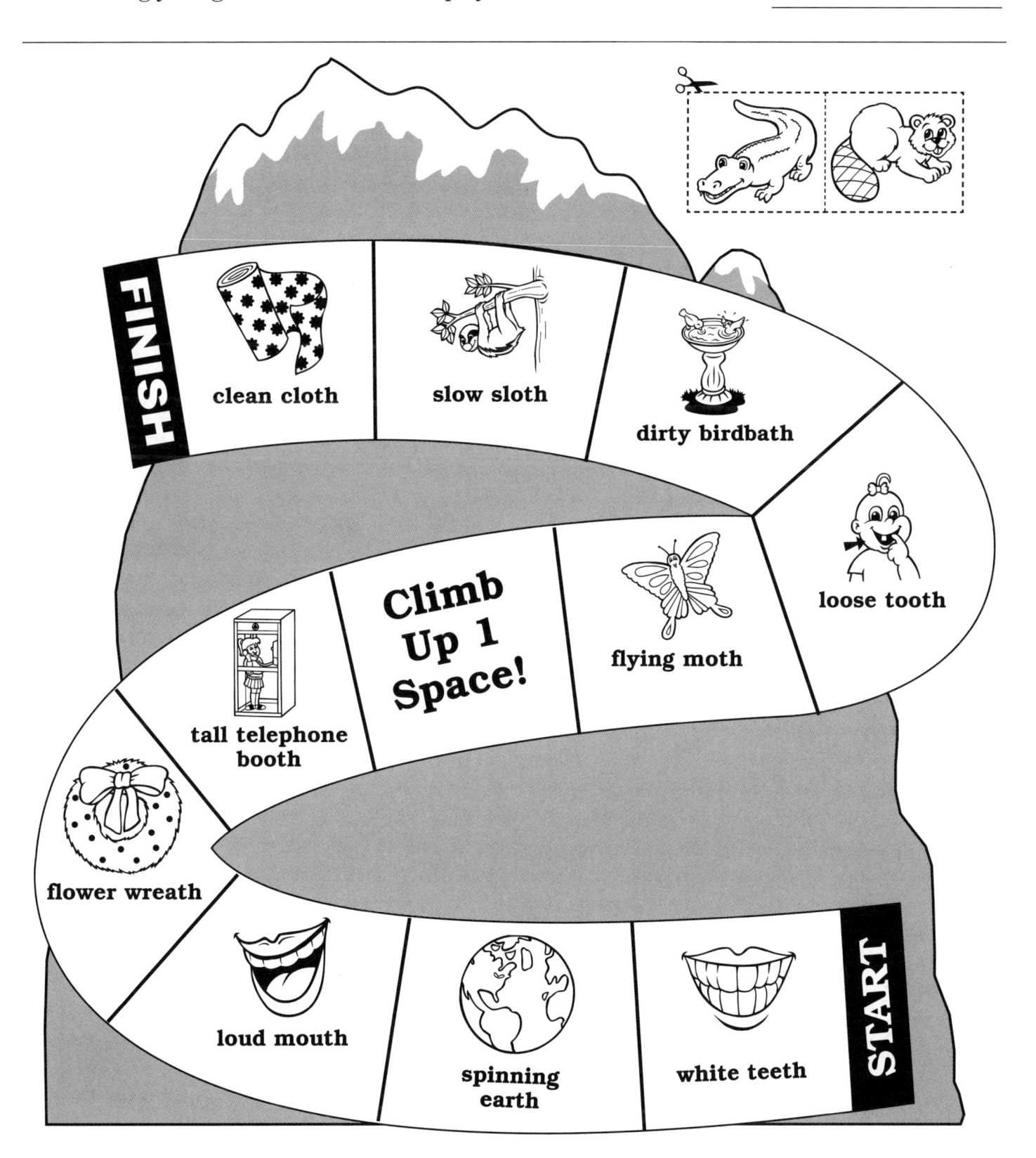

FINISH

- clean cloth
- slow sloth
- dirty birdbath
- loose tooth
- flying moth
- **Climb Up 1 Space!**
- tall telephone booth
- flower wreath
- loud mouth
- spinning earth
- white teeth

START

Homework Partner   Date   Speech-Language Pathologist

Final TH Phrases

Birdbath Splash

Directions: Cut out the birdbaths and birds below. Place a bird under each birdbath. Roll a die or spin a spinner. Lift the birdbath with the same number to reveal a bird phrase. Say the phrase aloud. Then, place the bird on top of the birdbath. Once all the phrases are on top of the birdbaths, read/say all the phrases again, using your good TH sound.

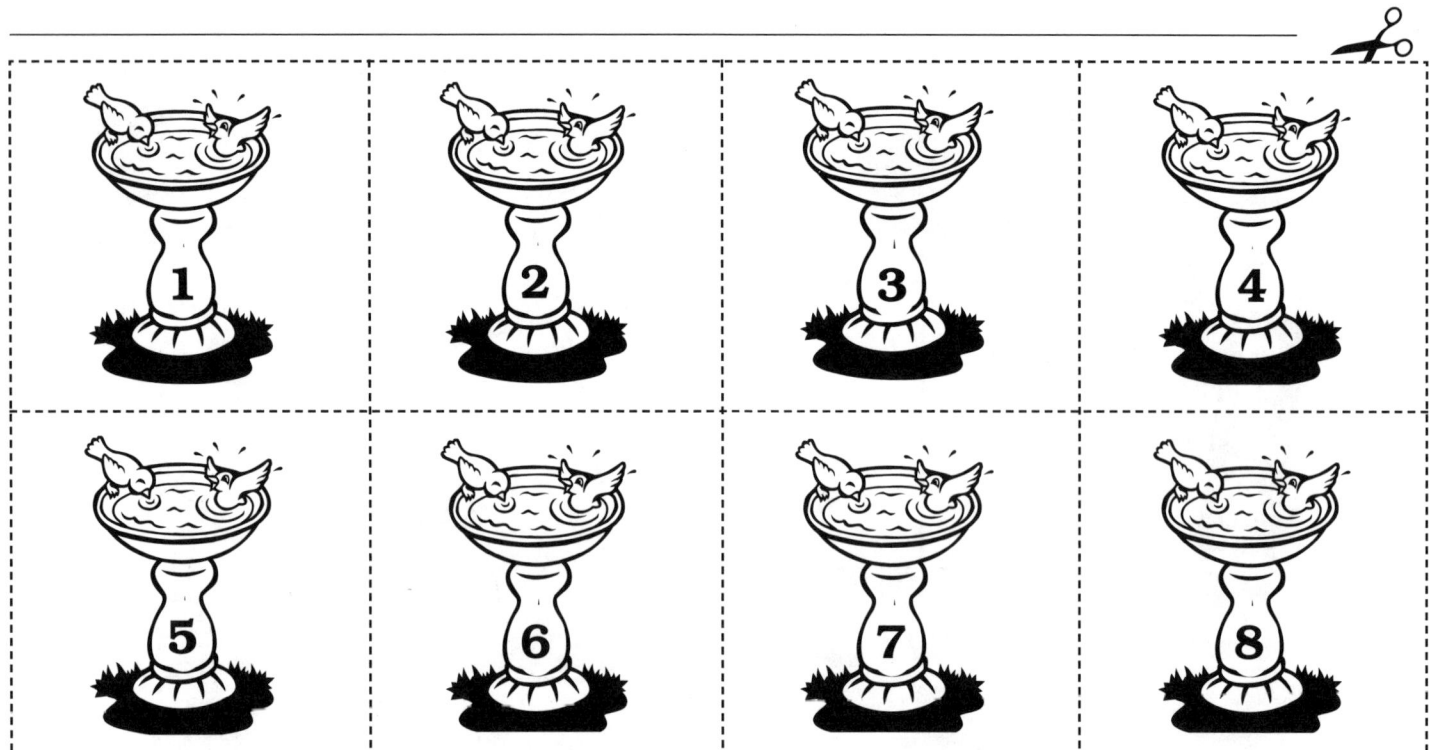

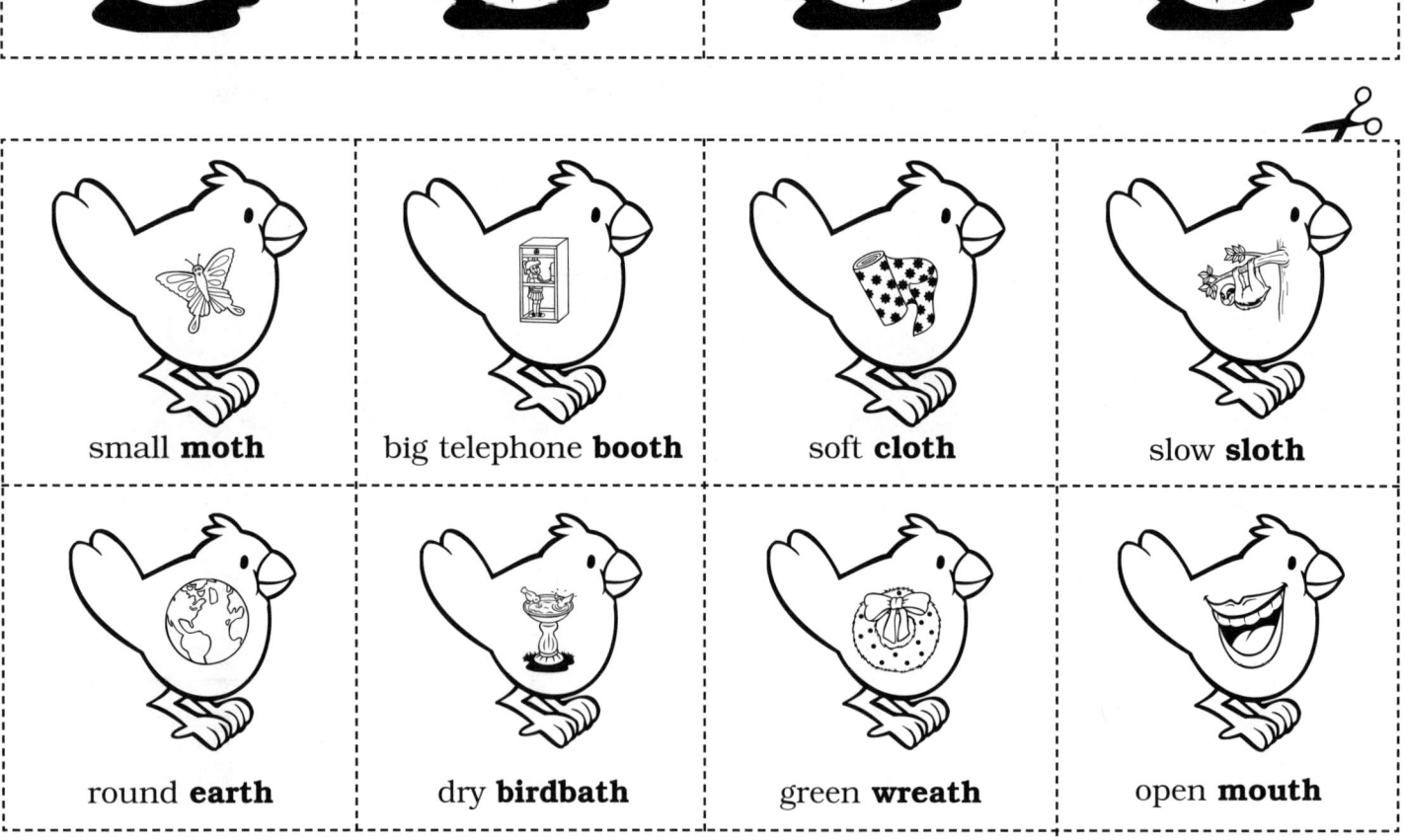

1	2	3	4
5	6	7	8

small **moth**	big telephone **booth**	soft **cloth**	slow **sloth**
round **earth**	dry **birdbath**	green **wreath**	open **mouth**

Homework Partner   Date   Speech-Language Pathologist

Final TH Phrases

Put the Tooth in the Mouth

Directions: Cut out the teeth below. Read/say the sentence on each tooth aloud and glue/tape or place the tooth in the mouth. Remember to use your good TH sound.

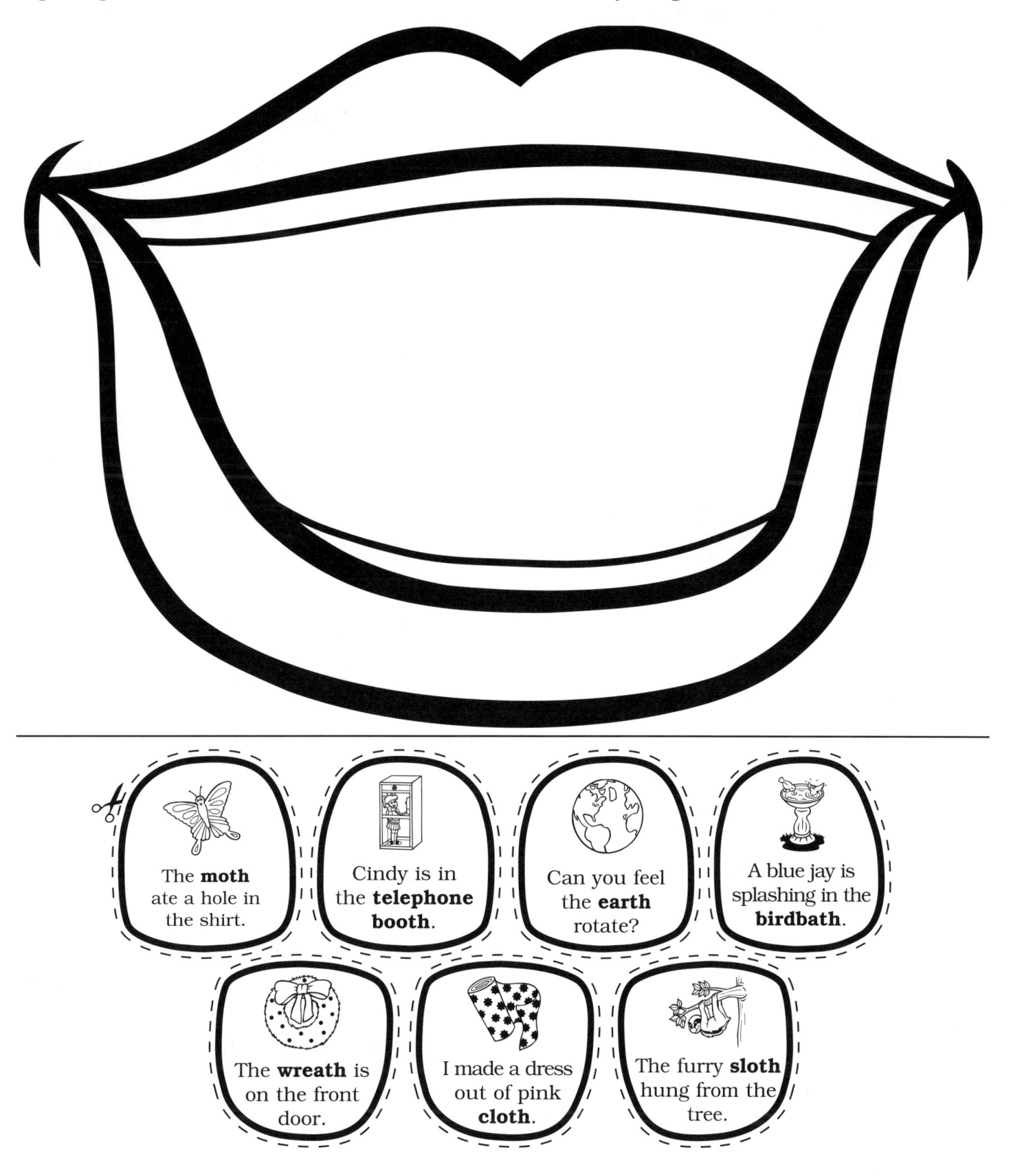

- The **moth** ate a hole in the shirt.
- Cindy is in the **telephone booth**.
- Can you feel the **earth** rotate?
- A blue jay is splashing in the **birdbath**.
- The **wreath** is on the front door.
- I made a dress out of pink **cloth**.
- The furry **sloth** hung from the tree.

Homework Partner   Date   Speech-Language Pathologist

Final TH Sentences

Crazy Crossword

Directions: Read/say the sentences below aloud. Using the words from the Word Bank, fill in the correct answers on the crossword puzzle. Remember to use your good TH sound when reading the target sentences.

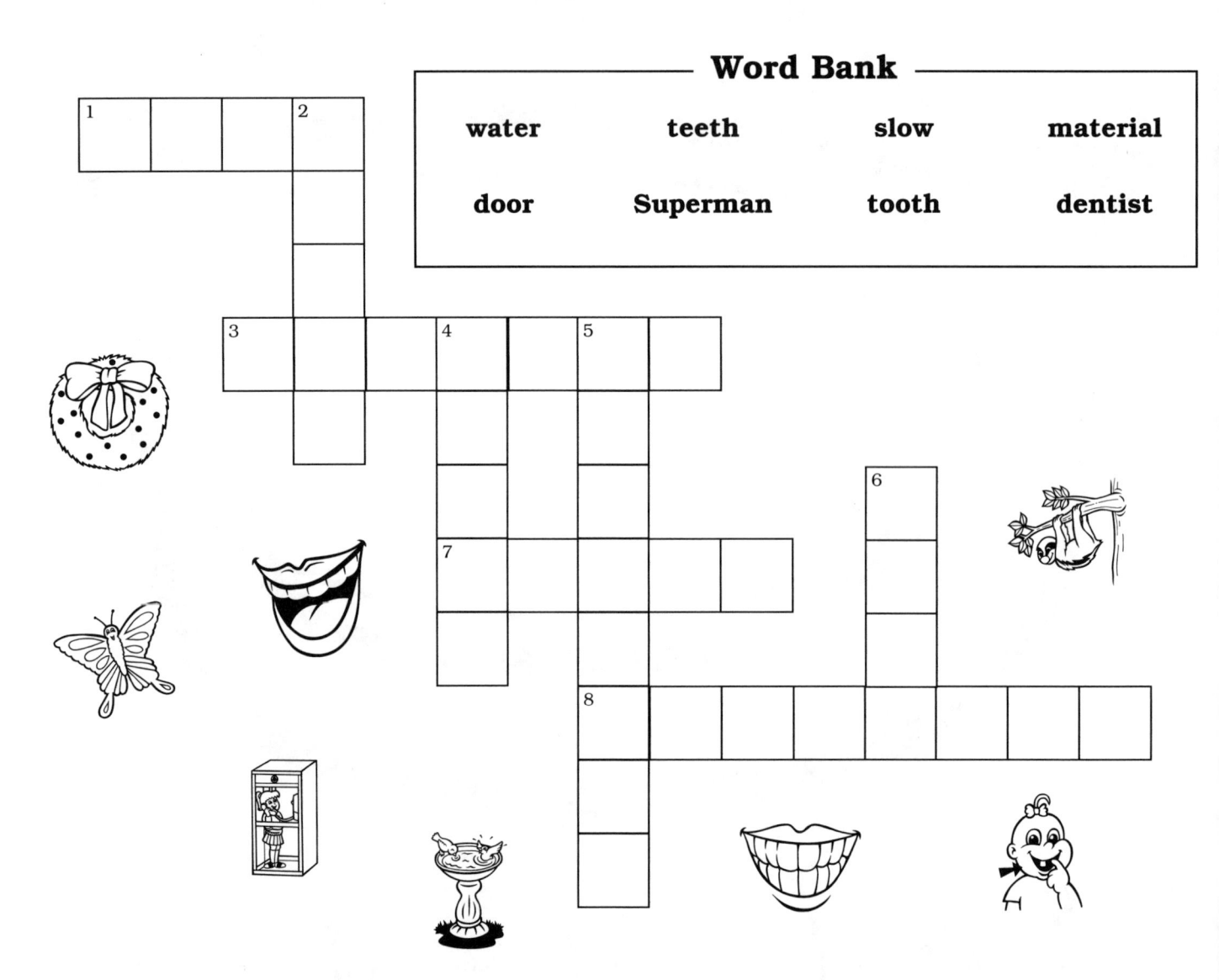

Word Bank

water   teeth   slow   material

door   Superman   tooth   dentist

Across

1. Does a **sloth** move fast or slow?
3. What doctor will fix your **mouth**?
7. Plural word for **tooth**.
8. A **moth** will eat _____.

Down

2. _____ is put in a **birdbath**.
4. Singular word for **teeth**.
5. What man jumps out of a **telephone booth**?
6. A **wreath** hangs here.

Answer Key on Page 279

Homework Partner   Date   Speech-Language Pathologist

Final TH Sentences

Story Loop

Directions: Read/say aloud each picture-word. Make up a story using all of the pictures in the circle. You can start anywhere in the circle and go in either direction, but you must always end where you started to complete the loop. Say your story aloud, using your good TH sound.

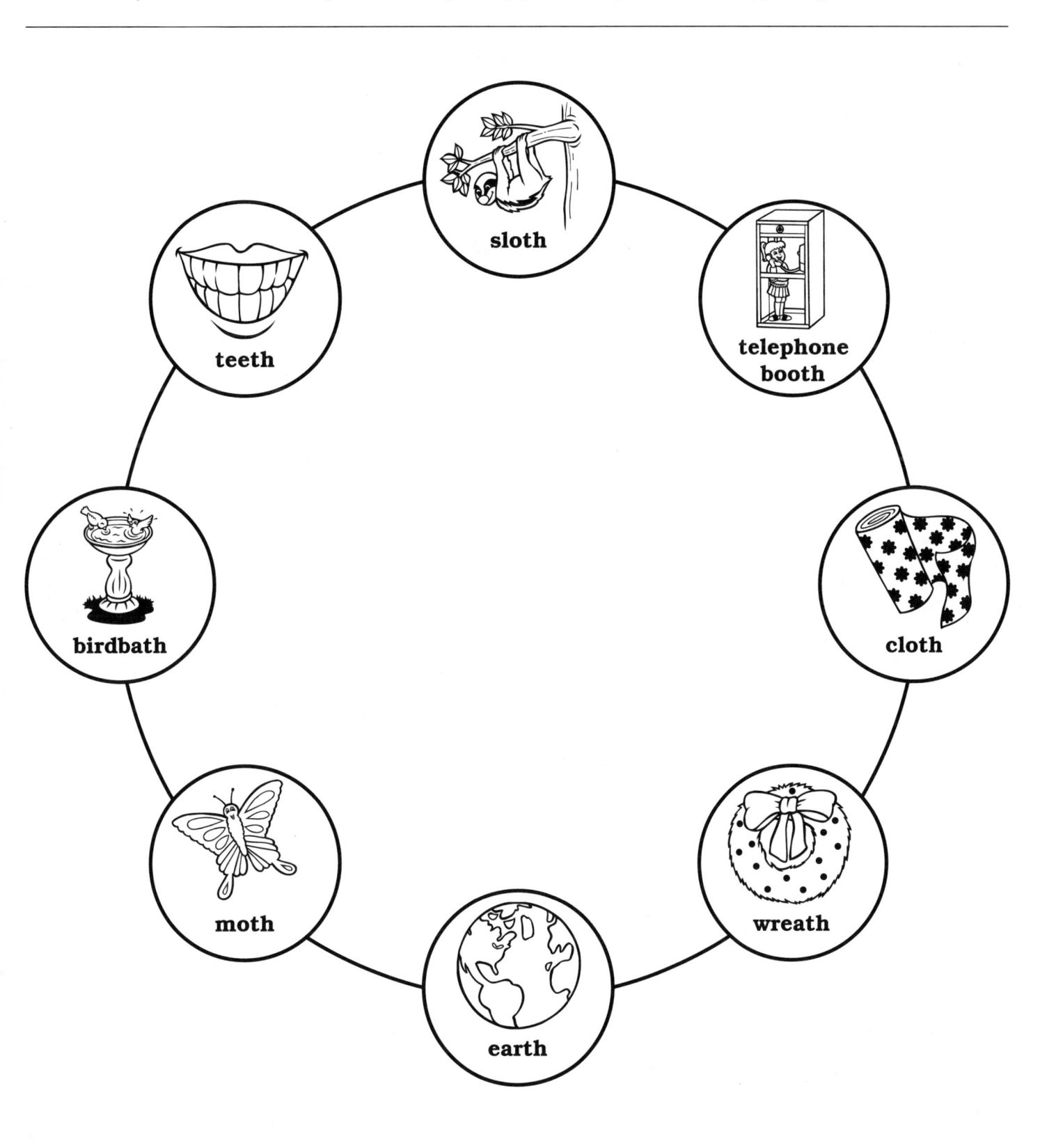

- sloth
- telephone booth
- cloth
- wreath
- earth
- moth
- birdbath
- teeth

_____ _____ _____

Homework Partner　　　　　Date　　　　　Speech-Language Pathologist

Final TH Sentences

Birthday Bash

Directions: Read/say aloud each picture-word. Cut out the candles below. Say the word on each candle, using your good TH sound. Then, place or glue each candle on the cake.

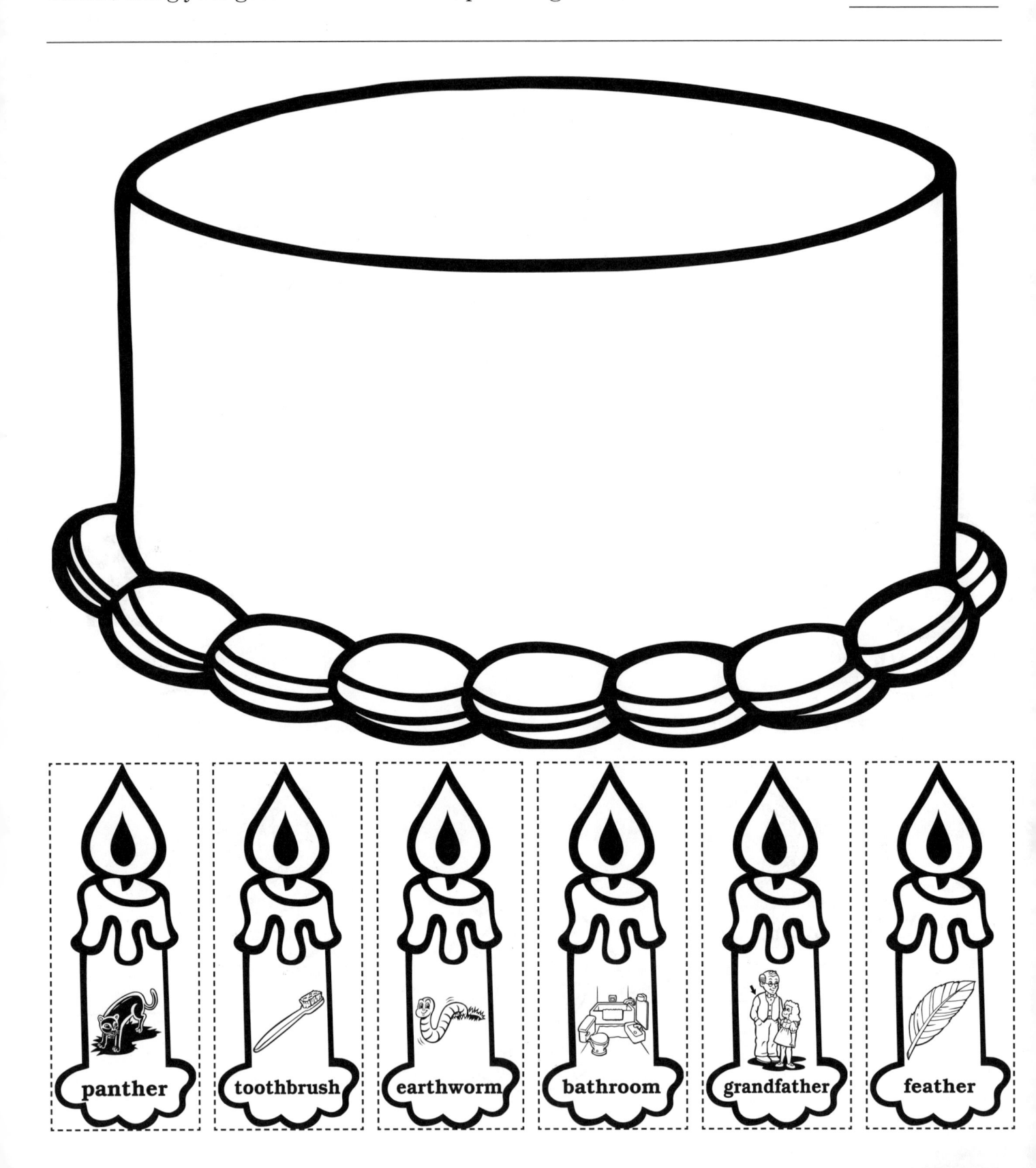

| panther | toothbrush | earthworm | bathroom | grandfather | feather |

Homework Partner   Date   Speech-Language Pathologist

Medial TH Words

Bait the Hook

Directions: Read/say the words on the earthworms. Then, draw a line from the hook to each earthworm as you read/say the words aloud.

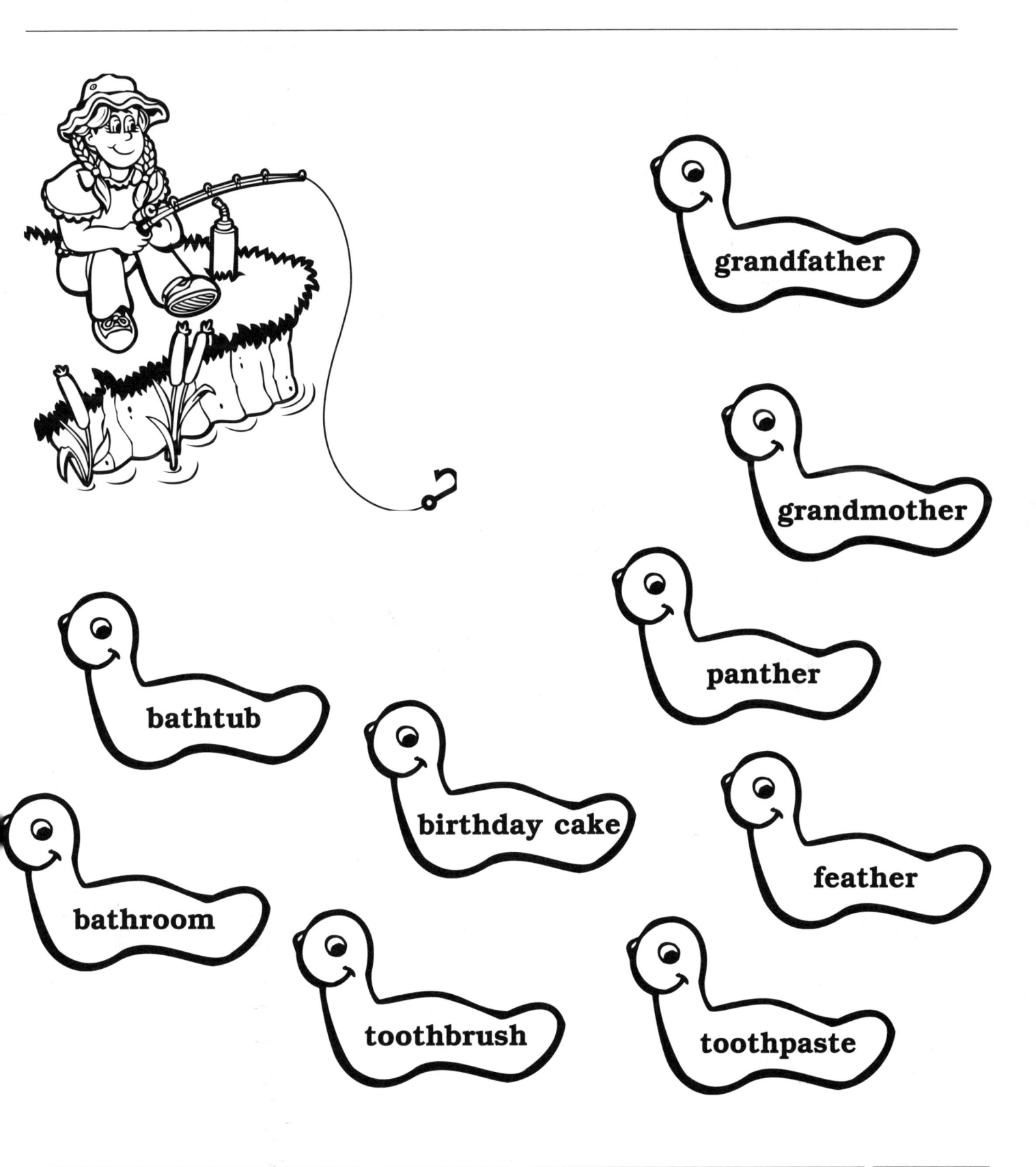

- grandfather
- grandmother
- panther
- bathtub
- birthday cake
- feather
- bathroom
- toothbrush
- toothpaste

Homework Partner   Date   Speech-Language Pathologist

Medial TH Words

Find the Feather

Directions: Tom Turkey needs to find his tail feathers. Cut out the feathers below. As you choose a feather, read/say aloud the picture–word and place/glue the feather on the turkey. Remember to use your good TH sound.

| birthday cake | earthworm | toothpaste | toothbrush | grandfather | panther |

Homework Partner   Date   Speech-Language Pathologist

Medial TH Words

TH Spinner Action

Directions: Read/say aloud the picture–words below. If you prefer, glue this page to construction paper for added durability. Cut out the arrow/dial. Use a brad to connect the dial to the circle. Spin the spinner. When you land on a picture, read/say the word aloud, using your best TH sound.

- birthday cake
- earthworm
- panther
- feather
- grandfather
- bathroom
- toothpaste
- bathtub

Homework Partner   Date   Speech-Language Pathologist

Medial TH Words

#BK-291 Webber® Artic Fun Sheets 2 • ©2002 Super Duper® Publications • www.superduperinc.com • 1-800-277-8737

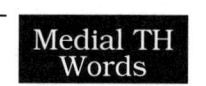

105

Give Me Another Word

Directions: Read/say aloud each picture–word below. Read the words in the middle and look at the picture–words around the page to find the one that best matches the words. Write the picture–word in the blank space. Remember to use your good TH sound.

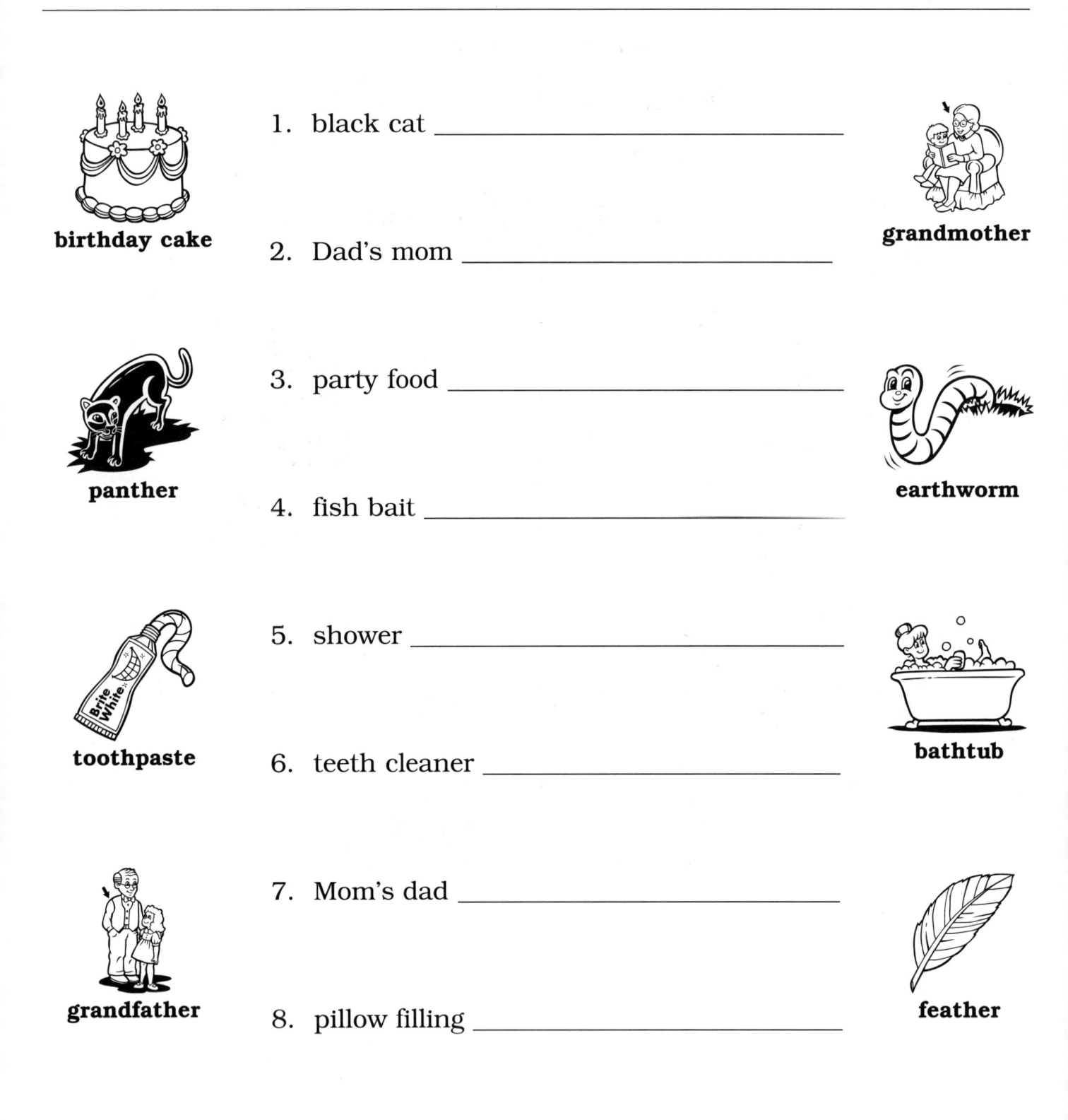

birthday cake

panther

toothpaste

grandfather

1. black cat _____
2. Dad's mom _____
3. party food _____
4. fish bait _____
5. shower _____
6. teeth cleaner _____
7. Mom's dad _____
8. pillow filling _____

grandmother

earthworm

bathtub

feather

Homework Partner   Date   Speech-Language Pathologist

Medial TH Words

106   #BK-291 Webber® Artic Fun Sheets 2 • ©2002 Super Duper® Publications • www.superduperinc.com • 1-800-277-8737

Word in a Word

Directions: Read/say aloud the picture–words on the left. Then, read a sentence and circle a word in the sentence that is part of the word on the left. (**feather:** You(eat)when you are hungry.) Then, say the picture–words again.

1. **bathroom**   You take a bath when you're dirty.

2. **birthday cake** The sun shines during the day.

3. **earthworm**   I hear things with my ear.

4. **panther**   An ant is a small bug that likes to build hills.

5. **grandmother**   A moth is a flying bug that might eat holes in clothes.

6. **feather**   You eat when you are hungry.

Answers: 1. bath, 2. day, 3. ear, 4. ant, 5. moth, 6. eat

Homework Partner   Date   Speech-Language Pathologist   Medial TH Words

Hide-and-Seek

Directions: Read/say aloud the picture–words. If you prefer, glue the pictures on a file folder/cardboard. Cut out the pictures and panther. Place the pictures face up. Have your partner hide the panther under a picture. Name the picture where you think the panther is hidden. (Bathtub?) First player to find the panther wins! Use your good TH sound.

bathroom	bathtub	grandmother
grandfather	toothpaste	toothbrush
earthworm	birthday cake	feather

Homework Partner   Date   Speech-Language Pathologist

Medial TH Words

Descripto Match

Directions: Read/say aloud the picture–words on the right. Then, draw a line from the describing word on the left to a picture–word it describes. There may be more than one describing word for each picture. Then, read/say each phrase aloud (tickly feather). Remember to use your good TH sound!

1. tickly

2. slimy

    birthday cake

3. full

    earthworm

4. messy

    feather

5. smiling

    bathtub

6. scary

7. green

    bathroom

8. yummy

    grandmother

9. shiny

10. cool

    panther

Homework Partner   Date   Speech-Language Pathologist

Medial TH Phrases

Mine or Yours?

Directions: Read/say each picture–word below. Cut out the pictures and place face down. First player picks up a card and flips a coin. Heads means the student keeps the pictures and says, "My _____" (My panther). Tails means that the student gives the picture to the player on his right and says, "Your _____" (Your panther). Play continues in turn. Player with the most pictures at the end wins.

birthday cake	**earthworm**
bathtub	**toothpaste**
panther	**grandmother**
feather	**grandfather**
toothbrush	**bathroom**

Homework Partner   Date   Speech-Language Pathologist

Medial TH Phrases

Fill It In!

Directions: Look at the cartoons below. Read/say the beginning of the phrase (mmm...). Choose a word from the Word Bank to fill in the blank to make a phrase. Read/say aloud, using your good TH sound (mmm...birthday cake).

Word Bank

birthday cake	toothbrush	grandmother
panther	earthworm	feather

mmm _____

slimy _____

ticklish _____

hungry _____

sleepy _____

big _____

Homework Partner   Date   Speech-Language Pathologist

Medial TH Phrases

To Grandmother's House We Go

Directions: Read/say aloud the picture–words below. Then, cut out the markers. Flip a coin (heads=1, tails=2) to determine how many spaces to move. As you move, use each word in a sentence aloud, using your good TH sound. First player to reach the finish wins.

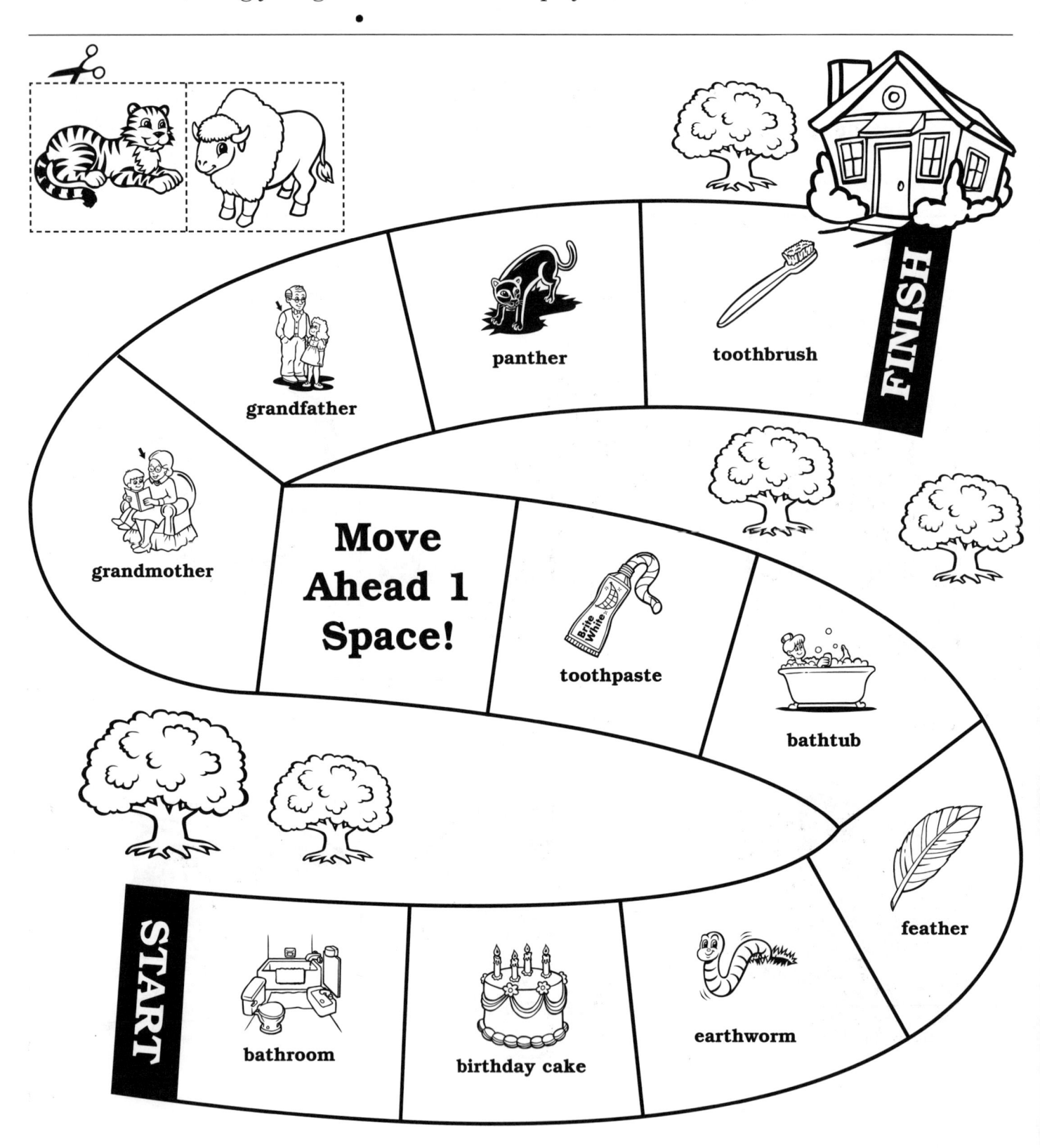

- grandfather
- panther
- toothbrush
- grandmother
- Move Ahead 1 Space!
- toothpaste
- bathtub
- feather
- earthworm
- birthday cake
- bathroom

START — FINISH

Homework Partner Date Speech-Language Pathologist

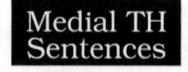

Medial TH Sentences

Sentence Scene

Directions: Cut out the picture scenes and picture cards below. Place cards face down in a pile. Pick a card and create a sentence by linking the picture to the scene. (The panther went down the snowy hill.) Remember to use your good TH sound.

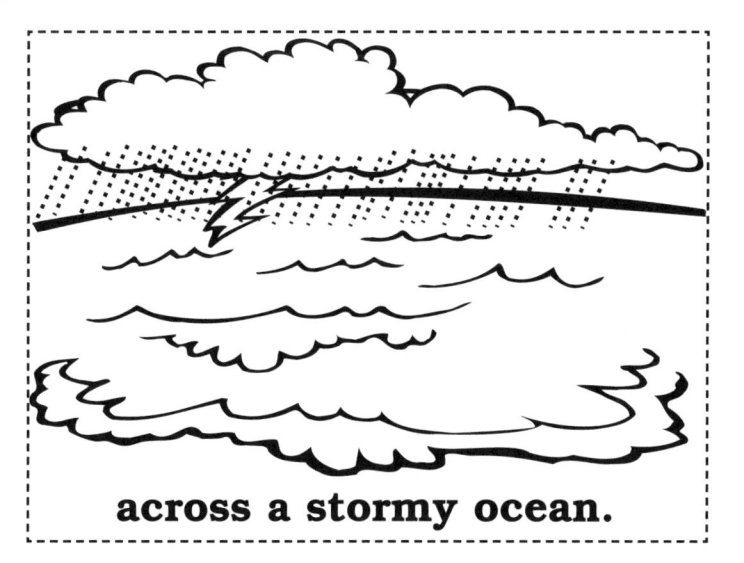

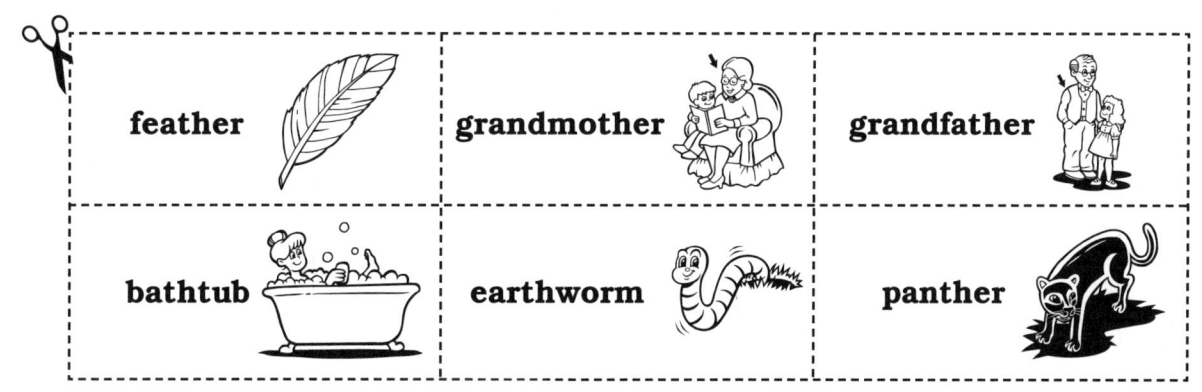

down the snowy hill.	in a dark jungle.
across a stormy ocean.	on a farm.

feather	grandmother	grandfather
bathtub	earthworm	panther

Homework Partner   Date   Speech-Language Pathologist

Medial TH Sentences

Grid a Sentence

Directions: Pick one word from the side of the grid, and one word from the top, and say or write a sentence using both words. (birthday cake/yummy: He had a yummy birthday cake.) Use your good TH sound.

	yummy	soft	busy
birthday cake			
earthworm			
feather			
bathtub			
toothbrush			
grandfather			

Homework Partner   Date   Speech-Language Pathologist

Medial TH Sentences

K Sound

K Cube Roll

Directions: Assemble the cube as follows: glue onto construction paper for added durability. Cut along the dotted lines. Fold on solid lines and glue as indicated. To play: roll the cube. Read/say aloud the word you see using your best K sound.

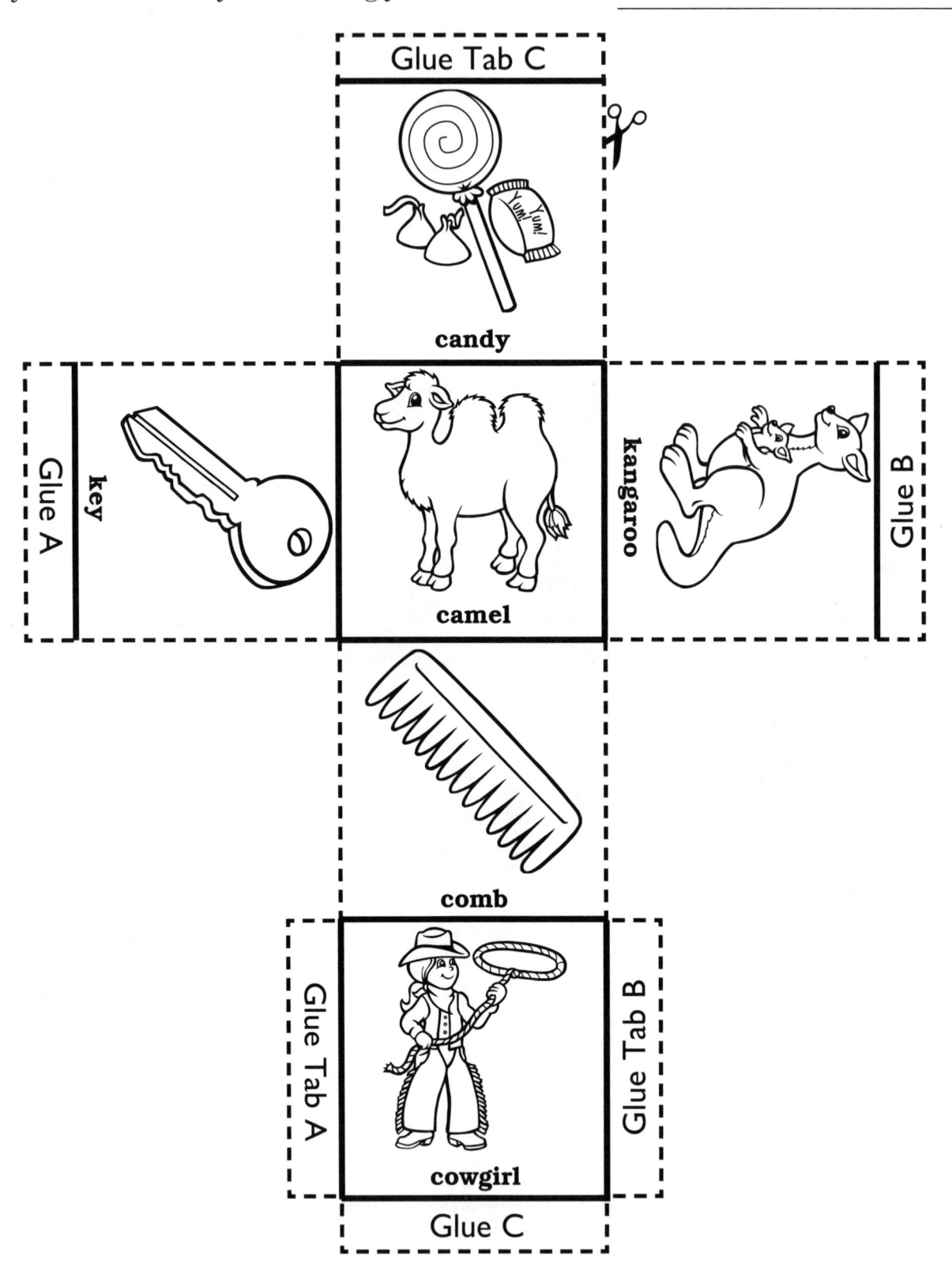

Glue Tab C

candy

Glue A | key | camel | kangaroo | Glue B

comb

Glue Tab A | cowgirl | Glue Tab B

Glue C

Homework Partner | Date | Speech-Language Pathologist

Initial K Words

116 #BK-291 Webber® Artic Fun Sheets 2 • ©2002 Super Duper® Publications • www.superduperinc.com • 1-800-277-8737

Football Mania!

Directions: Read/say aloud the picture–words. Cut out the footballs and place them at the 10 yard line on opposite ends of the field. First player flips a coin and moves 10 yards (heads) or 20 yards (tails). Say the word you land on aloud using your good K sound. Play continues in turn. First player to score a touchdown wins. Next time you play, switch ends.

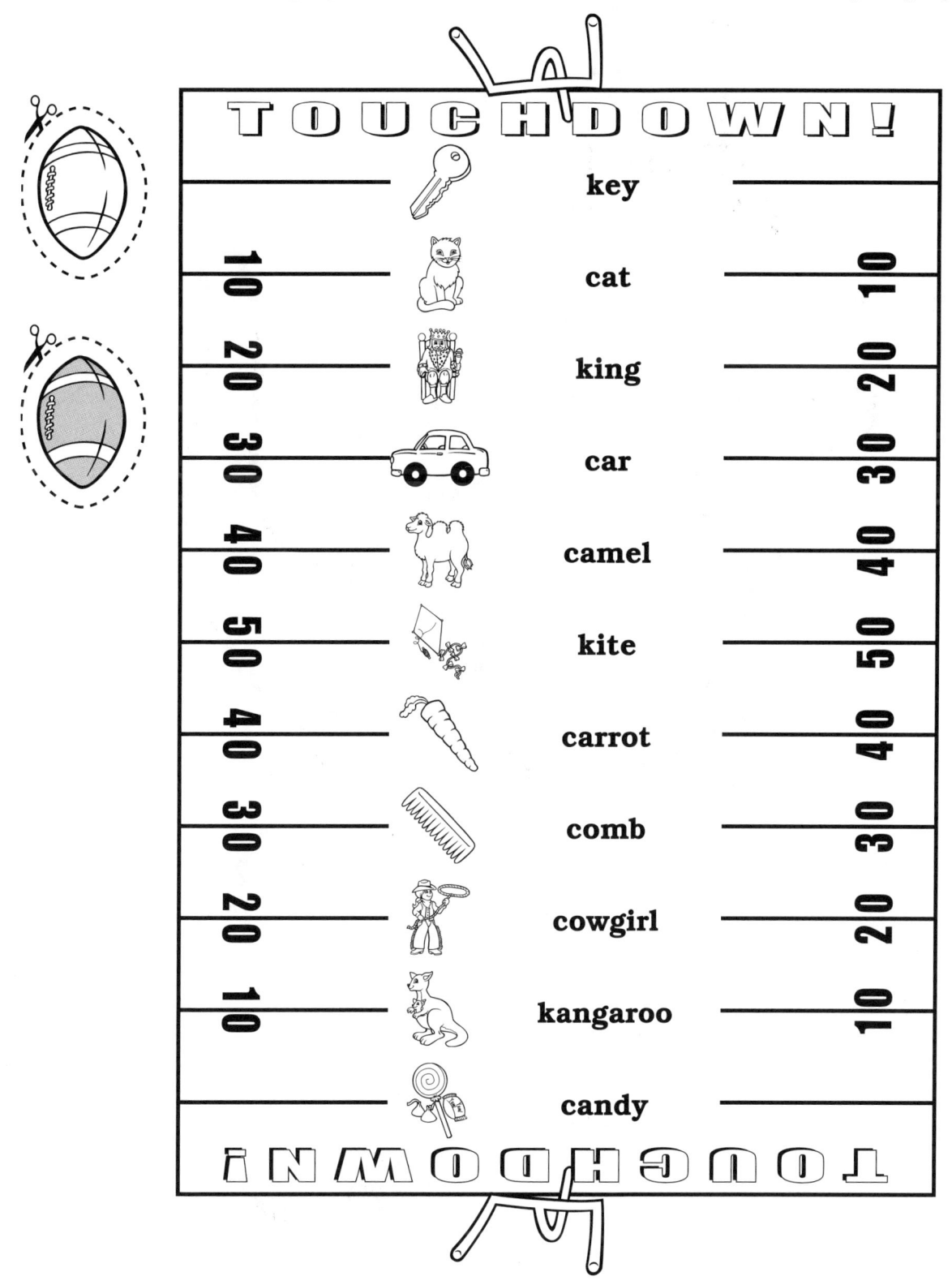

TOUCHDOWN!

key

cat

king

car

camel

kite

carrot

comb

cowgirl

kangaroo

candy

TOUCHDOWN!

Homework Partner   Date   Speech-Language Pathologist   Initial K Words

Kangaroo's Pouch

Directions: Cut out the picture–word cards below. Then, cut along the dotted line to make a pouch for the kangaroo. Read/say aloud each word as you place the cards into the kangaroo's pouch. Remember to use your good K sound.

candy	cow	comb	camel	king
cat	key	carrot	car	kite

Homework Partner   Date   Speech-Language Pathologist

Initial K Words

Hide-and-Seek

Directions: Read/say aloud the picture–words. If you prefer, glue the pictures on a file folder/cardboard. Cut out the pictures and key. Place the pictures face up. Have your partner hide the key under a picture. Name the picture where you think the key is hidden. (Comb?) First player to find the key wins! Use your good K sound.

cat	cow	candy
comb	cowgirl	carrot
camel	car	kite

_____   _____   _____
Homework Partner   Date   Speech-Language Pathologist

Initial K Words

Rhyming Matches

Directions: Read/say the words in column A. Then, find the rhyming words in column B (fat/cat). Draw a line to connect the pair and read/say the words in column B aloud. Use your good K sound.

A

parrot

fat

sing

star

bee

fight

Randy

foam

B

car

comb

key

kite

candy

carrot

king

cat

Answers: parrot/carrot, fat/cat, sing/king, star/car, bee/key, fight/kite, Randy/candy, foam/comb

Homework Partner   Date   Speech-Language Pathologist

Initial K Words

Ask and Answer

Directions: Cut along the dotted lines. Fold the paper flaps back along the solid black line to cover up the pictures. Read the questions and guess the answers. Read/say your answers aloud using your best K sound.

1. What animal says moo? — **cow**

2. What animal has a pouch and hops? — **kangaroo**

3. What person works with animals on a farm? — **cowgirl**

4. What does a rabbit eat? — **carrot**

5. What animal says meow? — **cat**

6. What animal has humps on its back? — **camel**

7. What rhymes with flea? — **key**

8. What do you fix your hair with? — **comb**

Fold here

Homework Partner   Date   Speech-Language Pathologist

Initial K Words

Get the Carrot

Directions: Read/say aloud the picture–words below. Then, cut out the markers. Flip a coin (heads=1, tails=2) to determine how many spaces to move. As you move, read/say each phrase aloud, using your good K sound. First player to reach the finish wins.

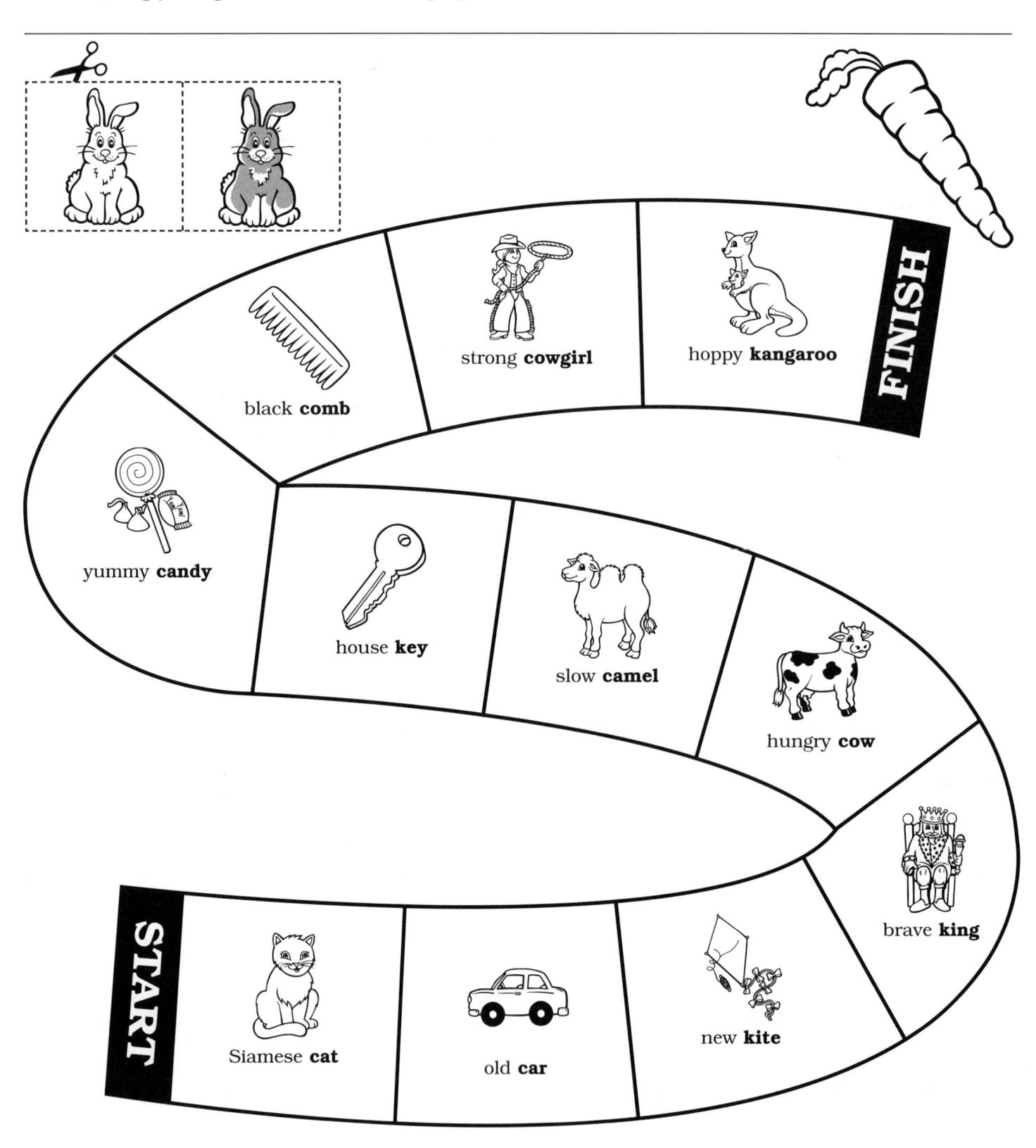

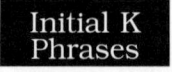

- black **comb**
- strong **cowgirl**
- hoppy **kangaroo**
- yummy **candy**
- house **key**
- slow **camel**
- hungry **cow**
- brave **king**
- Siamese **cat**
- old **car**
- new **kite**

START

FINISH

Homework Partner   Date   Speech-Language Pathologist

Initial K Phrases

Mouse & Cat

Directions: Cut out the cats and mice below. Choose a mouse and a cat. Combine the words to make a phrase (silly cow). Read/say the phrase aloud, using your good K sound.

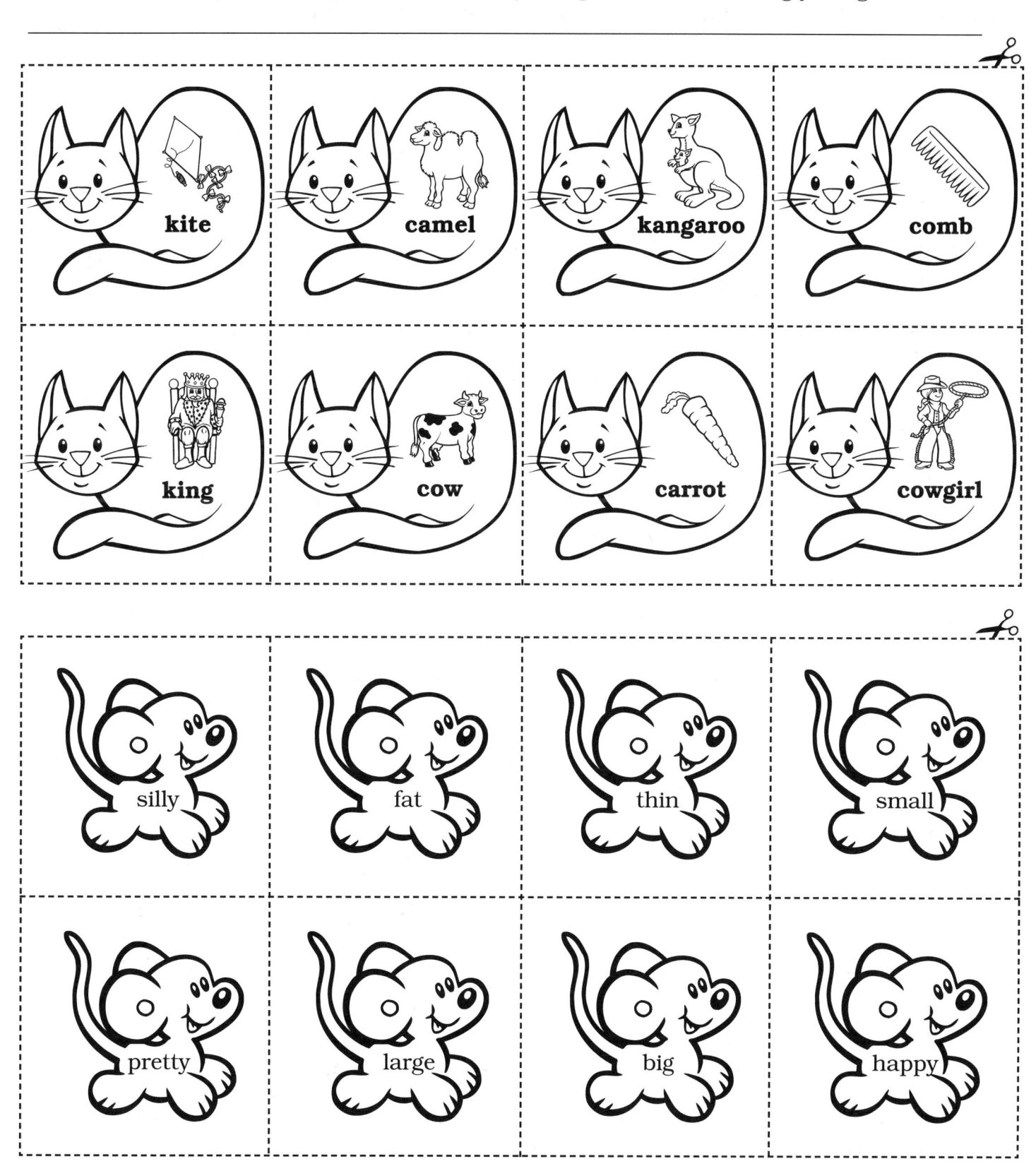

kite	camel	kangaroo	comb
king	cow	carrot	cowgirl

silly	fat	thin	small
pretty	large	big	happy

Homework Partner   Date   Speech-Language Pathologist

Initial K Phrases

#BK-291 Webber® Artic Fun Sheets 2 • ©2002 Super Duper® Publications • www.superduperinc.com • 1-800-277-8737

123

Search-a-Word

Directions: Read/say the picture–words aloud. Then, using the picture–words, complete the phrases below. Find and circle each picture–word in the word search box. Then, read/say the complete phrases aloud (horse and cow). Use your good K sound. _____

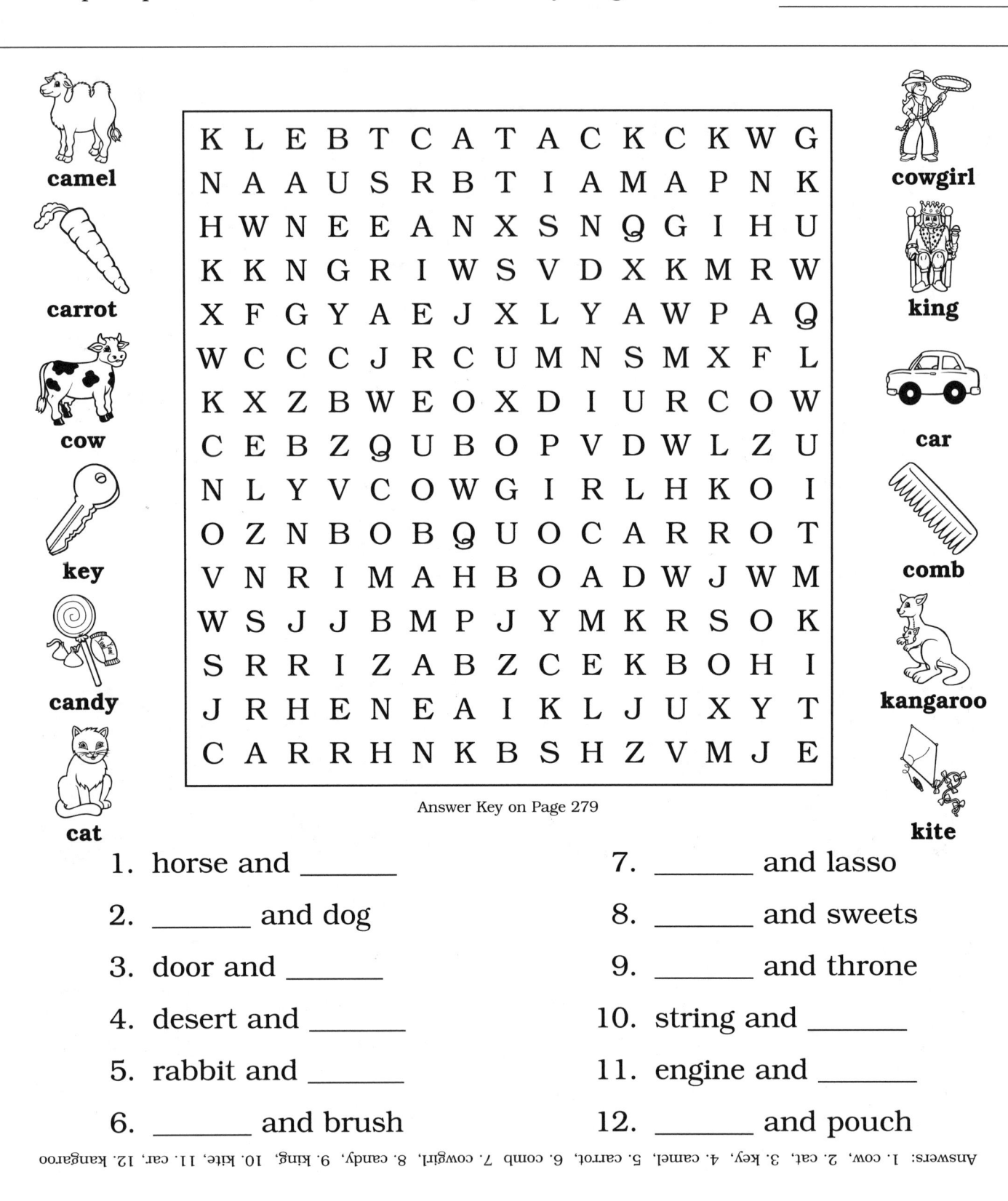

camel

carrot

cow

key

candy

cat

```
K L E B T C A T A C K C K W G
N A A U S R B T I A M A P N K
H W N E E A N X S N Q G I H U
K K N G R I W S V D X K M R W
X F G Y A E J X L Y A W P A Q
W C C C J R C U M N S M X F L
K X Z B W E O X D I U R C O W
C E B Z Q U B O P V D W L Z U
N L Y V C O W G I R L H K O I
O Z N B O B Q U O C A R R O T
V N R I M A H B O A D W J W M
W S J J B M P J Y M K R S O K
S R R I Z A B Z C E K B O H I
J R H E N E A I K L J U X Y T
C A R R H N K B S H Z V M J E
```

Answer Key on Page 279

cowgirl

king

car

comb

kangaroo

kite

1. horse and _____
2. _____ and dog
3. door and _____
4. desert and _____
5. rabbit and _____
6. _____ and brush

7. _____ and lasso
8. _____ and sweets
9. _____ and throne
10. string and _____
11. engine and _____
12. _____ and pouch

Answers: 1. cow, 2. cat, 3. key, 4. camel, 5. carrot, 6. comb 7. cowgirl, 8. candy, 9. king, 10. kite, 11. car, 12. kangaroo

_____ _____ _____   Initial K
Homework Partner   Date   Speech-Language Pathologist   Phrases

124   #BK-291 Webber® Artic Fun Sheets 2 • ©2002 Super Duper® Publications • www.superduperinc.com • 1-800-277-8737

Story Loop

Directions: Read/say aloud each picture–word. Make up a story using all of the pictures in the circle. You can start anywhere in the circle and go in either direction, but you must always end where you started to complete the loop. Say your story aloud, using your good K sound.

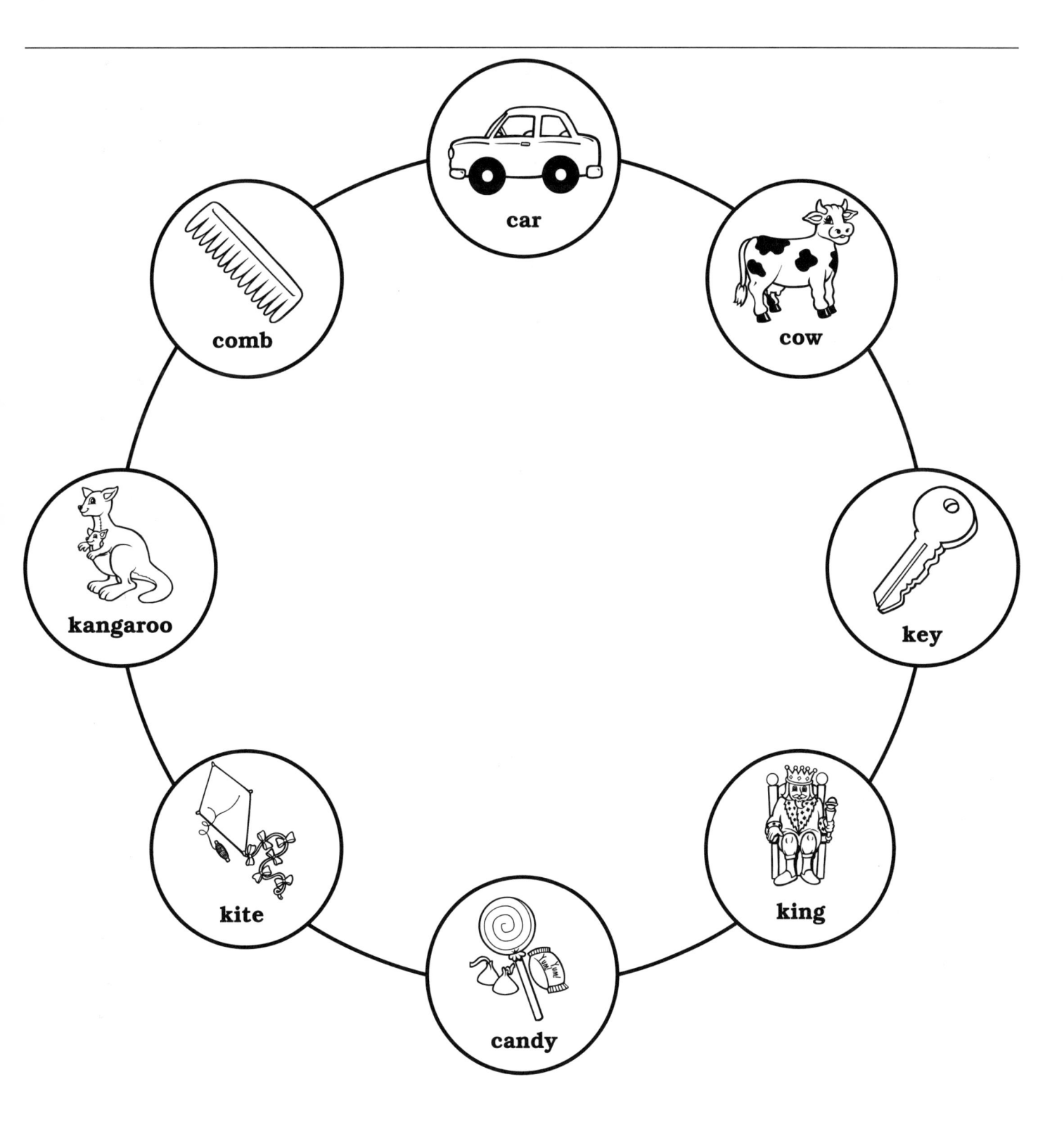

- car
- cow
- key
- king
- candy
- kite
- kangaroo
- comb

Homework Partner   Date   Speech-Language Pathologist

Initial K Sentences

I Like It!

Directions: Read/say aloud each picture–word. To make a sentence, choose an adjective from the middle of the page and then choose a picture–word. Begin your sentences with, "I like the..." (I like the shiny car.) Words can be used more than once. Remember to use your good K sound.

cow

comb

kite

car

carrot

Adjectives

sweet

paper

gold

shiny

big

old

dirty

red

orange

tall

candy

camel

king

key

cat

Homework Partner   Date   Speech-Language Pathologist

Initial K Sentences

126   #BK-291 Webber® Artic Fun Sheets 2 • ©2002 Super Duper® Publications • www.superduperinc.com • 1-800-277-8737

Make It Count

Directions: Roll a die or spin a spinner to determine a number. Begin a sentence with "I have...." Then, complete the sentence with the given number and a word chosen from the picture–words below. (I have one cow.) Read/say the sentence aloud, using your good K sound.

cat	candy	cow
key	kangaroo	kite
car	king	comb
camel	carrot	cowgirl

Homework Partner   Date   Speech-Language Pathologist

Initial K Sentences

3 Games in 1

Directions: Say aloud the picture–words below, using your good K sound. Then, play one of the following games:

☐ Lotto – Caller reads a word and student repeats the word and covers it with a token/chip.

☐ Tic–Tac–Toe – Each time you write an **X** or **O**, say the word you mark over.

☐ Memory – Cut out all the cards and place face down. Try to find matching pairs. Say aloud each word you find. Keep all matches.

duck	sock	bike
rake	pink	lipstick
snake	book	truck

book	truck	lipstick
duck	bike	rake
pink	sock	snake

Homework Partner Date Speech-Language Pathologist

Final K Words

Truck Stop

Directions: Read/say aloud the picture–words below. Then, cut out the markers. Flip a coin (heads=1, tails=2) to determine how many spaces to move. As you move, read/say each word aloud, using your good K sound. First player to reach the finish wins.

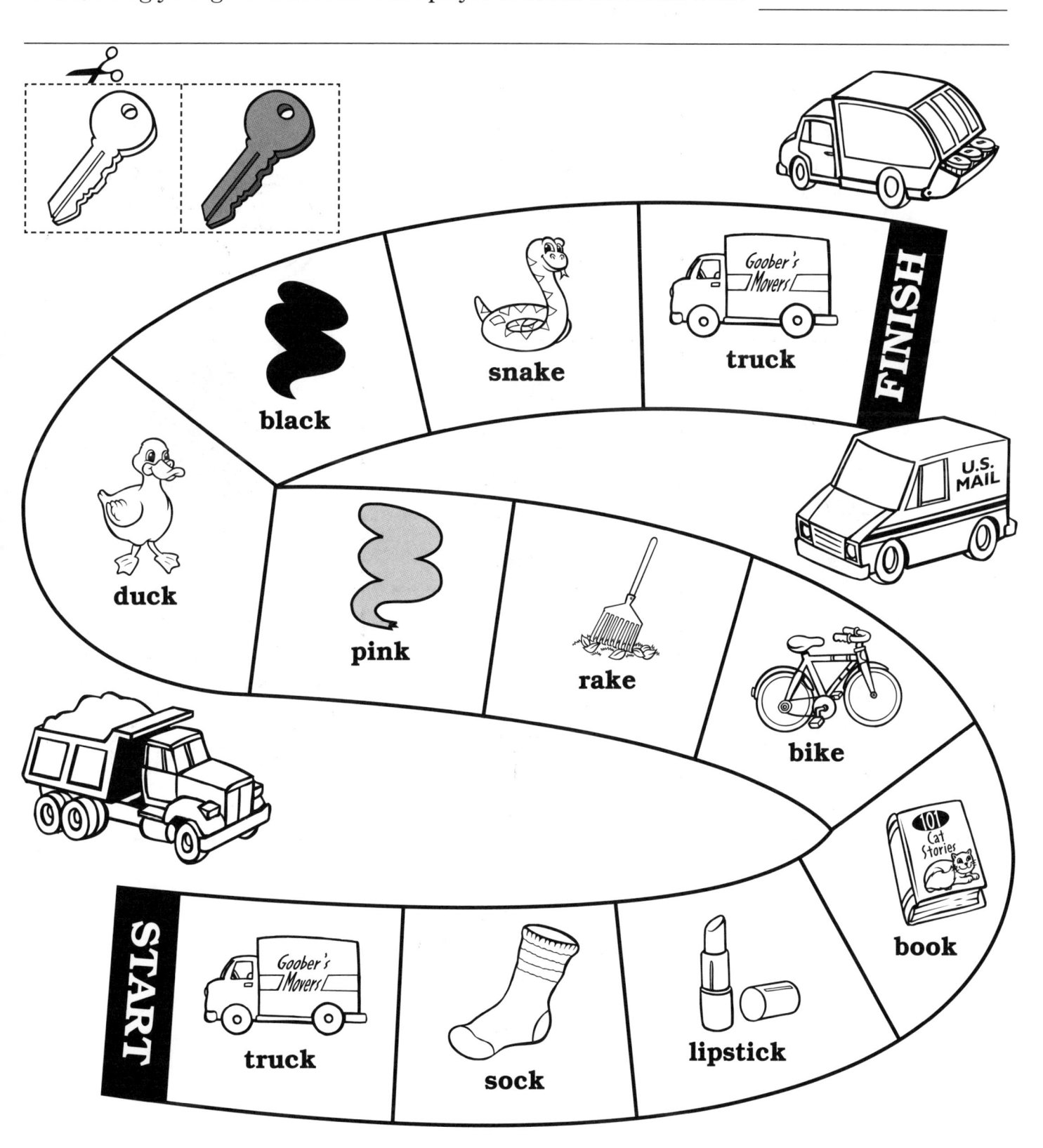

START — truck — sock — lipstick — book — bike — rake — pink — duck — black — snake — truck — **FINISH**

Homework Partner — Date — Speech-Language Pathologist

Final K Words

Hide-and-Seek

Directions: Read/say aloud the picture–words. If you prefer, glue the pictures on a file folder/cardboard. Cut out the pictures and sock. Place the pictures face up. Have your partner hide the sock under a picture. Read/say aloud the name of the picture to find the sock. (Rake?) Use your good K sound!

duck	pink	bike
rake	book	black
lipstick	snake	truck

Homework Partner   Date   Speech-Language Pathologist

Final K Words

What Am I?

Directions: Read/say aloud each picture–word below. Then, read each question. Fill in the blank with the appropriate word. Read/say each answer aloud, using your good K sound.

truck	duck	book	rake
snake	lipstick	sock	bike

1. I am yellow and have feathers. I am a _____.

2. I go on your foot to keep it warm. I am a _____.

3. Use me to pile up your leaves. I am a _____.

4. Girls put me on their lips. I am _____.

5. I hiss and slither. I am a _____.

6. I have two wheels and handlebars. I am a _____.

7. I have many pages and people read me. I am a _____.

8. I am bigger than a van and move things. I am a _____.

Answers: 1. duck, 2. sock, 3. rake, 4. lipstick, 5. snake, 6. bike, 7. book, 8. truck

Homework Partner   Date   Speech-Language Pathologist

Final K Words

#BK-291 Webber® Artic Fun Sheets 2 • ©2002 Super Duper® Publications • www.superduperinc.com • 1-800-277-8737

Duck, Duck, Goose!

Directions: Cut out the cards below, shuffle them, and place them in a pile. Sit in a circle around the cards. One student should go around the circle, lightly tapping each player's head while saying, "Duck, Duck, Goose." The last student tapped "Goose" draws a card and reads/says the picture–word aloud. Then, that student goes around the circle and play continues in turn. Remember to use your good K sound.

duck	pink	bike
rake	sock	black
lipstick	snake	truck

Homework Partner   Date   Speech-Language Pathologist

Final K Words

Read the Book!

Directions: The words below are all missing a letter. Use the picture clue to help you fill the letters in on the line provided. Then, read/say the words aloud, using your good K sound.

1. ____uck

2. ____nake

3. soc____

4. bi____e

5. tru____k

6. r____ke

Answers: 1. duck, 2. snake, 3. sock, 4. bike, 5. truck, 6. rake

Homework Partner   Date   Speech-Language Pathologist   Final K Words

Color It

Directions: Read/say the picture–words below. Then, color each crayon. Use a different color for each one. Then, say a phrase aloud about each crayon, using the color on that crayon (a pink book).

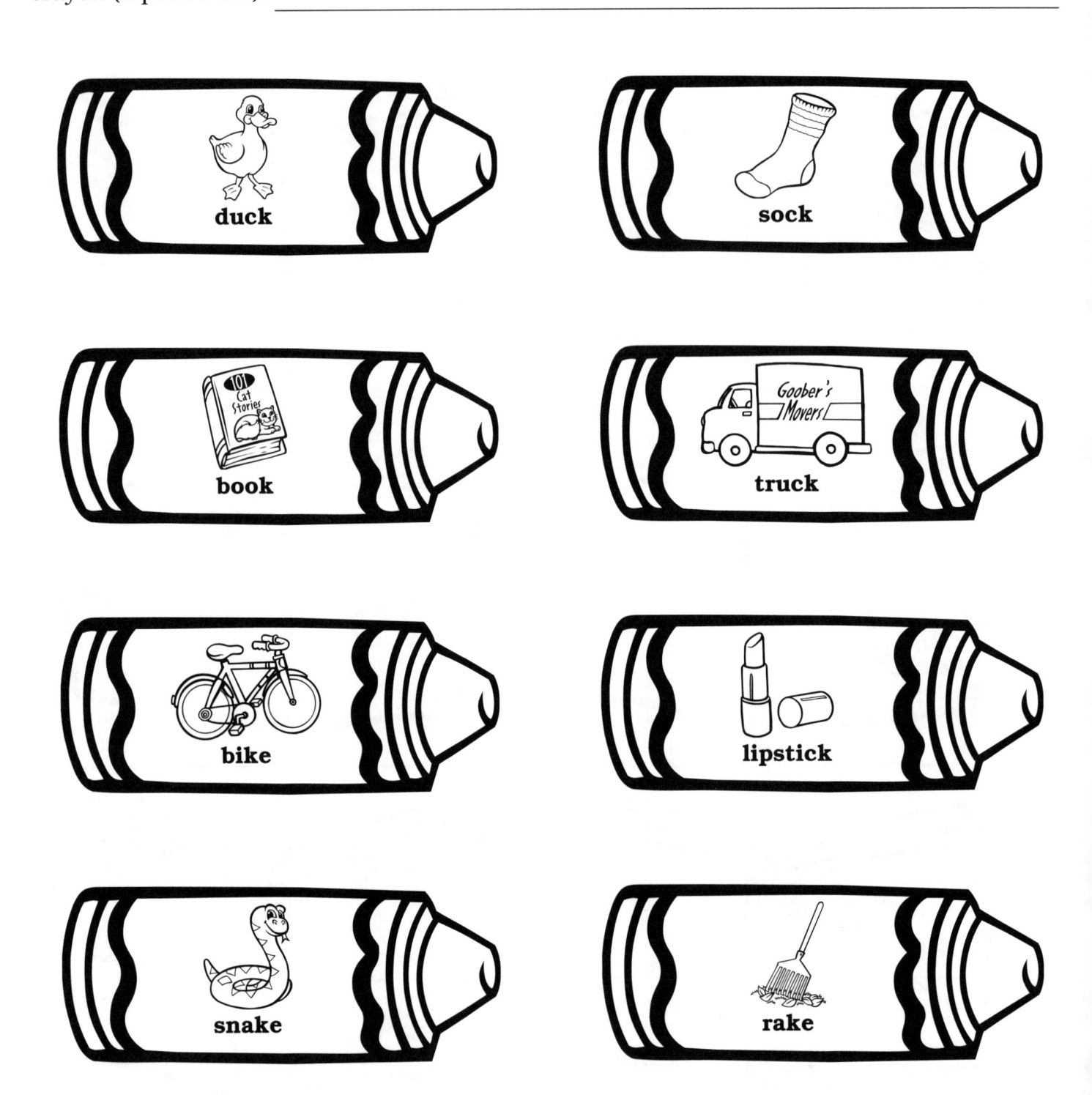

duck

sock

book

truck

bike

lipstick

snake

rake

Bonus
Name two colors that end with a K sound.

Answers: black, pink

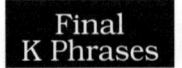

Homework Partner   Date   Speech-Language Pathologist

Final K Phrases

Phrase Racing

Directions: Cut out the cars. Give one to the student and one to a race partner. Begin at the starting line. Use a coin to determine the number of spaces to advance (heads=2, tails=1). Read/say aloud each phrase as you land on it. First one to the Finish wins! Play again.

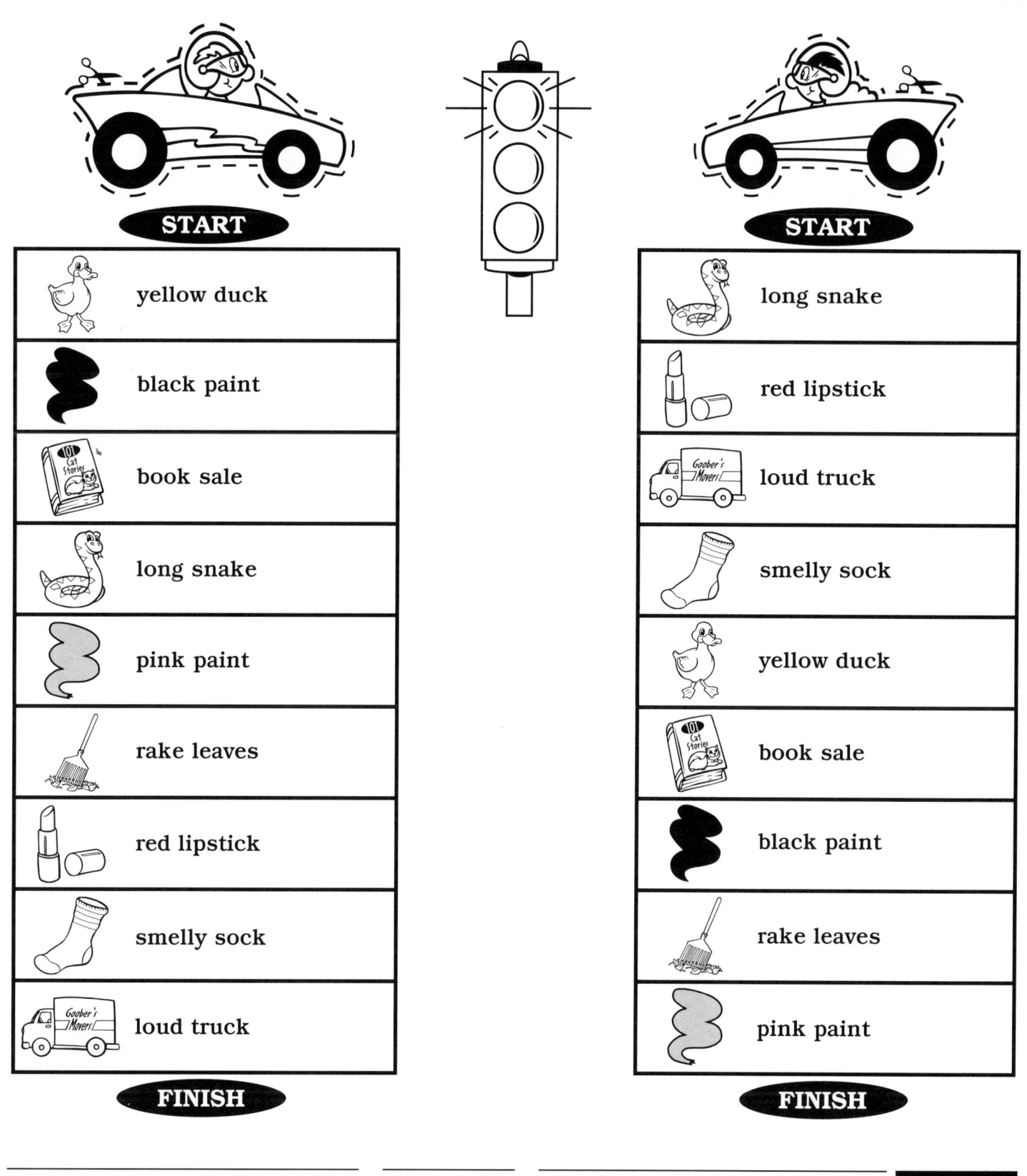

START

	yellow duck
	black paint
	book sale
	long snake
	pink paint
	rake leaves
	red lipstick
	smelly sock
	loud truck

FINISH

START

	long snake
	red lipstick
	loud truck
	smelly sock
	yellow duck
	book sale
	black paint
	rake leaves
	pink paint

FINISH

Homework Partner   Date   Speech-Language Pathologist

Final K Phrases

#BK-291 Webber® Artic Fun Sheets 2 • ©2002 Super Duper® Publications • www.superduperinc.com • 1-800-277-8737

135

Match Up Phrases

Directions: Read/say aloud each picture–word in column B. Then, draw a line from an adjective in column A that matches up to the words in column B (big book). Read/say the phrases aloud, using your good K sound. They can be silly or serious.

A	B
sleeping	duck
big	truck
red	lipstick
yellow	book
old	sock
new	bike
shiny	rake

Homework Partner   Date   Speech-Language Pathologist   Final K Phrases

Make It Fit!!

Directions: Circle the words that best finish the sentences below. Then, read/say the sentences aloud, using your good K sound.

1. Billy wants to ride his   **telephone**   **bike**   **chair** .

2. Mom put on her   **lipstick**   **beachball**   **car** .

3. The horn beeped on the   **dog**   **truck**   **candy** .

4. There are feathers on a   **bathtub**   **hot dog**   **duck** .

5. Before my shoe, I put on a   **buffalo**   **sock**   **flashlight** .

6. I heard the hissing   **ladder**   **fish**   **snake** .

7. I just read a great   **book**   **beaver**   **bug** .

Homework Partner   Date   Speech-Language Pathologist

Final K Sentences

A-Mazing Sentences!

Directions: Find the middle of the maze and begin reading the sentences. As you come to the end of a sentence, draw a line to separate the sentences. Read/say the sentences aloud, using your good K sound.

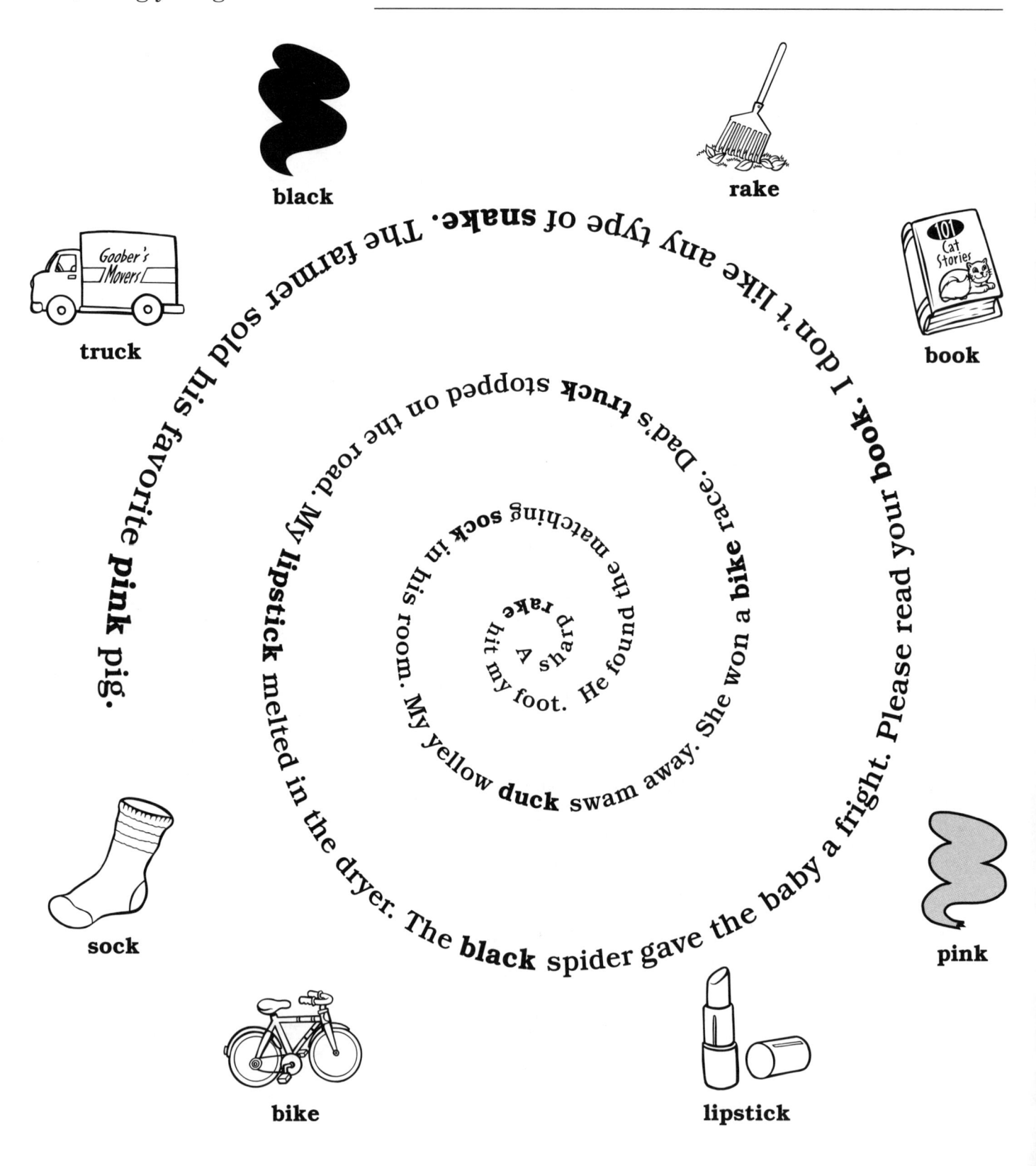

black

rake

truck

book

Sentences in spiral (from center outward):
A sharp **rake** hit my foot. He found the matching **sock** in his room. My yellow **duck** swam away. She won a **bike** race. Dad's **truck** stopped on the road. My **lipstick** melted in the dryer. The **black** spider gave the baby a fright. Please read your **book**. I don't like any type of **snake**. The farmer sold his favorite **pink pig**.

sock

pink

bike

lipstick

Homework Partner — Date — Speech-Language Pathologist

Final K Sentences

Story Loop

Directions: Read/say aloud each picture–word. Make up a story using all of the pictures in the circle. You can start anywhere in the circle and go in either direction, but you must always end where you started to complete the loop. Say your story aloud, using your good K sound.

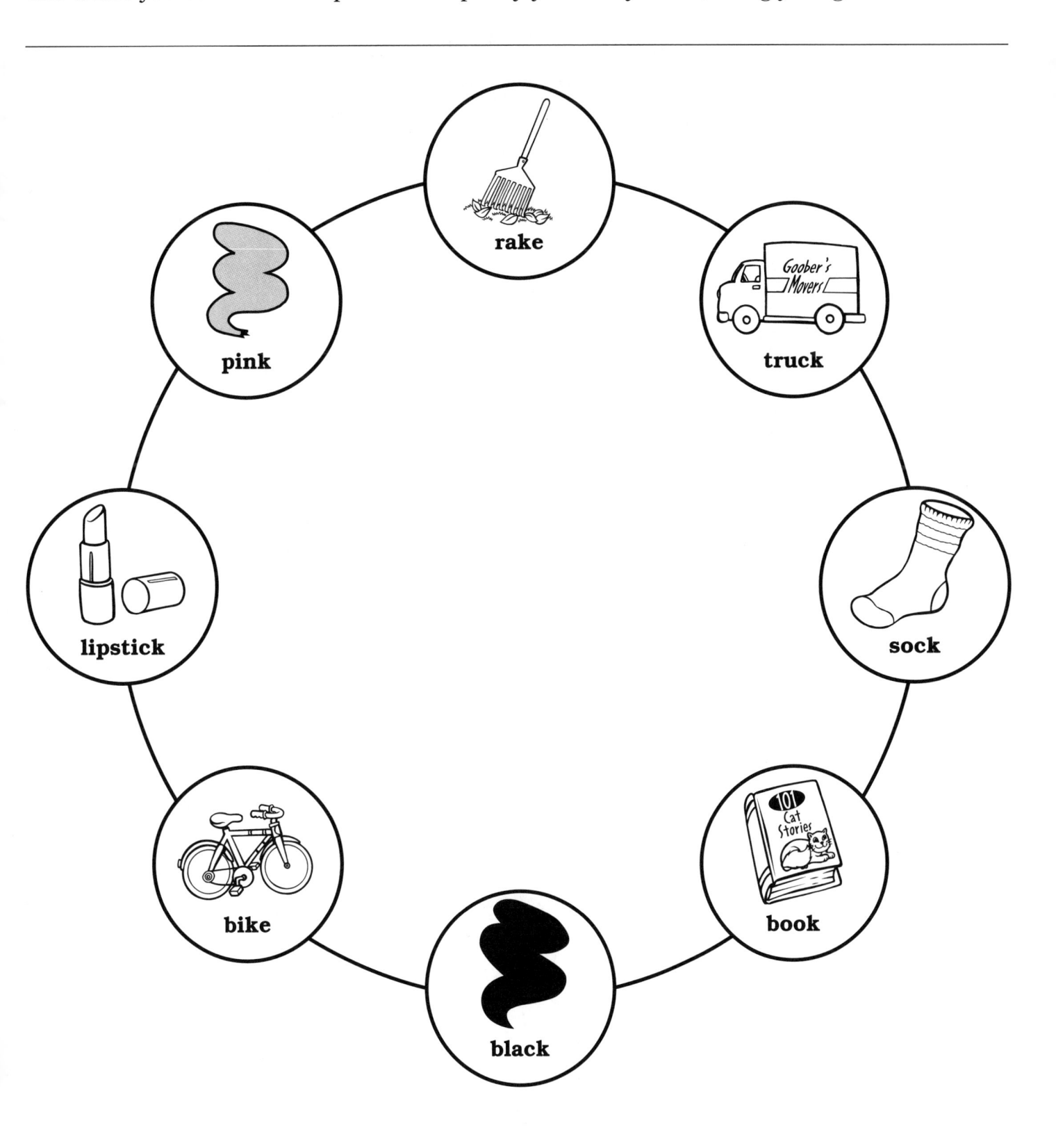

- rake
- truck
- sock
- book
- black
- bike
- lipstick
- pink

Homework Partner Date Speech-Language Pathologist

Final K Sentences

139

Pickles in a Jar

Directions: Cut out the pickles below and place them face down. As you choose a pickle, read/say aloud the picture–word on it and place the pickle onto the pickle jar. Remember to use your good K sound.

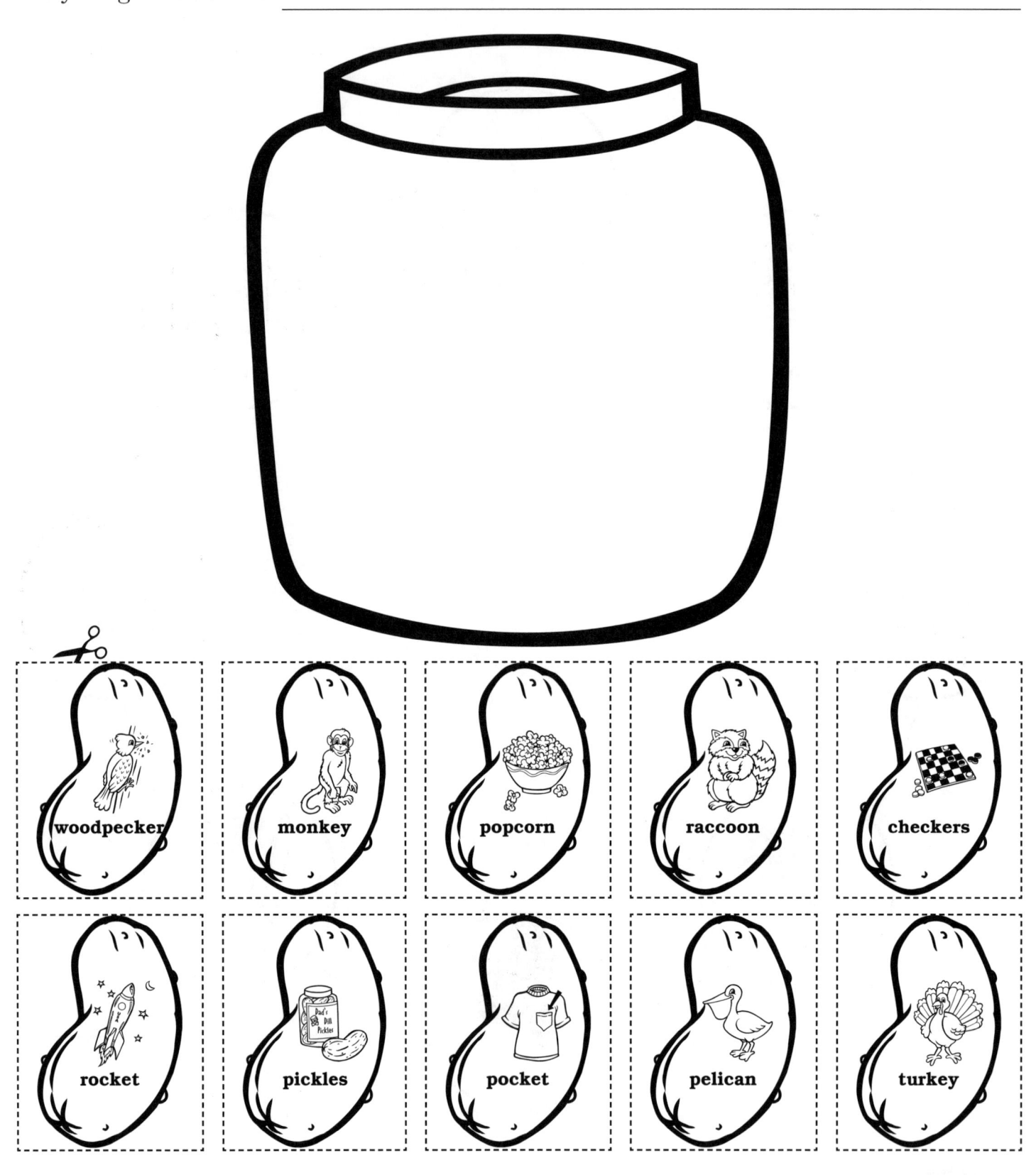

woodpecker	monkey	popcorn	raccoon	checkers
rocket	pickles	pocket	pelican	turkey

Homework Partner   Date   Speech-Language Pathologist

Medial K Words

Popcorn Popper

Directions: Toss a coin or roll a die on the page. Read/say aloud the word on the popcorn kernel nearest to where it lands. Then, color the popcorn. Remember to use your good K sound.

- turkey
- rocket
- monkey
- pocket
- raccoon
- pickles
- checkers
- pelican
- woodpecker

Homework Partner   Date   Speech-Language Pathologist

Medial K Words

X and O

Directions: Cut out each **X** and **O** below. Have each player/partner choose **X** or **O**. The first player reads/says a picture–word aloud and places an **X** or **O** on the square. Play continues in turn. The first person to get three in a row wins.

monkey	pickles	rocket
woodpecker	pelican	popcorn
checkers	pocket	turkey

X X X X X

O O O O O

Homework Partner   Date   Speech-Language Pathologist

Medial K Words

142   #BK-291 Webber® Artic Fun Sheets 2 • ©2002 Super Duper® Publications • www.superduperinc.com • 1-800-277-8737

Checkerboard

Directions: Cut out the checkers at the bottom of the page. Play checkers. Read/say aloud each picture–word you land on, using your good K sound.

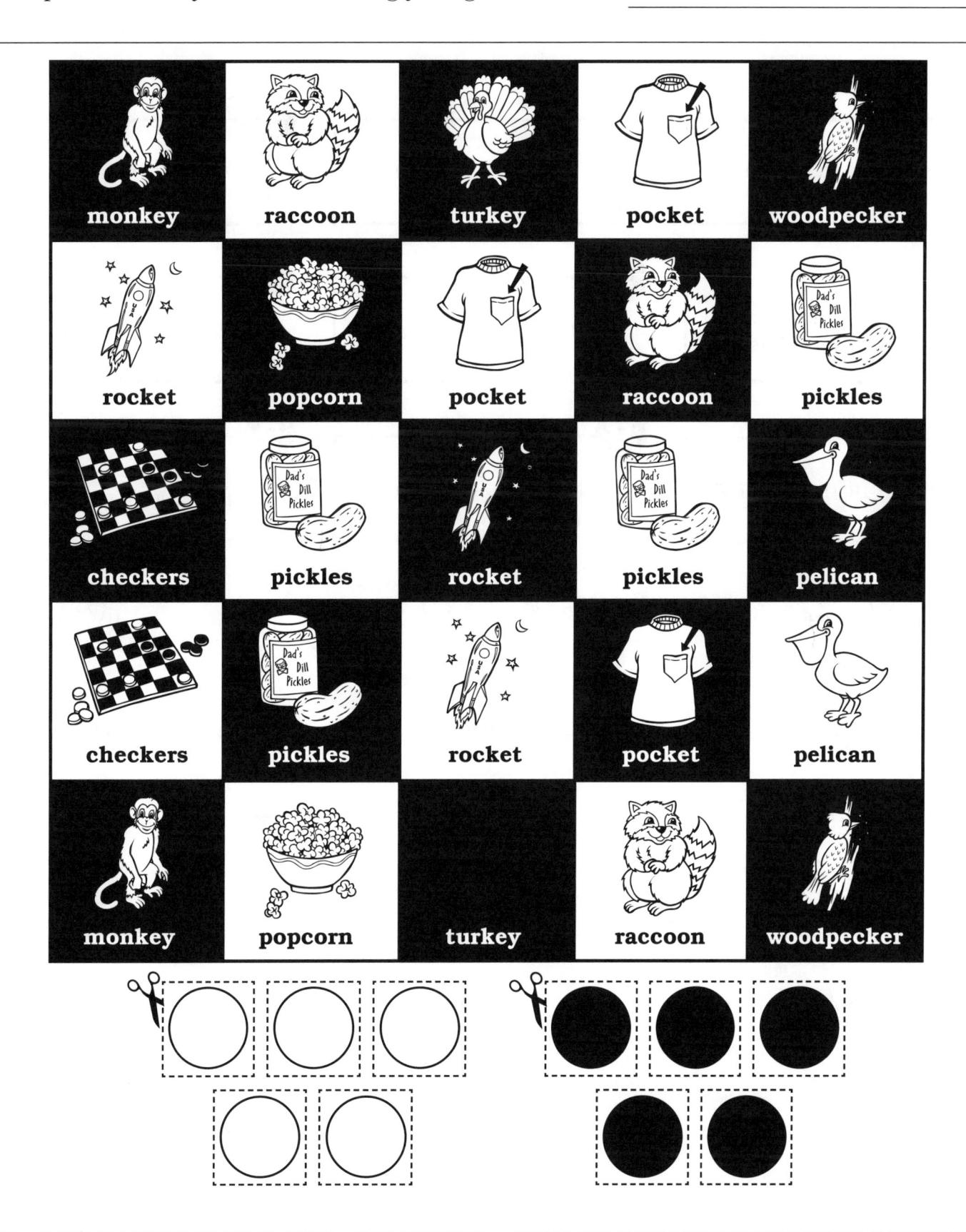

monkey	raccoon	turkey	pocket	woodpecker
rocket	popcorn	pocket	raccoon	pickles
checkers	pickles	rocket	pickles	pelican
checkers	pickles	rocket	pocket	pelican
monkey	popcorn	turkey	raccoon	woodpecker

Homework Partner   Date   Speech-Language Pathologist

Medial K Words

Make a Match

Directions: Read the statements. Then, find the correct answer below and write in the correct number in the blank space. Read/say the answers aloud, using your good K sound.

1. It's a bird that gobbles.
2. It is a board game.
3. It's a bird that eats fish.
4. It likes climbing and eating bananas.
5. It goes to the moon.
6. You put things in it.
7. Eat it at the movies.
8. It puts holes in trees.
9. It's an animal that looks like he wears a mask.

____ **pocket**

____ **monkey**

____ **turkey**

____ **pelican**

____ **rocket**

____ **woodpecker**

____ **popcorn**

____ **checkers**

____ **raccoon**

Homework Partner ____ Date ____ Speech-Language Pathologist

Medial K Words

What's in the Pocket?

Directions: Read each clue sentence aloud. Then, guess the answer from the Word Bank below. Say your answers, using your good K sound (monkey).

In the pocket I see...

1. ...an animal that eats bananas and swings from trees. What's in the pocket?

2. ...a game you play on a red and black board. What's in the pocket?

3. ...a food you eat with butter and salt at the movies. What's in the pocket?

4. ...an animal that has feathers and gobbles. What's in the pocket?

5. ...a snack in a jar that can be sweet or sour. What's in the pocket?

6. ...an ocean bird that eats fish with a big beak. What's in the pocket?

7. ...a furry animal that looks like he's wearing a mask. What's in the pocket?

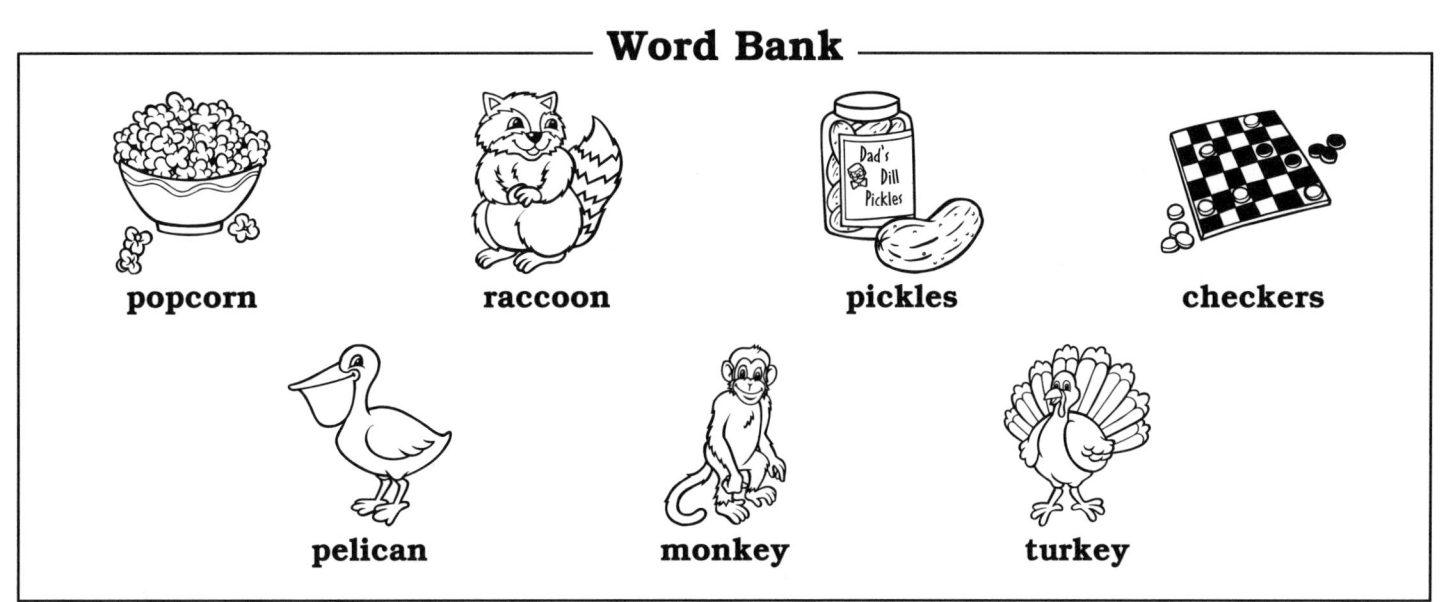

Word Bank

popcorn raccoon pickles checkers

pelican monkey turkey

Answers: 1. monkey, 2. checkers, 3. popcorn, 4. turkey, 5. pickles, 6. pelican, 7. raccoon

Homework Partner   Date   Speech-Language Pathologist

Medial K Words

Feed the Pelican

Directions: Read/say aloud each picture–word on the fish below. Cut out the fish, and place them face down. As you choose a fish word–picture, give it to one of the pelicans. Read/say the two words, saying the pelican word first (fast turkey). Remember to use your good K sound.

fast   silly   short

big   wet   green

turkey   pickles   popcorn   checkers

pelican   raccoon   woodpecker   rocket

Homework Partner   Date   Speech-Language Pathologist

Medial K Phrases

X and O

Directions: Cut out each **X** and **O** below. Have each player/partner choose **X** or **O**. The first player reads/says a picture–phrase aloud and places an **X** or **O** on the square. Play continues in turn. The first person to get three in a row wins.

gobbling turkey	shirt pocket	green pickles
flying pelican	huge rocket	jumping checkers
salty popcorn	loud woodpecker	sleepy raccoon

X X X X X

O O O O O

Homework Partner   Date   Speech-Language Pathologist

Medial K Phrases

Phrase Racing

Directions: Cut out the cars. Give one to the student and one to a race partner. Begin at the starting line. Use a coin to determine the number of spaces to advance (heads=2, tails=1). Read/say aloud each phrase as you land on it. First one to the Finish wins! Play again.

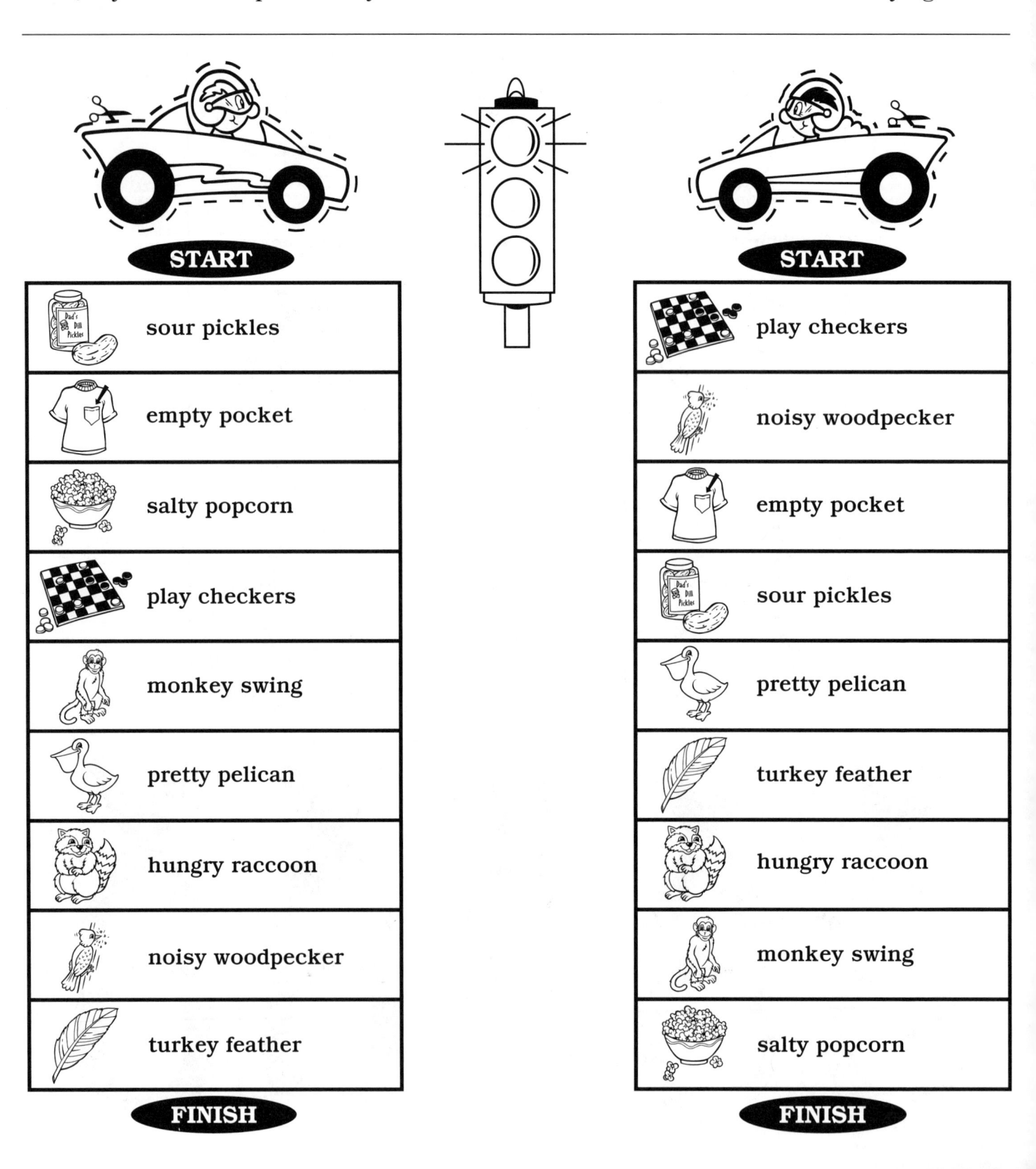

START

	sour pickles
	empty pocket
	salty popcorn
	play checkers
	monkey swing
	pretty pelican
	hungry raccoon
	noisy woodpecker
	turkey feather

FINISH

START

	play checkers
	noisy woodpecker
	empty pocket
	sour pickles
	pretty pelican
	turkey feather
	hungry raccoon
	monkey swing
	salty popcorn

FINISH

Homework Partner   Date   Speech-Language Pathologist

Medial K Phrases

Story Loop

Directions: Read/say aloud each picture–word. Make up a story using all of the pictures in the circle. You can start anywhere in the circle and go in either direction, but you must always end where you started to complete the loop. Say your story aloud, using your good K sound.

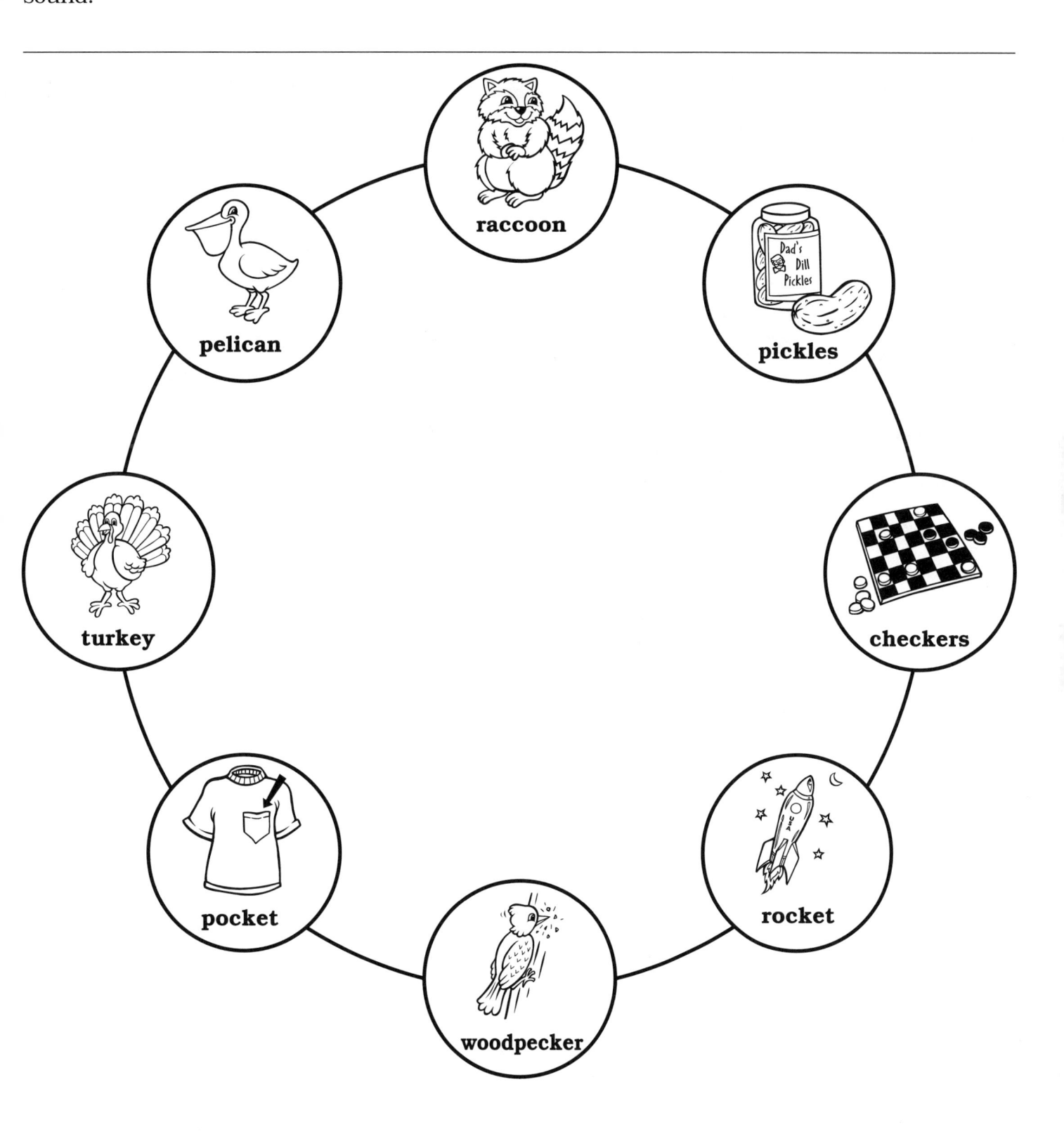

- raccoon
- pickles
- checkers
- rocket
- woodpecker
- pocket
- turkey
- pelican

Homework Partner   Date   Speech-Language Pathologist

Medial K Sentences

149

Pick a Pocket

Directions: Cut out the picture–word cards below. Also, cut on the dotted lines around each pocket so they can flip up. Hide one card under each pocket. Guess what is in each pocket using a sentence. (Is_____ in this pocket?) Use your good K sound. _____

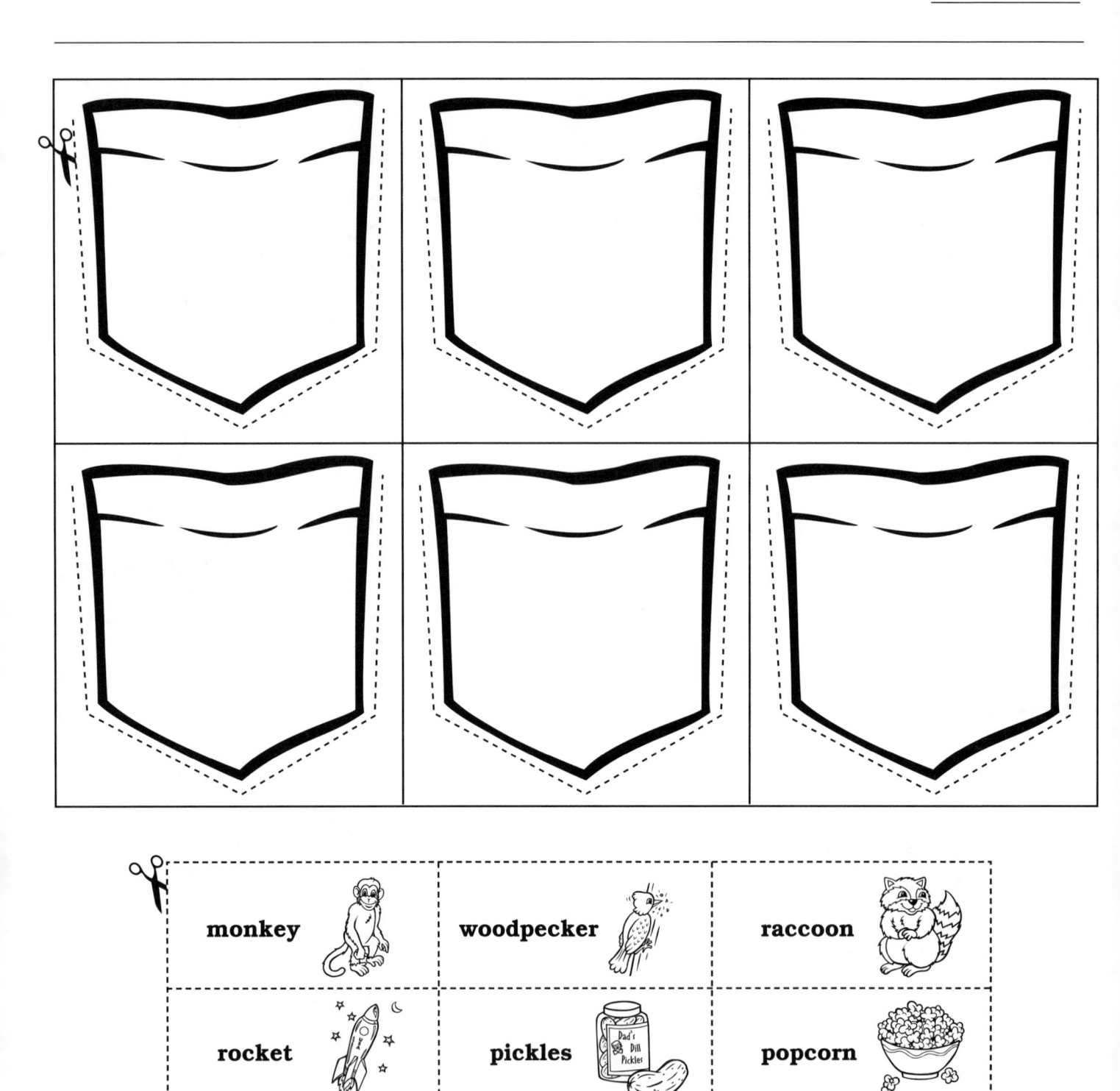

monkey	woodpecker	raccoon
rocket	pickles	popcorn

Homework Partner   Date   Speech-Language Pathologist

Medial K Sentences

150

To the Moon

Directions: Cut out the cards below. Shuffle the cards and place them face down. Have students sit around a table. Draw a card and read/say aloud the sentence on the rocket with that number. Then, pass the card around the table the number of times shown on the rocket's nose. The last person with the card reads/says the sentence aloud. Use your good K sound.

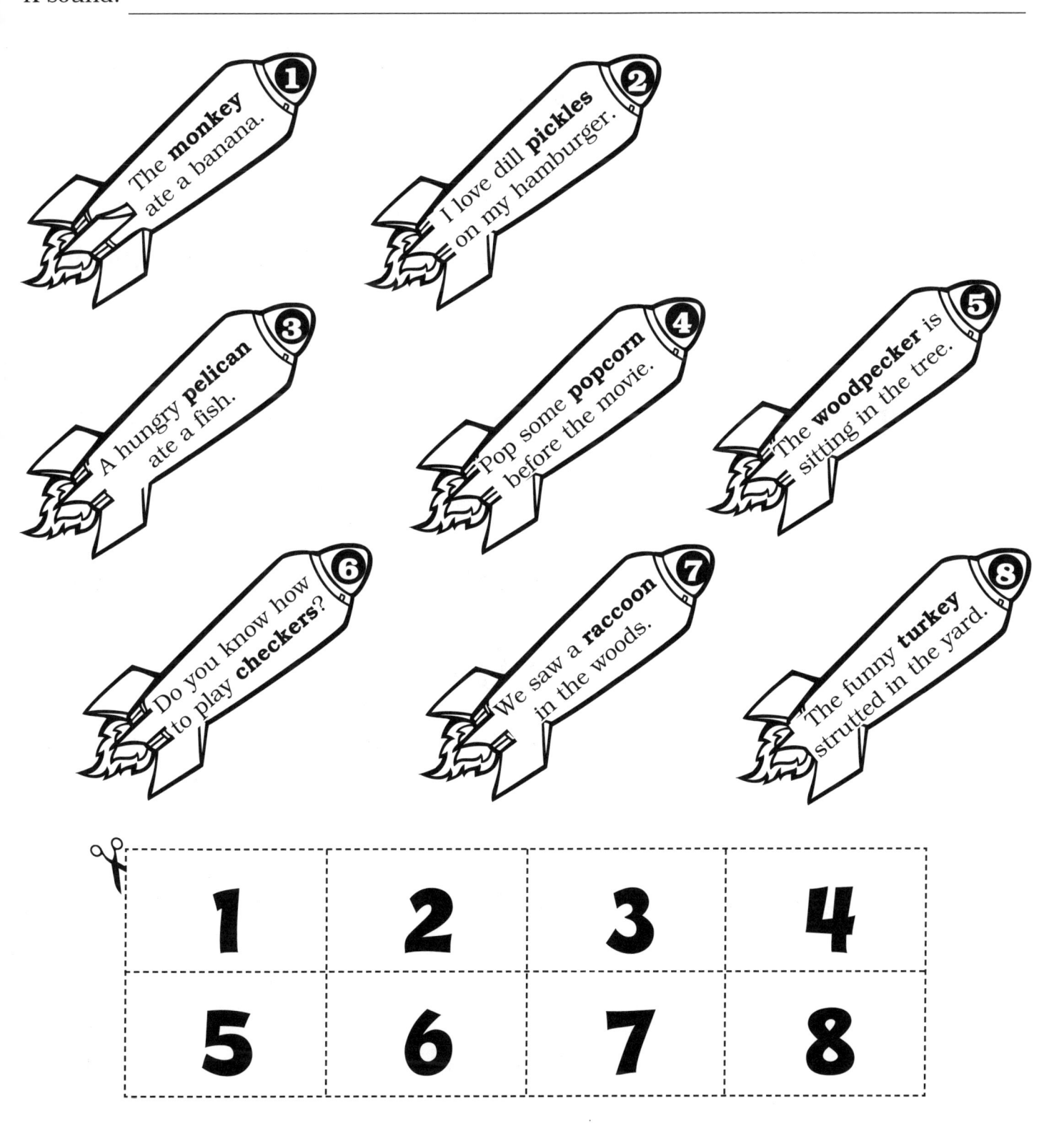

1. The **monkey** ate a banana.
2. I love dill **pickles** on my hamburger.
3. A hungry **pelican** ate a fish.
4. Pop some **popcorn** before the movie.
5. The **woodpecker** is sitting in the tree.
6. Do you know how to play **checkers**?
7. We saw a **raccoon** in the woods.
8. The funny **turkey** strutted in the yard.

1	2	3	4
5	6	7	8

Homework Partner   Date   Speech-Language Pathologist

Medial K Sentences

Make It Fit!!

Directions: Circle the words that best finish the sentences below. Then, read/say the sentences aloud, using your good K sound.

1. I put the dollar in my   **peach**   **cheese**   **pocket** .

2. I popped some   **popcorn**   **dishes**   **gown** .

3. I went to the zoo to see the   **leg**   **monkey**   **chair** .

4. I love to eat sour   **football**   **eyelashes**   **pickles** .

5. Let's play a game of   **checkers**   **gorilla**   **wrench** .

6. Let's go to Mars in a   **spider**   **rocket**   **fan** .

7. I heard a gobbling   **beachball**   **turkey**   **chair** .

Homework Partner   Date   Speech-Language Pathologist

Medial K Sentences

G Sound

Gopher Game

Directions: Cut out the gophers below and along the dotted lines on the holes. Poke a gopher halfway through each hole, enough so that the word is not showing. Choose a gopher to pull through hole and read/say each picture–word aloud, using your good G sound.

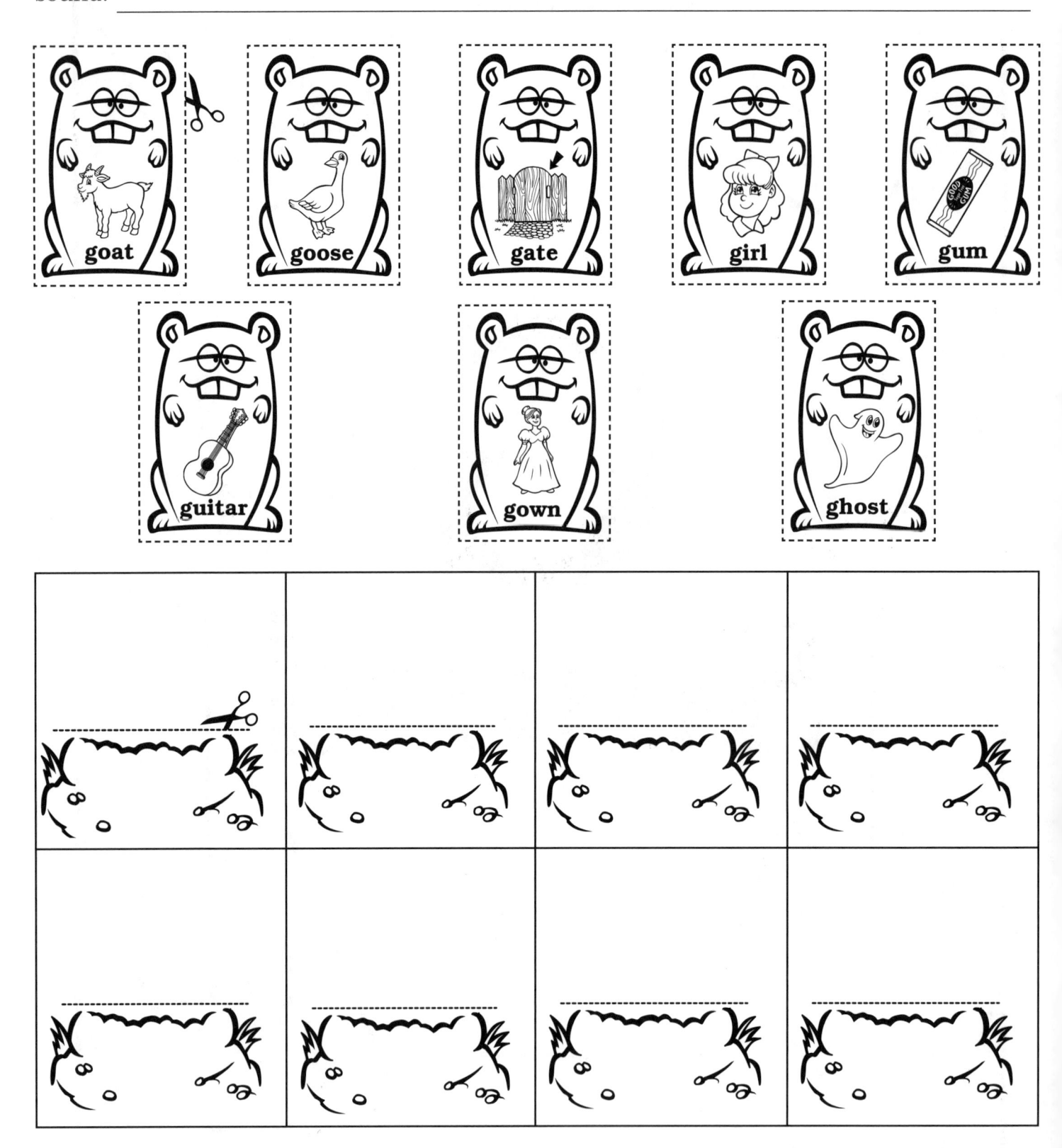

goat   goose   gate   girl   gum

guitar   gown   ghost

Homework Partner   Date   Speech-Language Pathologist

Initial G Words

The Most Ghosts

Directions: Cut out the ghosts, and spread out face down. Choose a ghost to flip over and name the picture–word. Remember to use your good G sound.

goat	goose	gate
girl	guitar	gum
gopher	goldfish	gown

Homework Partner   Date   Speech-Language Pathologist

Initial G Words

Flip the Fish

Directions: Cut out the fish cards below. Then, on the back, number them from 1-6. Place all the fish face down. Roll a die and select the fish with the same number as rolled. Read/say the word aloud, using your good G sound. (As a variation, say the word the same number of times as the number rolled.)

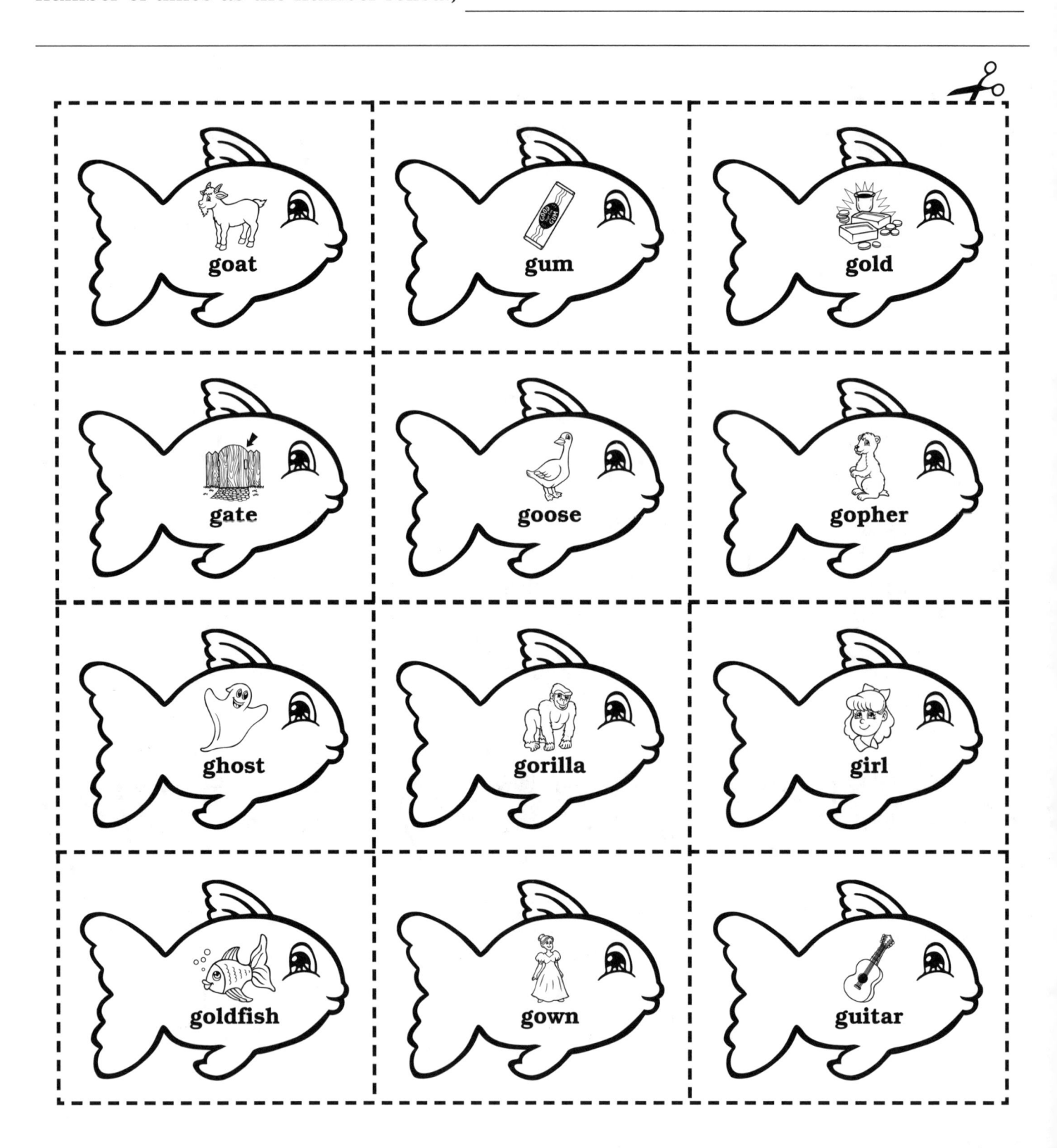

goat	gum	gold
gate	goose	gopher
ghost	gorilla	girl
goldfish	gown	guitar

Homework Partner   Date   Speech-Language Pathologist

Initial G Words

G Cube Roll

Directions: Assemble the cube as follows: glue onto construction paper for added durability. Cut along the dotted lines. Fold on solid lines and glue as indicated. To play: roll the cube. Read/say aloud the word you see using your good G sound.

Glue Tab C

goldfish

Glue A | goat | gopher | gorilla | Glue B

gown

Glue Tab A | girl | Glue Tab B

Glue C

Homework Partner | Date | Speech-Language Pathologist

Initial G Words

Gold Rush!

Directions: Cut out the picture–word cards and the gold pieces below. Arrange the cards face up, and hide various numbers of gold pieces under each card. First player reads/says a picture–word aloud, using his/her good G sound. He/she keeps the gold pieces. Play continues in turn. Player with the most gold wins.

goat	goose	girl	gate
gum	**gown**	**ghost**	**guitar**

Homework Partner Date Speech-Language Pathologist Initial G Words

Rhyming Matches

Directions: Read/say the words in column A. Then, find the rhyming words in column B (pearl/girl). Draw a line to connect the pair and read/say the rhyming words in column B aloud. Use your good G sound.

A	**B**
moose	goat
drum	gate
toast	goose
boat	gum
cold	gold
frown	gown
pearl	ghost
plate	girl

Answers: moose/goose, drum/gum, toast/ghost, boat/goat, cold/gold, frown/gown, pearl/girl, plate/gate

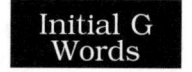

Homework Partner   Date   Speech-Language Pathologist   Initial G Words

Mine or Yours?

Directions: Read/say each picture–word below. Cut out the pictures. At each turn, flip a coin. Heads means the student keeps the pictures and says, "My _____" (My goat). Tails means that the student gives the picture to his partner and says, "Your _____" (Your goat). Player with the most pictures at the end wins.

goat	girl
gopher	gold
gorilla	gown
guitar	gate
goose	gum

Homework Partner   Date   Speech-Language Pathologist

Initial G Phrases

160   #BK-291 Webber® Artic Fun Sheets 2 • ©2002 Super Duper® Publications • www.superduperinc.com • 1-800-277-8737

Terrific Tunes

Directions: Pick a note and act out the phrase. Others guess what phrase is being acted out. One point awarded for every correct guess. Student with the most points wins. Remember to use your good G sound.

- hairy **gorilla**
- **gum** wrapper
- **ghost** town
- lovely **gown**
- little **gopher**
- white **goose**
- billy **goat**
- hidden **gold**
- **goldfish** pond

Homework Partner   Date   Speech-Language Pathologist

Initial G Phrases

Make a Phrase

Directions: Pick an adjective from column A and a noun from column B. Put them together to make a phrase in column C (happy ghost). Read/say your phrases aloud, using your good G sound.

A	B	C
1. shiny	gate	_____
2. happy	ghost	_____
3. scary	gold	_____
4. bubble	girl	_____
5. open	goat	_____
6. pretty	gown	_____
7. silly	gum	_____
8. evening	goose	_____

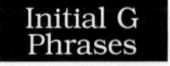

Homework Partner   Date   Speech-Language Pathologist

Initial G Phrases

Yo-De-Lay-De-Hoo Game

Directions: Read/say aloud the picture–words below. Then, cut out the markers. Flip a coin (heads=1, tails=2) to determine how many spaces to move. As you move, read/say each phrase aloud, using your good G sound. First player to reach the finish wins.

FINISH: wet goldfish — bubble gum — billy goat — silly goose — open gate — hairy gorilla — friendly ghost — Climb Up 1 Space! — happy girl — shiny gold — pretty gown — loud guitar — busy gopher — **START**

Homework Partner — Date — Speech-Language Pathologist

Initial G Phrases

#BK-291 Webber® Artic Fun Sheets 2 • ©2002 Super Duper® Publications • www.superduperinc.com • 1-800-277-8737

163

If...Then...

Directions: Read/say the following phrases aloud and make up an ending to complete each sentence. Remember to use your good G sound.

1. If a **guitar** would not play, then _____.

2. If the **gopher** made a hole, then _____.

3. If a **gorilla** escaped from the zoo, then _____.

4. If his **gate** did not shut, then _____.

5. If my **goldfish** fell asleep, then _____.

6. If the **girl** broke the lamp, then _____.

7. If the queen's **gown** was ripped, then _____.

8. If the **goat** ran away, then _____.

Homework Partner   Date   Speech-Language Pathologist

Initial G Sentences

One, Two, Three

Directions: Each student gets three turns to roll the die. Each turn represents a phrase to be used in a silly sentence. For example, a student who rolls a two, five, and one will make a sentence with the phrases: "The goose near the post is drinking milk." Read/say each sentence aloud using your good G sound.

	Roll One	Roll Two	Roll Three
1.	The **goat**	on a fence	is drinking milk.
2.	The **goose**	with a curl	is singing songs.
3.	A **gate**	in a boat	is jumping rope.
4.	A **girl**	on a trip	is eating fish.
5.	The **gum**	near the post	is happy.
6.	A **ghost**	on the train	is shaking hands.
7.	A **gorilla**	in a school	is making noises.
8.	The **gopher**	in a hole	is running wild.
9.	A **goldfish**	in the water	is asleep.
10.	The **gold**	on a bike	is very shiny.

Homework Partner   Date   Speech-Language Pathologist

Initial G Sentences

Pig Race

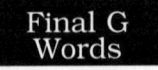

Directions: Read/say aloud the picture–words below. Then, cut out the markers. Flip a coin (heads=1, tails=2) to determine how many spaces to move. As you move, read/say each word aloud, using your good G sound. First player to reach the finish wins.

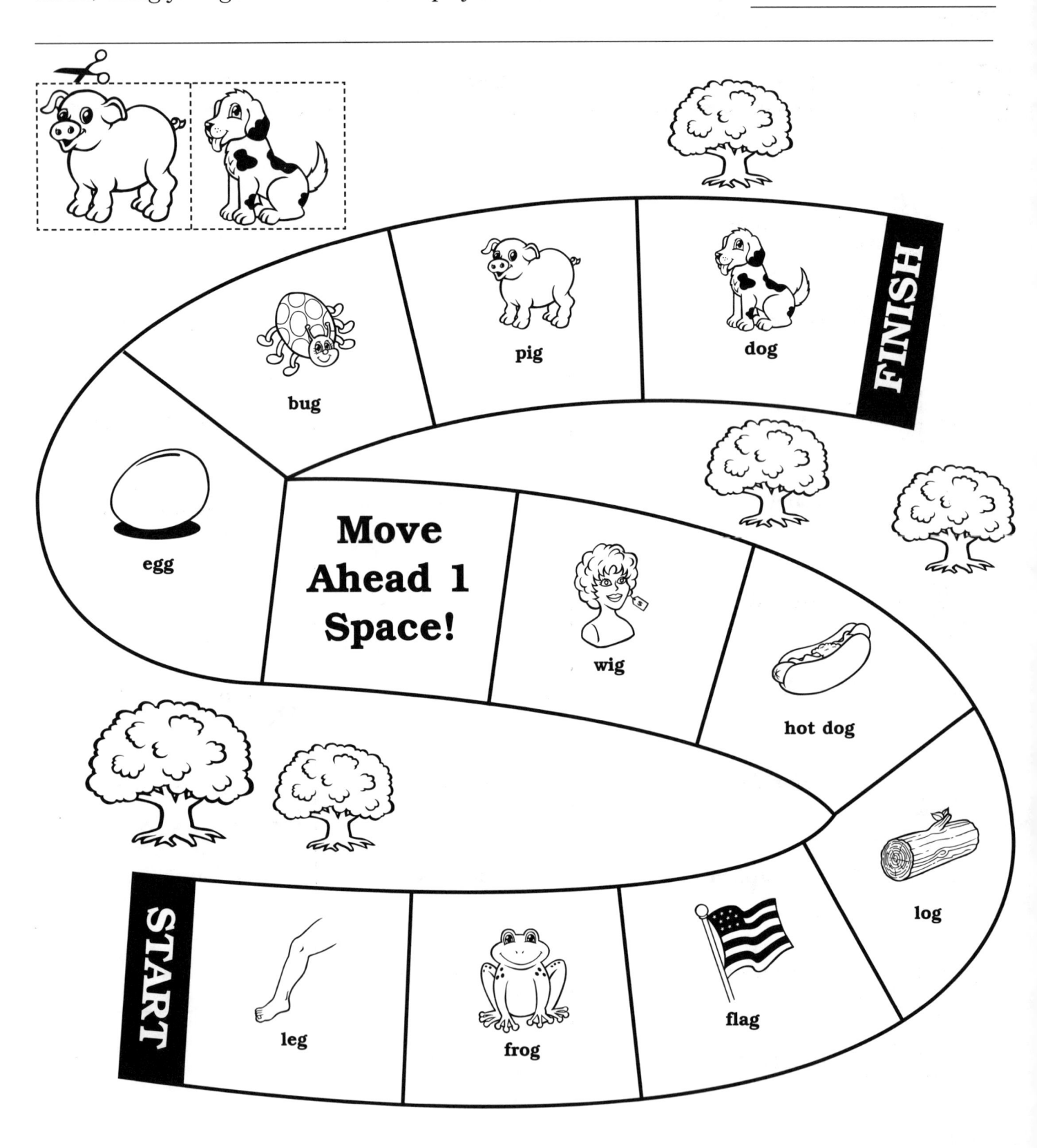

bug
pig
dog
FINISH
egg
Move Ahead 1 Space!
wig
hot dog
log
START
leg
frog
flag

Homework Partner   Date   Speech-Language Pathologist

Final G Words

3 Games in 1

Directions: Say aloud the picture–words below, using your good G sound. Then, play one of the following games:

- ☐ Lotto – Caller reads a word and student repeats the word and covers it with a token/chip.
- ☐ Tic–Tac–Toe – Each time you write an **X** or **O**, say the word you mark over.
- ☐ Memory – Cut out all the cards and place face down. Try to find matching pairs. Say aloud each word you find. Keep all matches.

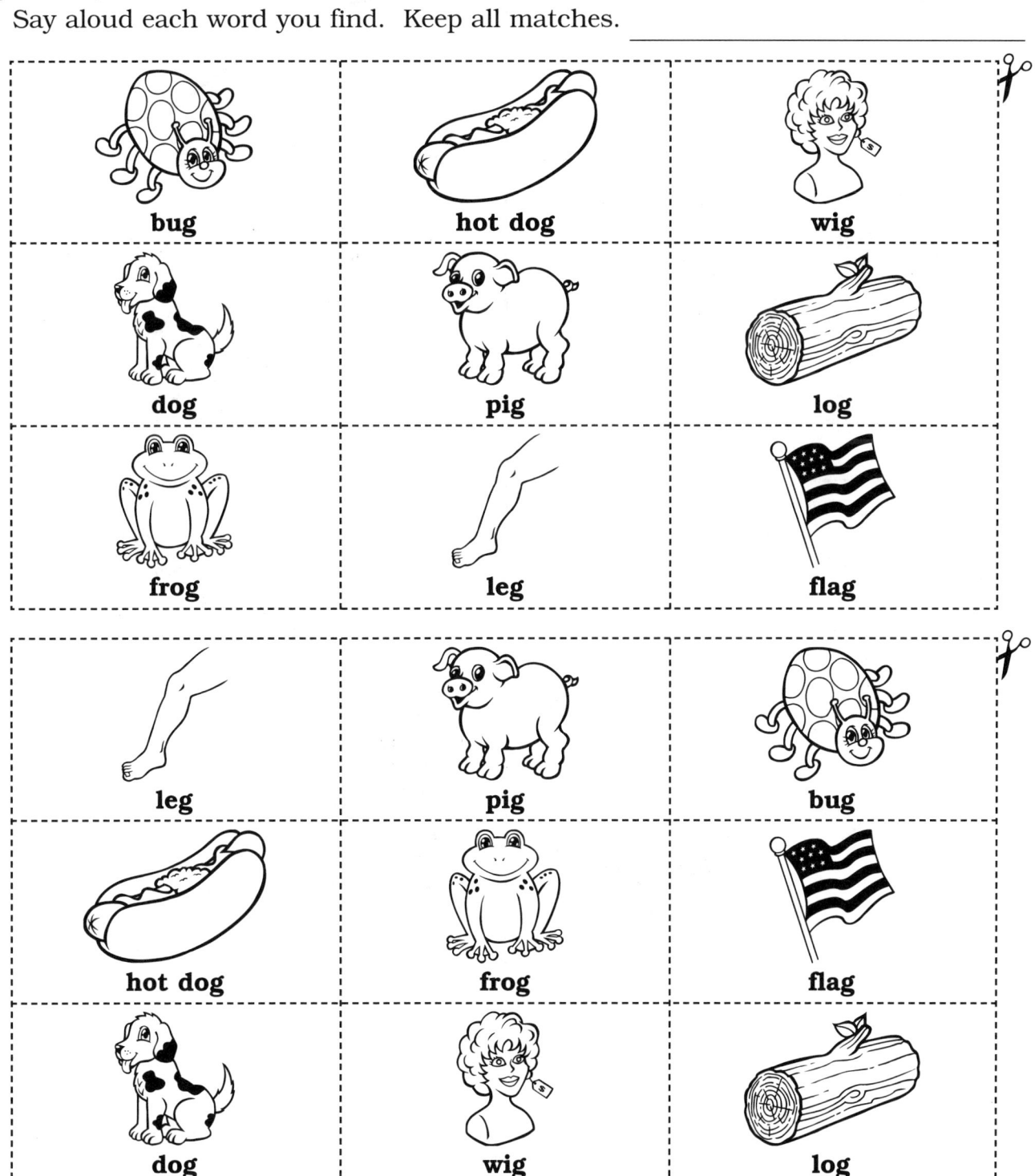

bug	hot dog	wig
dog	pig	log
frog	leg	flag
leg	pig	bug
hot dog	frog	flag
dog	wig	log

Homework Partner   Date   Speech-Language Pathologist

Final G Words

#BK-291 Webber® Artic Fun Sheets 2 • ©2002 Super Duper® Publications • www.superduperinc.com • 1-800-277-8737

167

G Spinner Action

Directions: Read/say aloud the picture–words below. If you prefer, glue this page to construction paper for added durability. Cut out the arrow/dial. Use a brad to connect the dial to the circle. Spin the spinner. When you land on a picture, read/say the word aloud, using your best G sound.

frog

pig

log

bug

wig

hot dog

egg

dog

Homework Partner   Date   Speech-Language Pathologist

Final G Words

Hide-and-Seek

Directions: Read/say aloud the picture–words. If you prefer, glue the pictures on a file folder/cardboard. Cut out the pictures and bug. Place the pictures face up. Have your partner hide the bug under a picture. Name the picture where you think the bug is hidden. (Hot dog?) Use your good G sound.

dog	pig	wig
flag	hot dog	leg
log	egg	frog

Homework Partner   Date   Speech-Language Pathologist

Final G Words

Read the Book!

Directions: The words below are all missing a letter. Use the picture clue to help you fill the letters in on the line provided. Then, read/say the words aloud, using your good G sound.

1. d___g
2. l___g
3. p___g
4. w___g
5. ___gg
6. hot d___g

Answers: 1. dog, 2. log, 3. pig, 4. wig, 5. egg, 6. hot dog

Homework Partner   Date   Speech-Language Pathologist

Final G Words

Change It!

Directions: Read/say aloud the picture–words below. Try to change the first word into the second word by changing one letter per line (dog, do<u>t</u>, <u>c</u>ot, c<u>a</u>t). You must do it in three lines. Each line must be a real word.

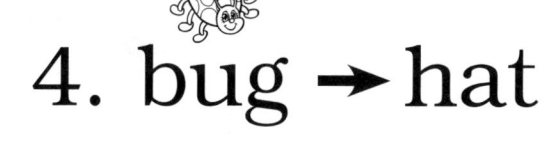

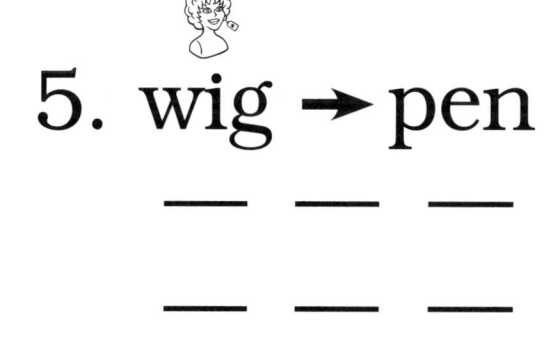

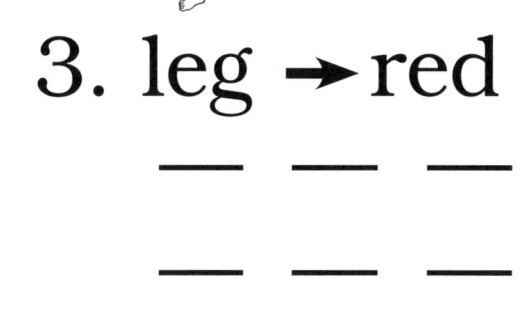

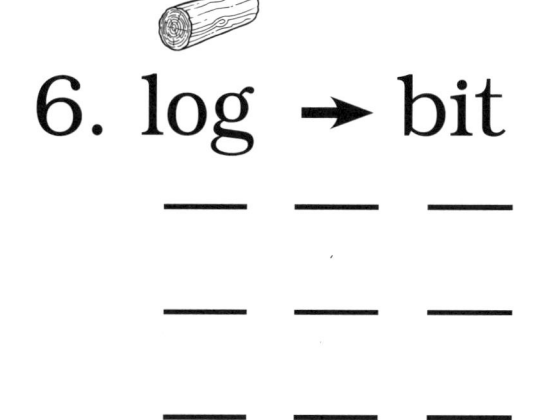

1. dog → cat

2. pig → ton

3. leg → red

4. bug → hat

5. wig → pen

6. log → bit

Answer Key on Page 279

Homework Partner   Date   Speech-Language Pathologist

Final G Words

Q & A Match Up

Directions: Read the questions and find the answers at the bottom. Write the question number on the line of the matching answer. Then, read/say each answer aloud (a little turtle). Use your good G sound!

1 What is good for breakfast?

2 What barks a lot?

3 What hops on lily pads?

4 What is small, red, and black?

5 What helps someone walk?

6 What eats and oinks?

7 What covers your head?

8 What do you salute?

9 What goes in a fireplace?

_____ **yippy dog**

_____ **expensive wig**

_____ **hoppy frog**

_____ **fried egg**

_____ **fat pig**

_____ **hairy leg**

_____ **American flag**

_____ **ladybug**

_____ **pine log**

Homework Partner   Date   Speech-Language Pathologist

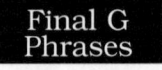

Final G Phrases

Egg Connection

Directions: Cut out the egg halves. Find each missing half, and say/read the phrase aloud. Keep any matches. Student with the most matches wins. Remember to use your good G sound.

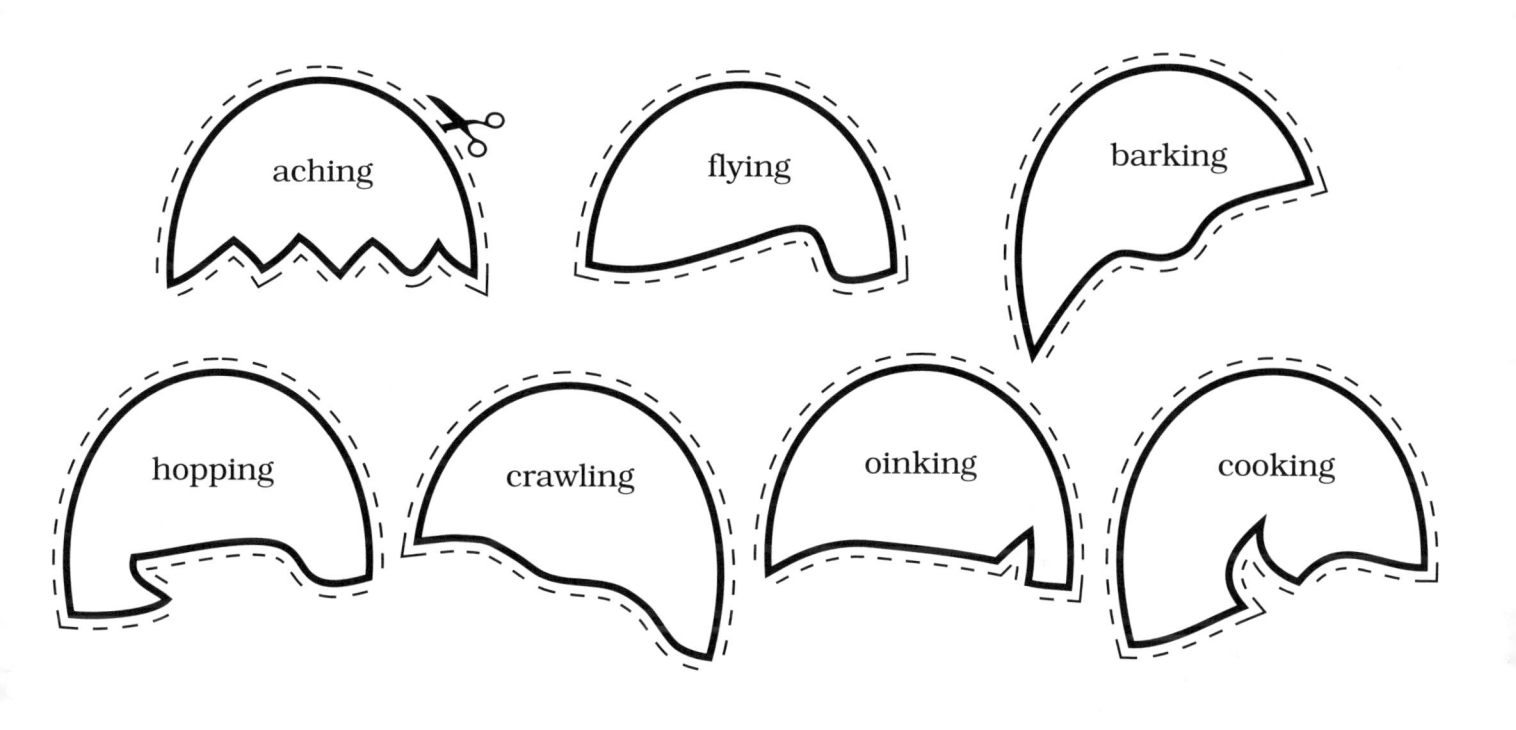

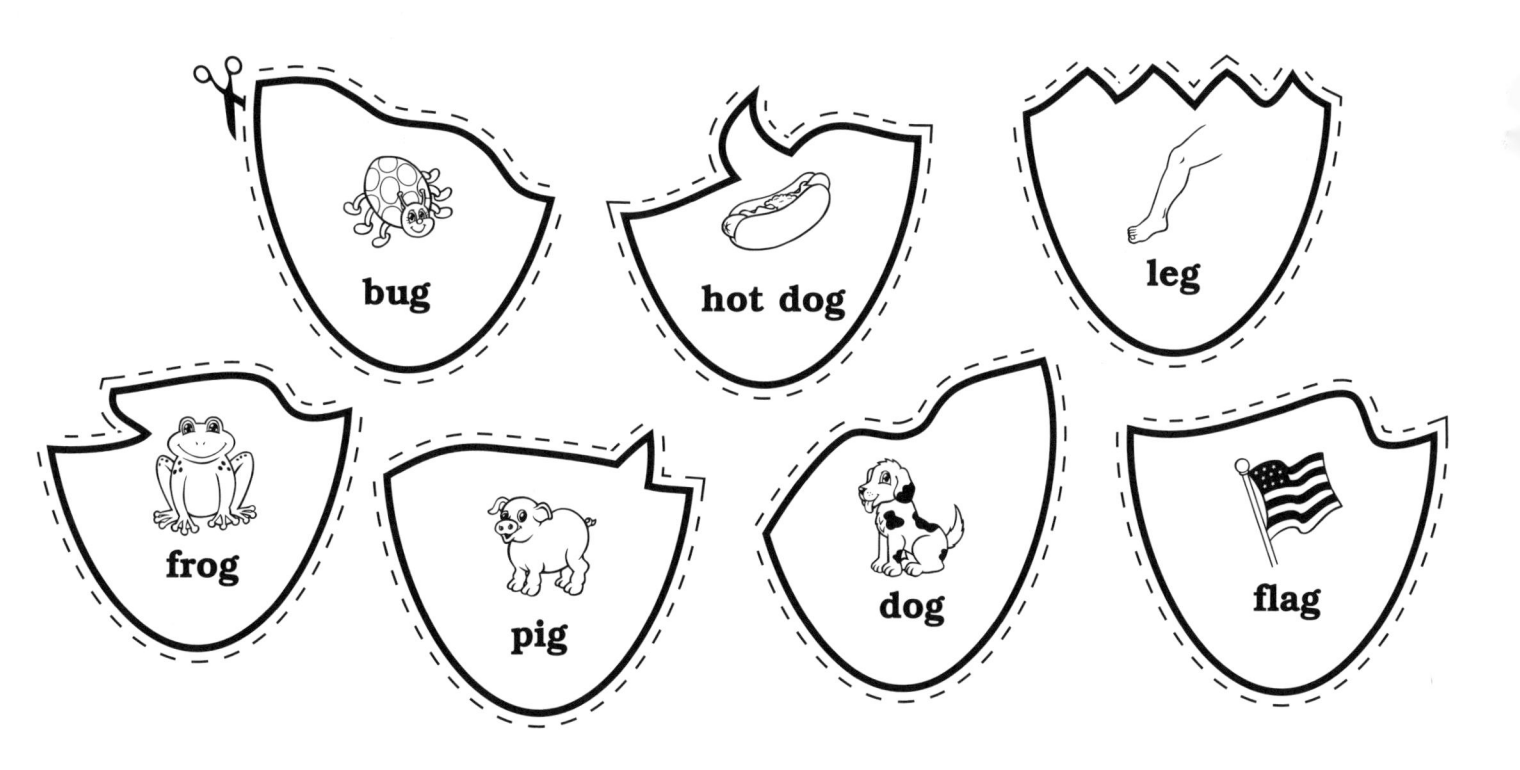

Top egg halves:
- aching
- flying
- barking
- hopping
- crawling
- oinking
- cooking

Bottom egg halves:
- bug
- hot dog
- leg
- frog
- pig
- dog
- flag

Homework Partner   Date   Speech-Language Pathologist

Final G Phrases

Search-a-Word

Directions: Read/say the picture–words aloud. Then, complete the phrases below. Use the picture–words for hints. Find and circle each word answer in the word search box. Then, read/say the complete phrases aloud. Use your good G sound. _____

_____

flag

wig

pig

log

egg

```
E L E B T I X H A C K C L O G
N G A U S R B O I A K A P A E
H W G E E A N T S N Q G J H U
K K N E R I W D V D X O M R W
X F G Y Z E J O L Y A W P A Q
W C F C J P I G M N S M X F L
K X Z B W E I X D I U R C O E
C E B Z Q F L A G V D W L Z G
N L Y V S U R W I D L H K O I
O Z N S O B Q U D C W I G S T
B N R I M A H B O S D W J W M
U S J J B F P J Y U K F S O K
G R R I Z R B Z C E K B R H K
J R H E N O A I K Y J U X O T
C X R R H G K B S H Z V D O G
```

bug

hot dog

dog

frog

leg

Answer Key on Page 280

1. ____ ____ bun
2. Easter ____
3. ____ collar
4. curly ____
5. dirty ____

6. hopping ____
7. broken ____
8. creepy ____
9. ____ cabin
10. salute the ____

Answers: 1. hot dog, 2. egg, 3. dog, 4. wig, 5. pig, 6. frog, 7. leg, 8. bug, 9. log, 10. flag

_____   _____   _____   Final G
Homework Partner   Date   Speech-Language Pathologist   Phrases

174   #BK-291 Webber® Artic Fun Sheets 2 • ©2002 Super Duper® Publications • www.superduperinc.com • 1-800-277-8737

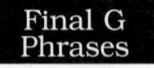

Finish the Sentence

Directions: Complete each sentence by telling what you would do. Say the complete sentence aloud, using your good G sound.

1. If I could be any **bug**... _____
_____.

2. If I only had one **leg**... _____
_____.

3. If I hatched from an **egg**... _____
_____.

4. If I had a pet **pig**... _____
_____.

5. If I lived in a **log**... _____
_____.

6. If I had to wear a **wig**... _____
_____.

7. If I could have anything on my **hot dog**... _____
_____.

8. If my **dog** could talk... _____
_____.

_____   _____   _____
Homework Partner   Date   Speech-Language Pathologist

Final G Sentences

Where's the Bun?

Directions: Read the phrase with the hot dog on the left. Then, find the phrase on the bun on the right that best matches to make a sentence. Read/say the complete sentence aloud, and draw a line connecting the phrases. Use your good G sound.

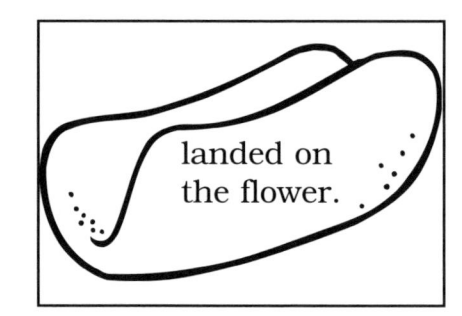

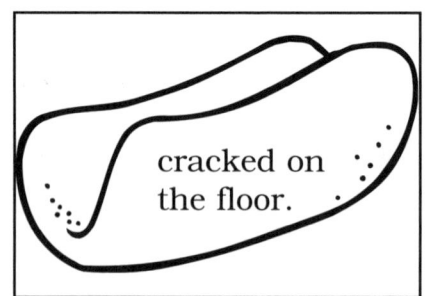

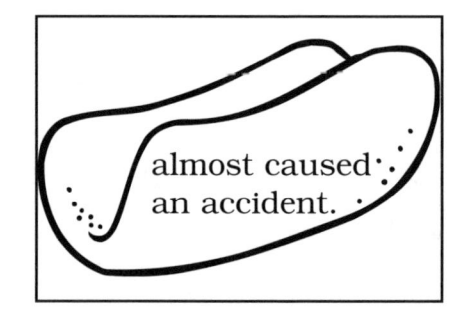

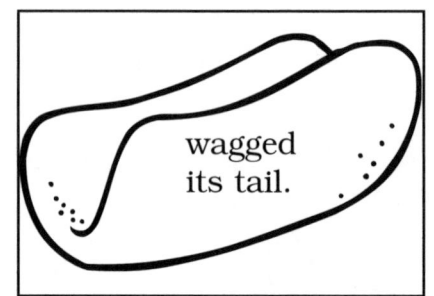

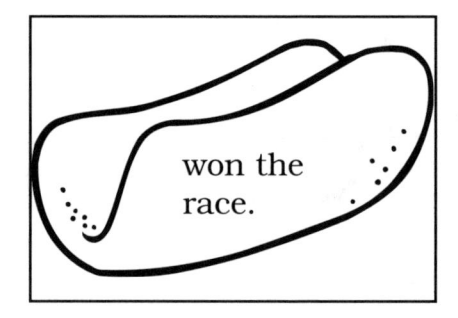

Left (hot dogs):
- The cute **dog**
- Our green **frog**
- The new **egg**
- The big **log** in the road
- The orange **bug**

Right (buns):
- landed on the flower.
- cracked on the floor.
- almost caused an accident.
- wagged its tail.
- won the race.

Homework Partner   Date   Speech-Language Pathologist

Final G Sentences

Story Loop

Directions: Read/say aloud each picture–word. Make up a story using all of the pictures in the circle. You can start anywhere in the circle and go in either direction, but you must always end where you started to complete the loop. Say your story aloud, using your good G sound.

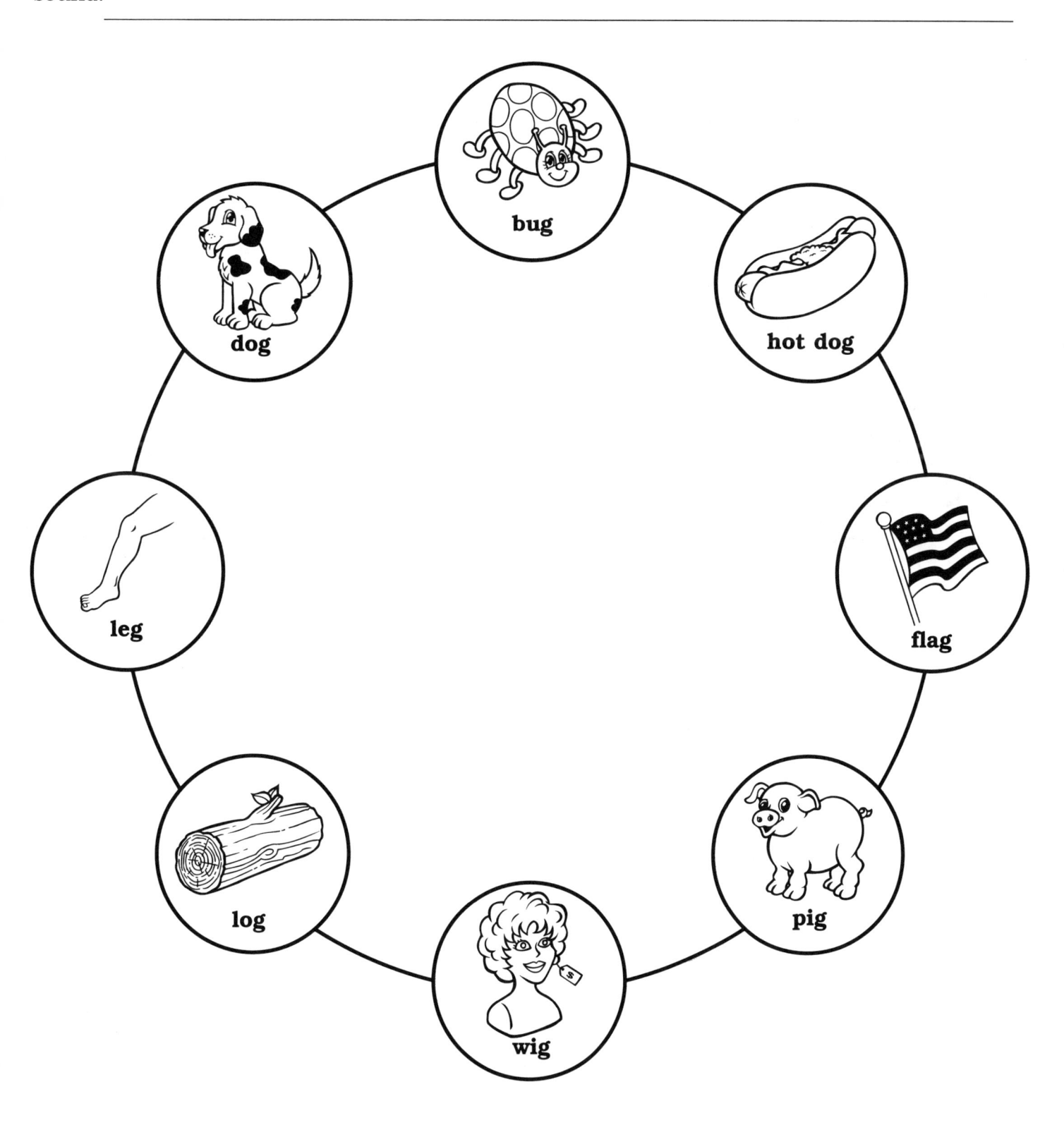

- bug
- hot dog
- flag
- pig
- wig
- log
- leg
- dog

Homework Partner   Date   Speech-Language Pathologist

Final G Sentences

Meatball Mountain

Directions: Cut out the plates of spaghetti and meatballs below. Read/say the picture-words on the meatballs. Then, place the meatballs on the spaghetti. Remember to use your good G sound.

- alligator
- eagle
- tiger
- wagon
- finger
- spaghetti
- seagull
- hamburger
- igloo
- luggage

Homework Partner   Date   Speech-Language Pathologist

Medial G Words

Alligator!

Directions: Read/say aloud the picture–words below. Then, cut out the markers. Flip a coin (heads=1, tails=2) to determine how many spaces to move. As you move, read/say each word aloud, using your good G sound. First player to reach the finish wins. _____

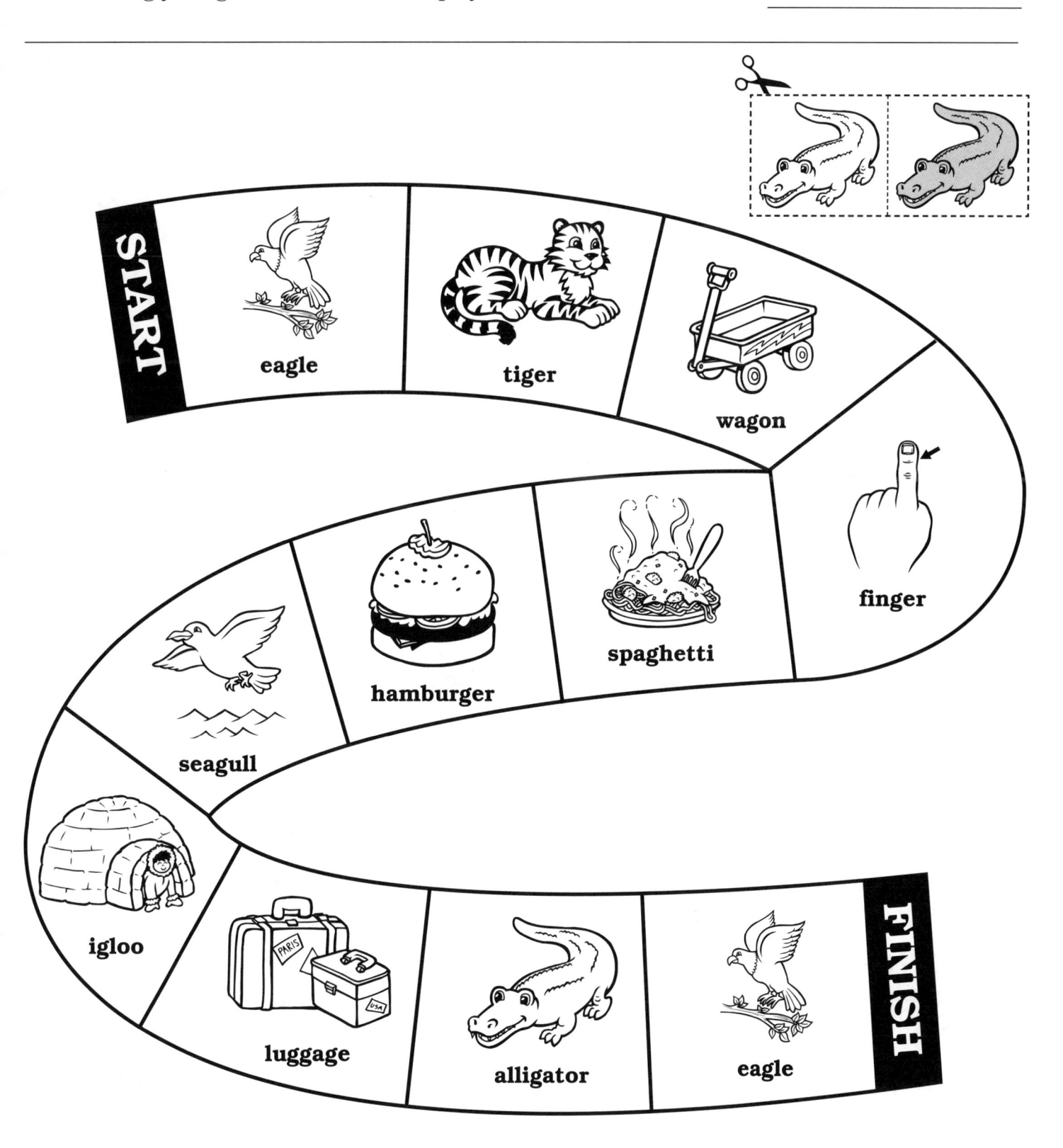

START

eagle

tiger

wagon

finger

spaghetti

hamburger

seagull

igloo

luggage

alligator

eagle

FINISH

_____ _____ _____ Medial G Words
Homework Partner   Date   Speech-Language Pathologist

Who's in the Igloo?

Directions: Copy and cut out igloos and cards below. Place one card under each igloo. Lift an igloo and read/say the picture–word card underneath it aloud, using your good G sound.

alligator	eagle	luggage	seagull
tiger	wagon	finger	spaghetti

Homework Partner   Date   Speech-Language Pathologist

Medial G Words

Duck, Duck, Goose!

Directions: Cut the squares out and place them face down in a pile. Arrange students in a circle around the pile. The first player chooses a card, reads/says the word–picture aloud and then walks around the circle tapping a different child for each syllable in the word (alligator: tap four children on the shoulder). The player sits beside the last person he/she taps. That player chooses a card, taps, etc.

alligator	eagle	igloo
hamburger	spaghetti	finger
luggage	seagull	tiger

Homework Partner Date Speech-Language Pathologist

Medial G Words

Check it Out!

Directions: Read/say aloud the picture-words. Choose a word from the Word Bank and write it in the correct alphabetical space, or say the word aloud that goes in the correct space. Read/say the G word again, using your best G sound.

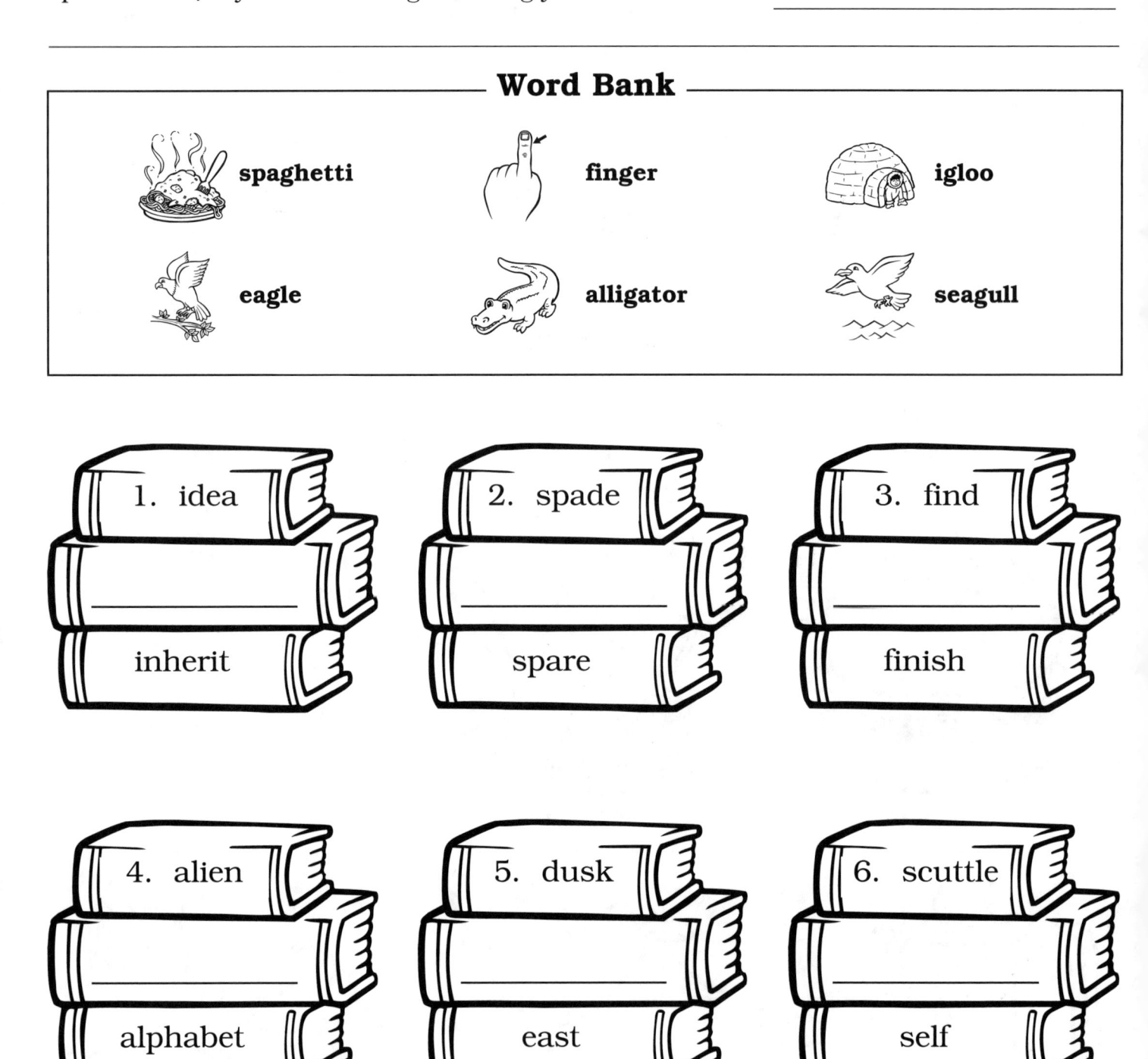

Word Bank

- spaghetti
- finger
- igloo
- eagle
- alligator
- seagull

1. idea
   _____
   inherit

2. spade
   _____
   spare

3. find
   _____
   finish

4. alien
   _____
   alphabet

5. dusk
   _____
   east

6. scuttle
   _____
   self

Answer key: 1. igloo, 2. spaghetti, 3. finger, 4. alligator, 5. eagle, 6. seagull

Homework Partner Date Speech-Language Pathologist

Medial G Words

Word in a Word

Directions: Read/say aloud the picture–words on the left, using your good G sound. Then, read the clues to find the words inside the target words (alligator–all). Write it on the line.

1. **alligator** Another word for everyone. _____

2. **wagon** A dog's tail does this. _____

3. **finger** A fish has this on its side. _____

4. **hamburger** I am a type of meat. _____

5. **luggage** Another word for how old a person is. _____

6. **seagull** An ocean. _____

Answers: 1. all, 2. wag, 3. fin, 4. ham, 5. age, 6. sea

Homework Partner   Date   Speech-Language Pathologist

Medial G Words

Paint the Tiger

Directions: Read/say aloud the G phrases below. Then, cut out the stripes at the bottom. As you read/say each phrase again, glue/tape or place them on the tiger.

- heavy luggage
- cold igloo
- wagon wheel
- eagle eye
- alligator tail
- hamburger bun
- spaghetti sauce
- index finger

Homework Partner Date Speech-Language Pathologist **Medial G Phrases**

Pack It Up

Directions: Cut out the picture–word cards and place in a pile. Cut out the slot in the suitcase. Pick a card, read/say the phrase, and pack it through the slot into the suitcase. Remember to use your good G sound.

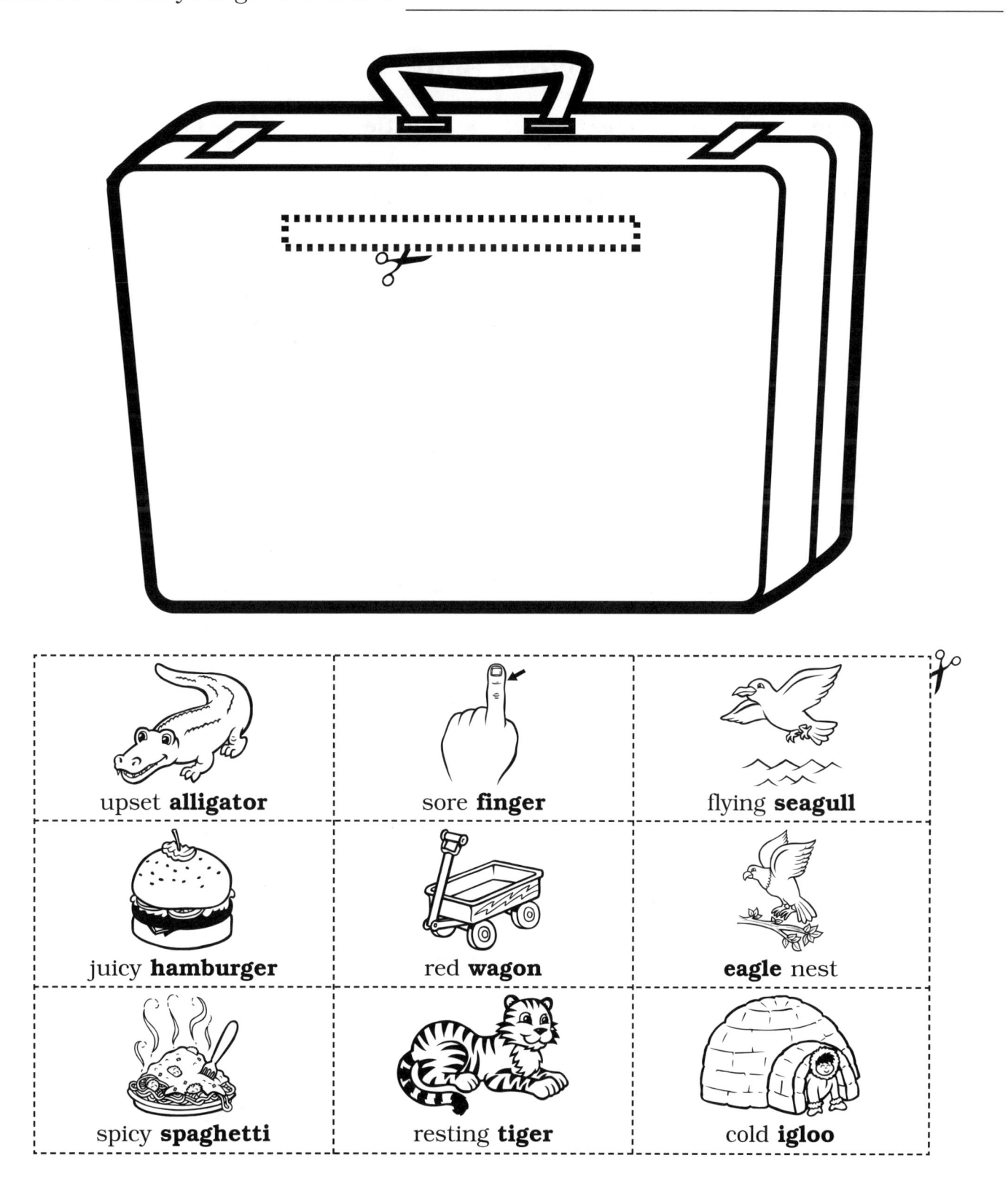

upset **alligator**	sore **finger**	flying **seagull**
juicy **hamburger**	red **wagon**	**eagle** nest
spicy **spaghetti**	resting **tiger**	cold **igloo**

Homework Partner   Date   Speech-Language Pathologist

Medial G Phrases

Descripto Fill In!

Directions: Read/say the picture–words aloud. Choose a describing word from the Word Bank to fill in the phrase. Then, read/say the word aloud, using your good G sound.

Word Bank

| hiding | mean | little | heavy |
| flying | yummy | cold | |

1. _____ alligator

2. _____ finger

3. _____ seagull

4. _____ igloo

5. _____ luggage

6. _____ hamburger

7. _____ tiger

Homework Partner   Date   Speech-Language Pathologist

Medial G Phrases

Number It Up!

Directions: Read/say aloud the picture–words. Number the words in the Word Bank below from 1-8 in any order you desire. Then, put the words on the lines below that match the corresponding numbers. Read/say the silly sentences aloud using your good G sound.

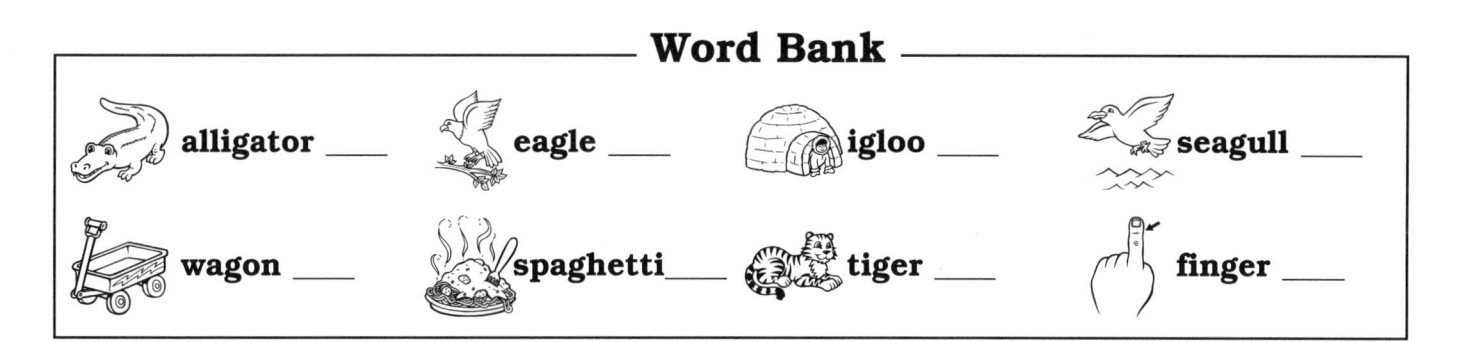

Word Bank

alligator ____   eagle ____   igloo ____   seagull ____

wagon ____   spaghetti ____   tiger ____   finger ____

---

1. A soaring _____ flew.

2. I ate a heaping plate of _____.

3. My little red _____ is sore.

4. Sleep in the freezing _____.

5. A(n) _____ is on the hunt.

6. Don't point your _____.

7. It's a(n) _____ in the swamp.

8. I hear a squawking _____.

Homework Partner   Date   Speech-Language Pathologist

Medial G Sentences

X and O

Directions: Cut out each **X** and **O** below. Have each player/partner choose **X** or **O**. The first player reads/says a picture–sentence aloud and places an **X** or **O** on the square. Play continues in turn. The first person to get three in a row wins.

The **alligator** is happy.	The **eagle** is ready to fly.	The **wagon** can hold toys.
He is pointing his **finger**.	The **spaghetti** is hot.	I want a **hamburger**.
The **seagull** flies over the water.	The **eskimo** is in the **igloo**.	I packed my **luggage**.

X X X X X

O O O O O

Homework Partner   Date   Speech-Language Pathologist

Medial G Sentences

Camping Trip

Directions: Read/listen to the story and fill in the blanks with the picture–words from the Word Bank. Then, read/repeat the completed sentences aloud, using your good G sound.

Word Bank

- eagle
- wagon
- alligator
- hamburger
- luggage
- spaghetti
- finger

One spring weekend my family and I packed our _____(1)_____ to go camping. We jumped in the van and headed for the campsites. On the way, we stopped and bought a _____(2)_____ for lunch. My brother spilled mustard on his _____(3)_____ so he licked it off. When we arrived, we loaded our stuff in a red _____(4)_____ to haul it to the nearby stream. In the tree we saw an _____(5)_____. Its nest looked like a bunch of _____(6)_____ noodles. An _____(7)_____ was swimming in the stream. We pitched our tent and settled in before dark. Whew! What a day.

Answers: 1. luggage, 2. hamburger, 3. finger, 4. wagon, 5. eagle, 6. spaghetti, 7. alligator

Homework Partner   Date   Speech-Language Pathologist

Medial G Sentences

Crazy Crossword

Directions: Read/say the picture–words below. Then, complete the crossword puzzle by reading and answering the clues. Use the pictures to help you. Then, use your good G sound and read/say the G sentences aloud, as you fill in your answers.

tiger

spaghetti

alligator

wagon

sea gull

luggage

eagle

igloo

Across

3. Put your toys in the _____.
6. The _____ swims in the water.
7. A _____ has stripes and whiskers.
8. I pack _____ for a trip.

Down

1. An eskimo lives in an _____.
2. I like meatballs in my _____.
4. An _____ soars in the sky.
5. The _____ likes to be at the beach.

Answer Key on Page 279

Homework Partner   Date   Speech-Language Pathologist

Medial G Sentences

F Sound

To the Rescue!

Directions: Help Fireman Tony put out the fires by saying the picture–words correctly. Cut out the fires below. Place fires in a single line. Choose a fire to "put out." Say the picture–word on the fire aloud, and turn it over to "put the fire out." Remember to use your good F sound.

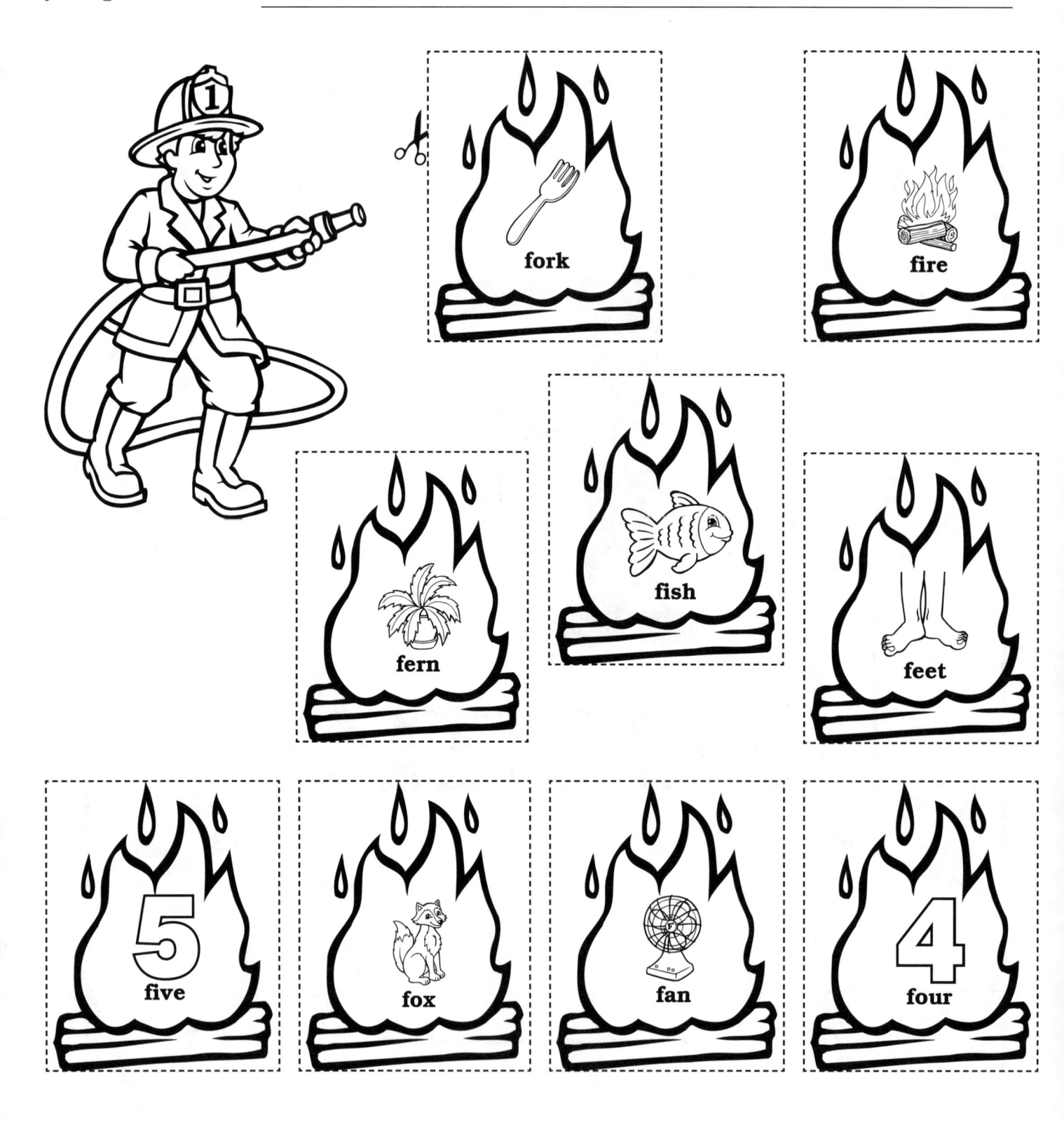

fork

fire

fern

fish

feet

five

fox

fan

four

Homework Partner Date Speech-Language Pathologist Initial F Words

192 #BK-291 Webber® Artic Fun Sheets 2 • ©2002 Super Duper® Publications • www.superduperinc.com • 1-800-277-8737

Football Mania!

Directions: Read/say aloud the picture–words. Cut out the footballs and place them at the 10 yard line on opposite ends of the field. First player flips a coin and moves 10 yards (heads) or 20 yards (tails). Say the word you land on aloud. Play continues in turn. First player to score a touchdown wins. Next time you play, switch ends.

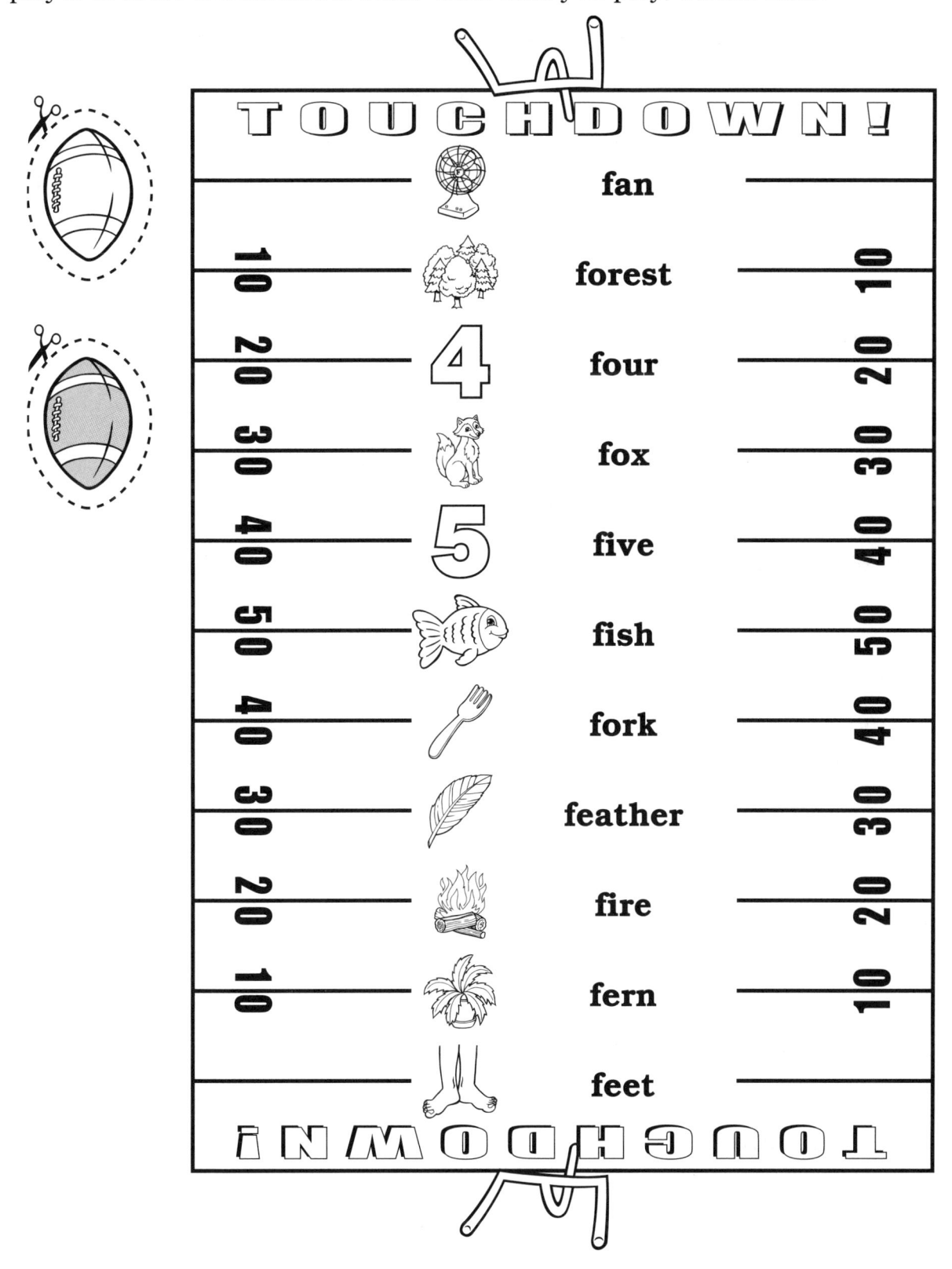

TOUCHDOWN!

- fan
- forest
- four
- fox
- five
- fish
- fork
- feather
- fire
- fern
- feet

TOUCHDOWN!

Homework Partner   Date   Speech-Language Pathologist

Initial F Words

#BK-291 Webber® Artic Fun Sheets 2 • ©2002 Super Duper® Publications • www.superduperinc.com • 1-800-277-8737

Give Me Another Name

Directions: Read/say aloud the picture–words aloud. Read/say the phrases on the page. Fill in the blank with the correct answer from the Word Bank. Read/say the word aloud using your good F sound. _____

Word Bank

| fish | forest | fox | feather |
| fork | fan | football | fern |

1. A green plant _____

2. A land animal _____

3. Part of a bird _____

4. A sea animal _____

5. A utensil _____

6. The woods _____

7. A sport _____

8. Cooling machine _____

Answers: 1. fern, 2. fox, 3. feather, 4. fish, 5. fork, 6. forest, 7. football, 8. fan

Homework Partner   Date   Speech-Language Pathologist

Initial F Words

Which Is?

Directions: Read/say the following questions aloud. Say the answers aloud, using your best F sound.

1. Which is bigger - a **fox** or a **fish**?

2. Which is lighter - a **feather** or a **fork**?

3. Which is higher - a **four** or a **five**?

4. Which is cooler - a **fire** or a **fan**?

5. Which is quicker - a **fox** or a **fern**?

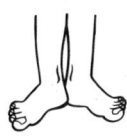

6. Which is longer - **feet** or a **football**?

7. Which is hotter - a **fire** or a **fan**?

8. Which is quieter - a **fish** or a **fox**?

Answers: 1. fox, 2. feather, 3. five, 4. fan, 5. fox, 6. football, 7. fire, 8. fish

Homework Partner   Date   Speech-Language Pathologist

Initial F Words

F Cube Roll

Directions: Assemble the cube as follows: glue onto construction paper for added durability. Cut along the dotted lines. Fold on solid lines and glue as indicated. To play: roll the cube. Read/say aloud the word you see using your best F sound.

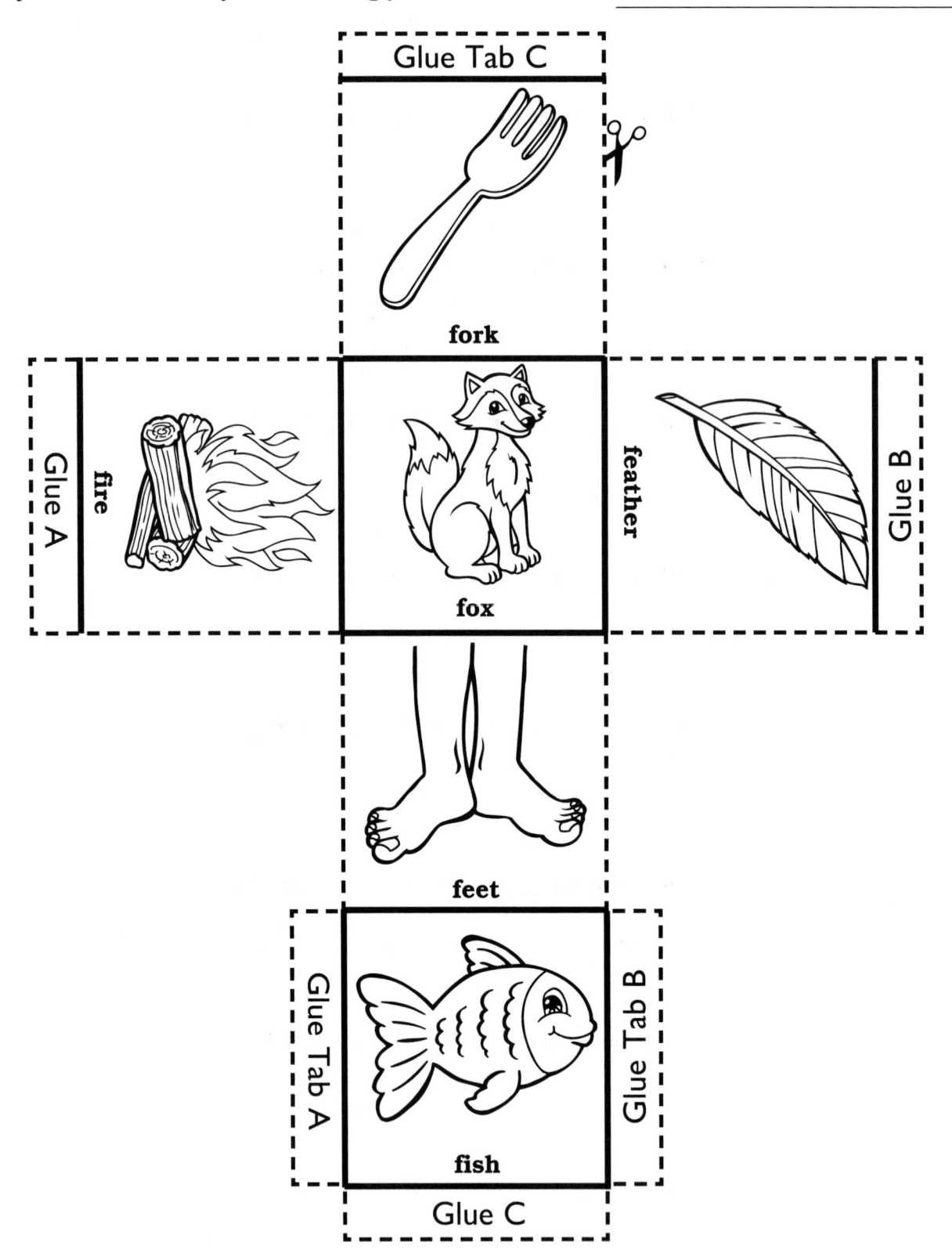

Glue Tab C

fork

Glue A | fire | fox | feather | Glue B

feet

Glue Tab A | fish | Glue Tab B

Glue C

Homework Partner | Date | Speech-Language Pathologist

Initial F Words

196 #BK-291 Webber® Artic Fun Sheets 2 • ©2002 Super Duper® Publications • www.superduperinc.com • 1-800-277-8737

Find It in the Forest!

Directions: Follow the Clue Map to find the picture–words in the forest. Circle and/or color each picture–word as you find it. Read/say each picture–word aloud, using your good F sound.

fan

fish

football

fern

four

feather

feet

fork

Clue Map

1. I am used in a game.
2. You eat with me.
3. I am a plant.
4. I keep you cool.
5. I help you walk.
6. I am on a bird.
7. I swim in the water.
8. I am a number.

Homework Partner   Date   Speech-Language Pathologist

Initial F Words

#BK-291 Webber® Artic Fun Sheets 2 • ©2002 Super Duper® Publications • www.superduperinc.com • 1-800-277-8737

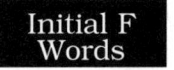

197

Go-Together Match-Ups

Directions: Read/say aloud the picture words on the right. Then find the words that "Go Together." Draw a line from the word in column A to the word in column B that goes together best. Read/say each phrase aloud (sly fox). Use your good F sound!

A	**B**
sly	fish
hot	football
brown	fox
green	fern
sharp	fire
wet	fork

Homework Partner   Date   Speech-Language Pathologist

Initial F Phrases

X and O

Directions: Cut out each **X** and **O** below. Have each player/partner choose **X** or **O**. The first player reads/says the picture phrase aloud and places an **X** or **O** on the square. Play continues in turn. The first person to get three in a row wins.

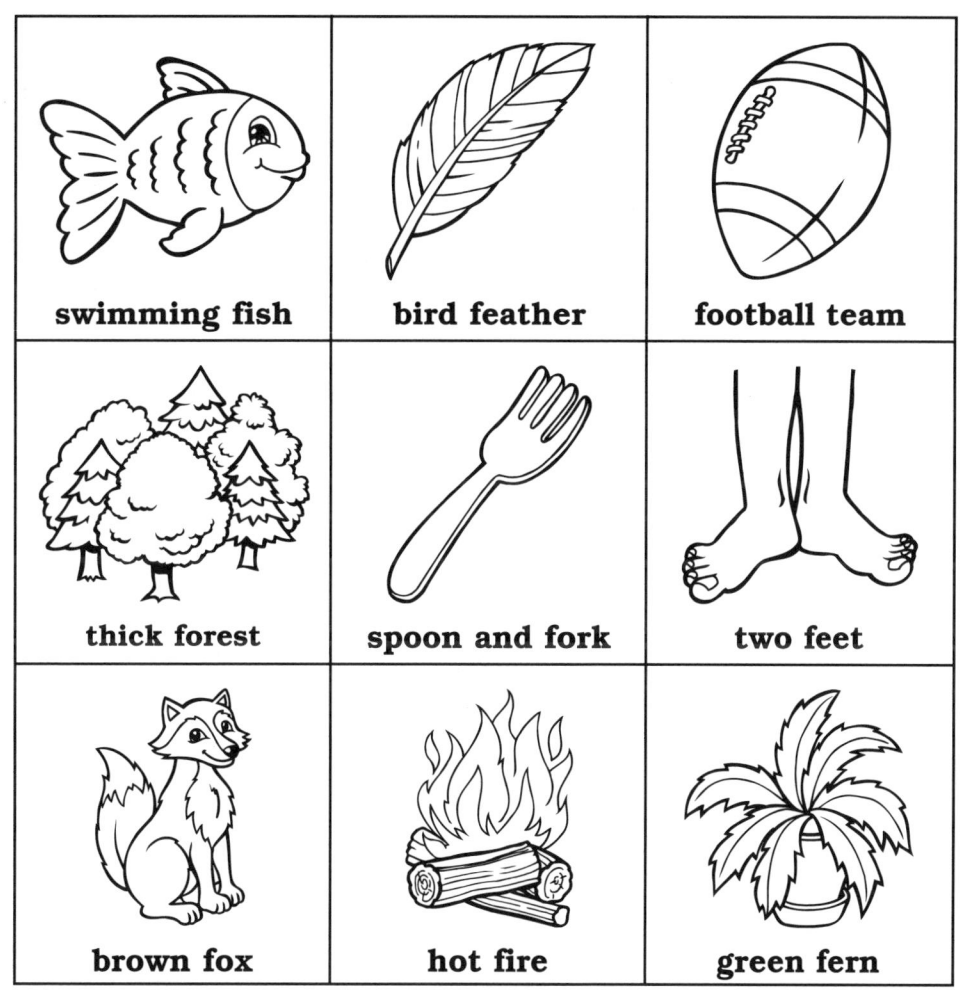

swimming fish	bird feather	football team
thick forest	spoon and fork	two feet
brown fox	hot fire	green fern

X X X X X

O O O O O

Homework Partner   Date   Speech-Language Pathologist

Initial F Phrases

F Phrase It

Directions: Assemble the cube as follows: glue onto construction paper for added durability. Cut along the dotted lines. Fold on solid lines and glue as indicated. To play: roll both cubes. Read/say the words and pictures together aloud to make up a phrase (metal fork). Use your good F sound.

Cube 1 faces: fish, football, fire, fork, forest, feet

Cube 2 faces: hot, two, metal, slippery, yummy, dark

Initial F Phrases

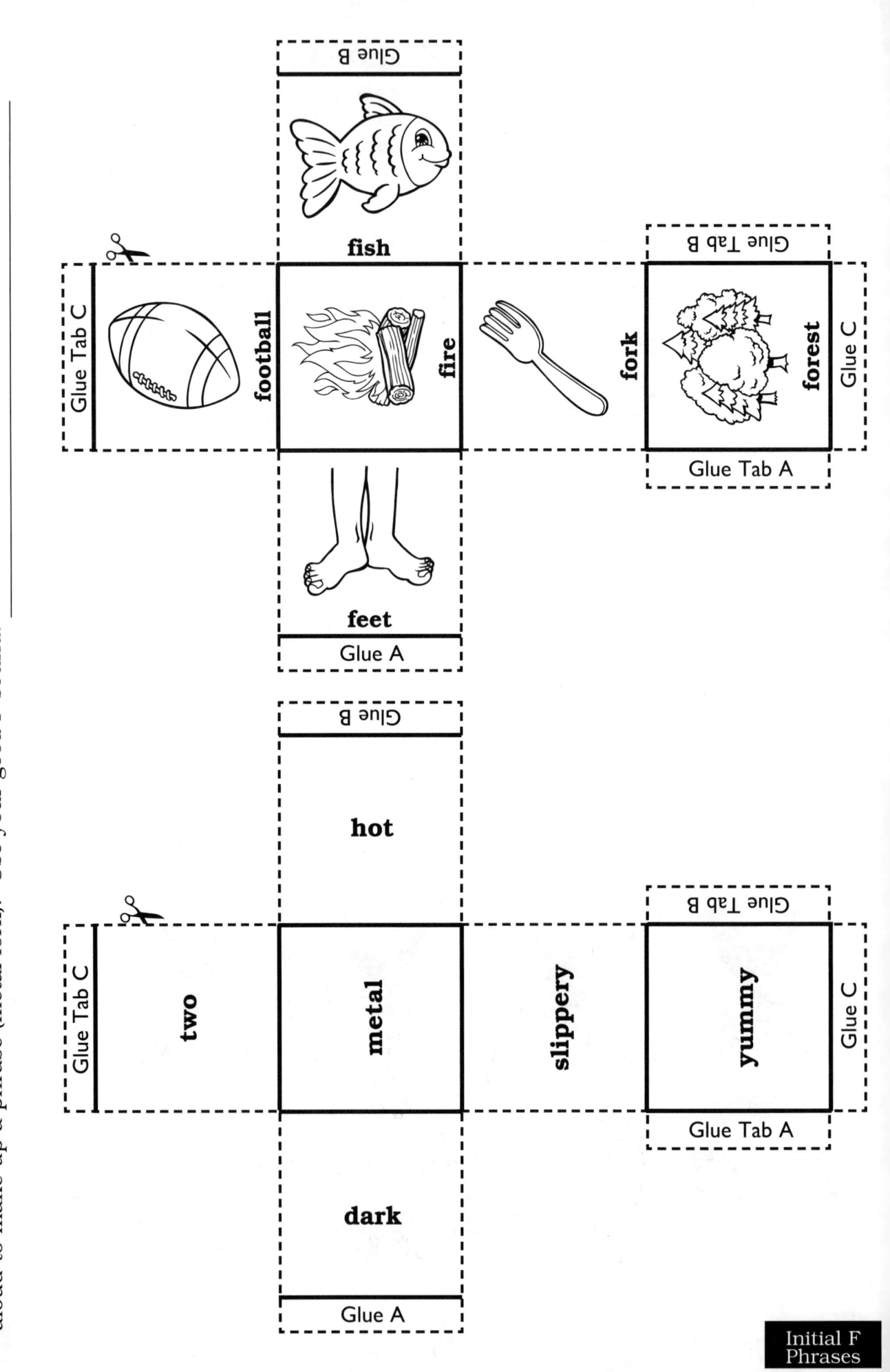

Something's Fishy!

Directions: Read/say aloud each sentence. Change the sentence so it makes sense using clues from the pictures on the page. Then, read/say the correct sentence aloud. _____

football

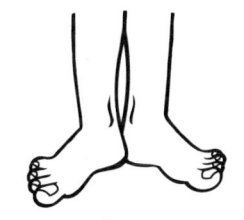

forest

fork

1. At the lake, he caught a <u>candy bar</u>.
   At the lake, he caught a _____.

2. I camped in the <u>porridge</u>.
   I camped in the _____.

3. I run with two <u>noses</u>.
   I run with two _____.

4. The player threw the <u>banana</u>.
   The player threw the _____.

5. The water put out the <u>marbles</u>.
   The water put out the _____.

6. She turned the spaghetti on her <u>stick</u>.
   She turned the spaghetti on her _____.

feet

fire

fish

Homework Partner   Date   Speech-Language Pathologist

Initial F Sentences

Scrambled Sentences

Directions: Try to unscramble each sentence. Write it on the line below the egg. Then read/say the sentence aloud using your best F sound. _____

1. _____.

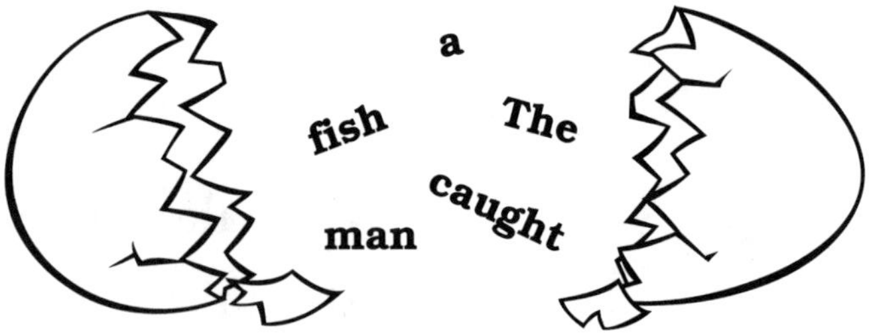

2. _____.

3. _____.

4. _____.

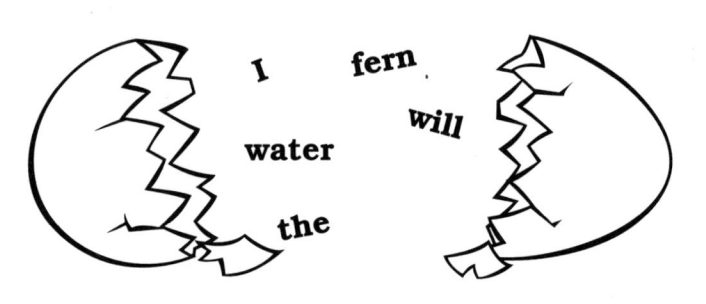

5. _____.

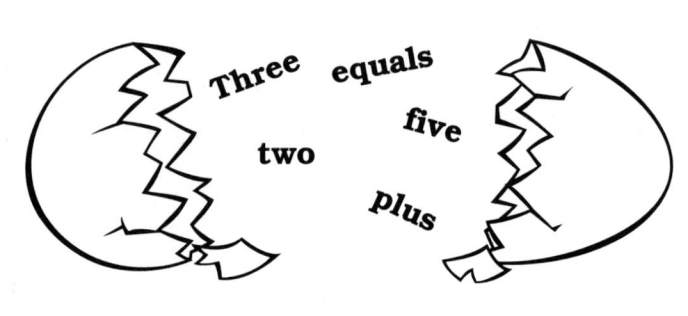

6. _____.

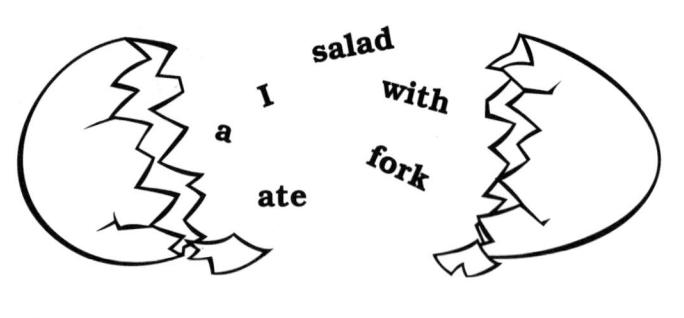

7. _____.

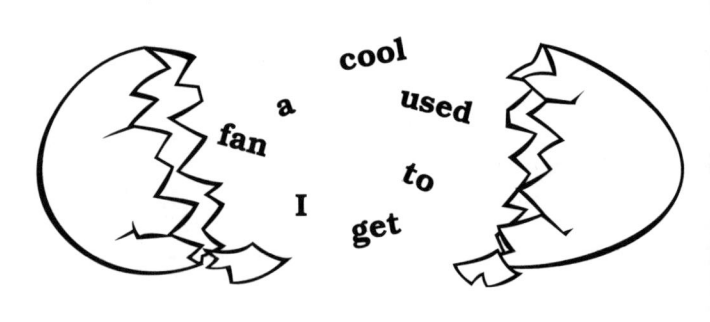

8. _____.

Answer Key on Page 279

Homework Partner   Date   Speech-Language Pathologist

Initial F Sentences

202   #BK-291 Webber® Artic Fun Sheets 2 • ©2002 Super Duper® Publications • www.superduperinc.com • 1-800-277-8737

Think Alikes

Directions: Read the incomplete sentences, or repeat them after your helper reads them. Then, write down the first word or words you think of. Do not tell anyone your answer. When everyone has completed the lists, compare answers one at a time. Read/say your answers using complete sentences. (Feather makes me think about tickle.) If you match anyone else, you get a point. Use your good F sound.

1. **Fan** makes me think about _____.

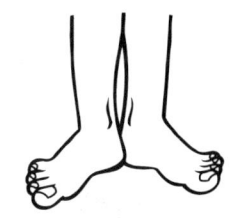

2. **Fern** makes me think about _____.

3. **Four** makes me think about _____.

4. **Fish** makes me think about _____.

5. **Forest** makes me think about _____.

6. **Five** makes me think about _____.

7. **Feather** makes me think about _____.

8. **Football** makes me think about _____.

9. **Feet** make me think about _____.

10. **Fire** makes me think about _____.

Homework Partner   Date   Speech-Language Pathologist   Initial F Sentences

Wacky Wolf

Directions: Read/say aloud the picture–words below. Then, cut out the markers. Flip a coin (heads=1, tails=2) to determine how many spaces to move. As you move, read/say each word aloud, using your good F sound. First player to reach the finish wins.

START — cuff — elf — roof — leaf — thief — wolf — giraffe — knife — chief — calf — elf — FINISH

Homework Partner Date Speech-Language Pathologist

Final F Words

204 #BK-291 Webber® Artic Fun Sheets 2 • ©2002 Super Duper® Publications • www.superduperinc.com • 1-800-277-8737

What's Under the Roof?

Directions: Cut out the cards below. Place one card under each house with a roof. Lift a roof card and read/say the picture–word card underneath it. Remember to use your good F sound.

giraffe	knife	leaf	wolf
elf	calf	thief	cuff

Homework Partner   Date   Speech-Language Pathologist

Final F Words

Colorful Spots

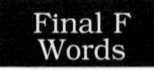

Directions: Read/say aloud each picture–word below. As you say each word, color the word–picture and the same number spot on the giraffe the color shown. Read/say the words aloud again, using your good F sound. _____

1.
chief
(Color brown)

2.
cuff
(Color red)

3.
giraffe
(Color green)

4.
leaf
(Color orange)

5.
calf
(Color yellow)

6.
roof
(Color black)

7.
thief
(Color light blue)

8.
elf
(Color purple)

9.
wolf
(Color pink)

10.
knife
(Color dark blue)

Homework Partner   Date   Speech-Language Pathologist

Final F Words

206   #BK-291 Webber® Artic Fun Sheets 2 • ©2002 Super Duper® Publications • www.superduperinc.com • 1-800-277-8737

Paper Chain

Directions: Read/say aloud each picture–word below. Cut out the word strips. Turn them face down. Pick up a strip and read/say the word aloud. Then, staple/glue the strips to make a chain link. Remember to use your good F sound as you make your chain.

- cuff
- thief
- wolf
- giraffe
- leaf
- knife
- calf
- roof
- elf

Homework Partner   Date   Speech-Language Pathologist   Final F Words

Who Said That?

Directions: Read/say each F picture–word aloud. Read the statements in the middle. Then, ask, **"Who said that?"** Answer with the correct word, using your good F sound. Then, draw a line from the sentence to the correct picture.

roof

giraffe

knife

chief

"I am a baby cow."

"I can cut vegetables."

"I cover the top of a house."

"I grow on trees."

"I am on the end of a sleeve."

"I am the head of a tribe."

"I have a long neck and spots."

"I am a little person with pointy ears."

cuff

calf

leaf

elf

Homework Partner   Date   Speech-Language Pathologist

Final F Words

Analogies

Directions: Read/say aloud the picture-words below. Then, read each analogy and choose an answer from the Word Bank. Read/say your answer aloud using your best F sound.

Word Bank

knife   wolf   elf

leaf   giraffe   calf

1. _____ is to steak as spoon is to soup.

2. Neck is to _____ as trunk is to elephant.

3. _____ is to Santa Claus as worker is to boss.

4. _____ is to tree as needle is to cactus.

5. Cow is to _____ as horse is to pony.

6. Howl is to _____ as meow is to cat.

Answers: 1. knife, 2. giraffe, 3. elf, 4. leaf, 5. calf, 6. wolf

Homework Partner   Date   Speech-Language Pathologist

Final F Words

X and O

Directions: Cut out each **X** and **O** below. Have each player/partner choose **X** or **O**. The first player reads/says a phrase aloud and places an **X** or **O** on the square. Play continues in turn. The first person to get three in a row wins. _____

hungry giraffe	howling wolf	green elf
steep roof	happy calf	sneaky thief
tall chief	pretty leaf	butter knife

X X X X X

O O O O O

_____ _____ _____
Homework Partner   Date   Speech-Language Pathologist

Final F Phrases

210   #BK-291 Webber® Artic Fun Sheets 2 • ©2002 Super Duper® Publications • www.superduperinc.com • 1-800-277-8737

Amaze Me

Directions: Try to solve the maze. Say aloud each F phrase you come across as you try to solve the maze. Remember to use your good F sound.

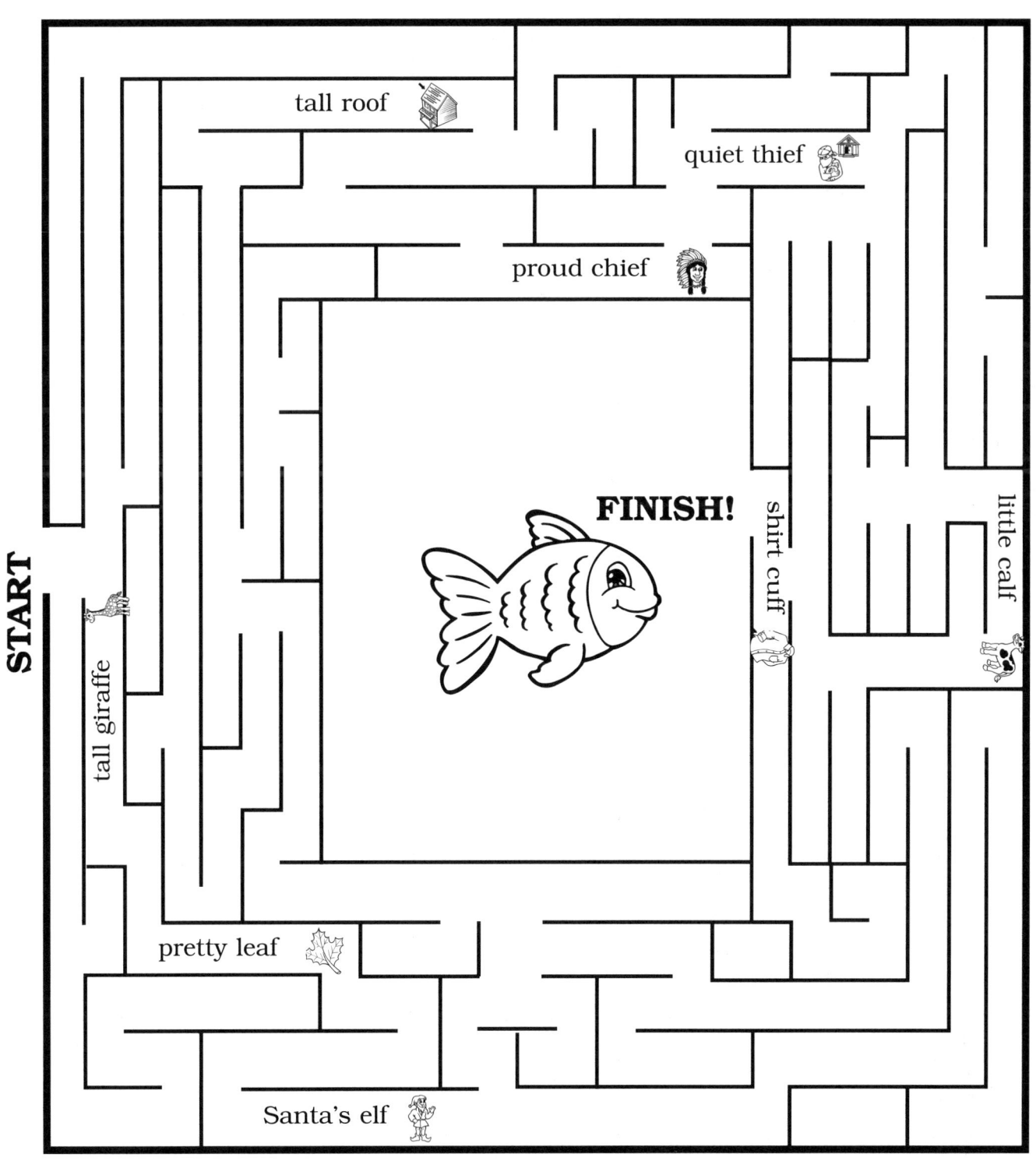

- tall roof
- quiet thief
- proud chief
- FINISH!
- shirt cuff
- little calf
- START
- tall giraffe
- pretty leaf
- Santa's elf

Answer Key on Page 280

Homework Partner   Date   Speech-Language Pathologist

Final F Phrases

F Phrase It

Directions: Assemble the cube as follows: glue onto construction paper for added durability. Cut along the dotted lines. Fold on solid lines and glue as indicated. To play: roll both cubes. Read/say the word and picture together aloud to make up a phrase (silly wolf). Use your good F sound.

Cube 1 (pictures):
- wolf
- cuff
- thief
- giraffe
- leaf
- elf

Cube 2 (words):
- sad
- happy
- silly
- young
- large
- old

Final F Phrases

212 #BK-291 Webber® Artic Fun Sheets 2 • ©2002 Super Duper® Publications • www.superduperinc.com • 1-800-277-8737

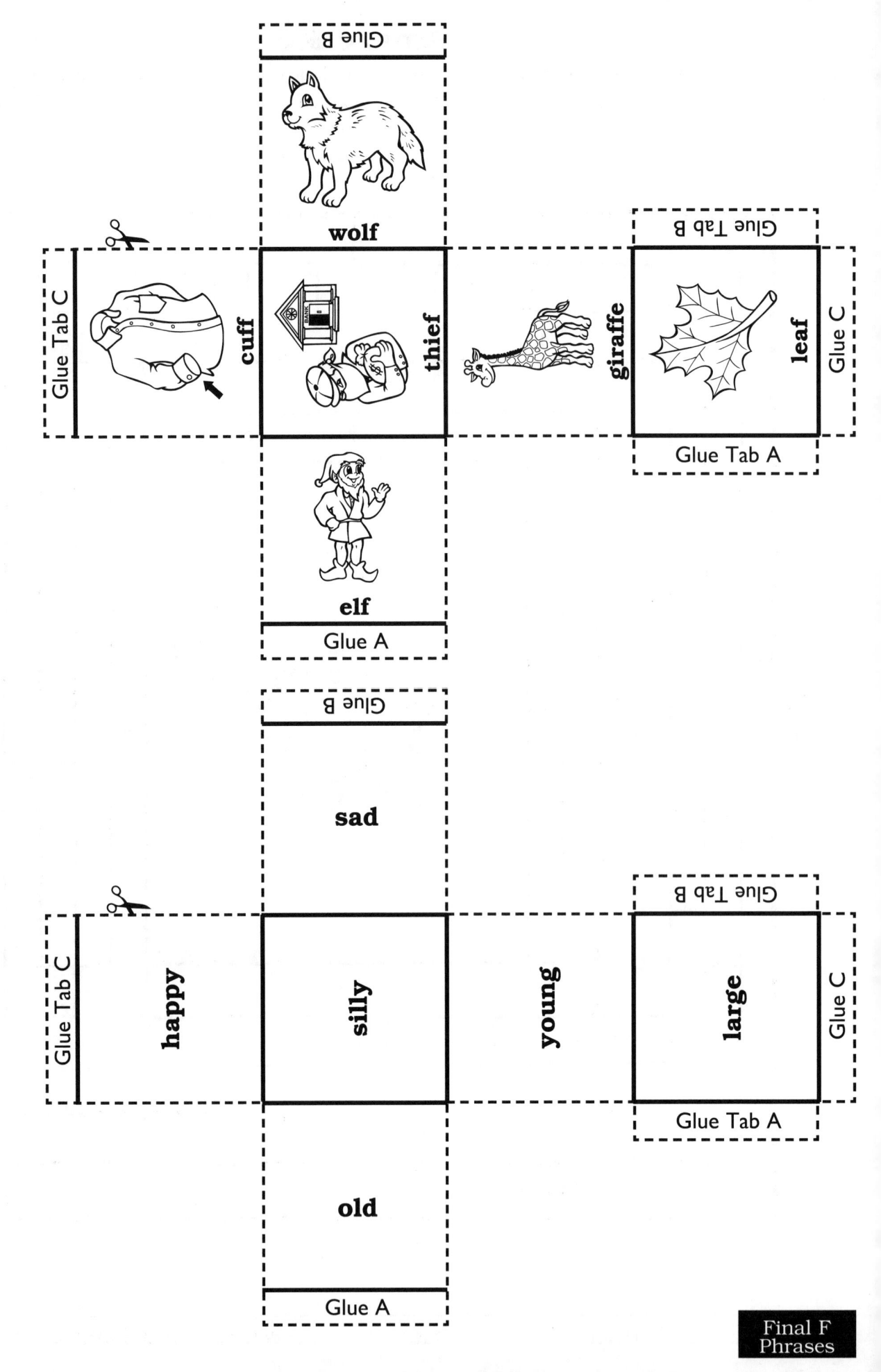

Where Do You See?

Directions: Read/say aloud each question from 1–8. Then, pick a place at the bottom of the page where you would see each item. Write the places on the blank lines. Then, read each sentence aloud. (You see a calf on the farm.) Use your good F sound. _____
_____

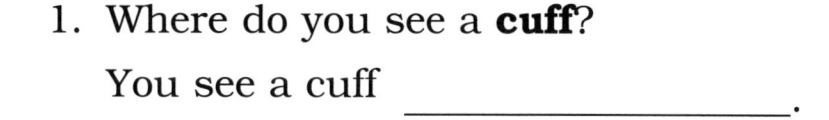

1. Where do you see a **cuff**?
   You see a cuff _____.

2. Where do you see a **leaf**?
   You see a leaf _____.

3. Where do you see a **roof**?
   You see a roof _____.

4. Where do you see a **knife**?
   You see a knife _____.

5. Where do you see a **wolf**?
   You see a wolf _____.

6. Where do you see an **elf**?
   You see an elf _____.

7. Where do you see a **giraffe**?
   You see a giraffe _____.

8. Where do you see a **calf**?
   You see a calf _____.

A. in a kitchen   C. at the North Pole   E. on the farm   G. on a tree

B. at the zoo   D. on a sleeve   F. on a house   H. in the woods

Answers: 1.D, 2.G, 3.F, 4.A, 5.H, 6.C, 7.B, 8.E

_____   _____   _____
Homework Partner   Date   Speech-Language Pathologist

Final F Sentences

Listen Up!

Directions: Practice saying aloud each F picture–word. Answer the following questions using the pictures as clues. Read/say each word answer aloud, using your good F sound. Then, follow the directions.

wolf

chief

1. What animal has a long neck?
   (Circle it.)

2. What is another name for a robber?
   (Draw a line through it.)

knife

giraffe

3. What animal howls at the moon?
   (Underline it.)

4. What grows on a tree?
   (Put an X next to it.)

elf

roof

5. Who wears a headdress and is in charge of the tribe?
   (Draw a square around it.)

6. What utensil do we cut with?
   (Color it blue.)

leaf

thief

7. What is the top of a house called?
   (Draw a circle over it.)

8. Who is small and wears pointy shoes?
   (Draw a circle on it.)

Homework Partner   Date   Speech-Language Pathologist

Final F Sentences

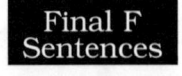

Answer with a Question

Directions: Read/say aloud each statement below. Then, ask a question about the statement. (This animal has a long neck. What has a long neck?) Use the pictures as hints. Read/say each question aloud. Each correct question earns one point. The student with the most points wins.

Answer

1. This is part of your shirt.

2. This grows on a tree.

3. This is something you cut with.

4. This is someone who steals.

5. This is Santa's helper.

6. This animal travels in packs.

7. This is the top of a house.

8. This animal has a long neck.

Question

_____

_____

_____

_____

_____

_____

_____

_____

wolf   **elf**   **leaf**   **knife**

roof   **thief**   **cuff**   **giraffe**

Homework Partner   Date   Speech-Language Pathologist

Final F Sentences

#BK-291 Webber® Artic Fun Sheets 2 • ©2002 Super Duper® Publications • www.superduperinc.com • 1-800-277-8737

215

Eli Elephant

Directions: Read/say aloud the picture–words below. Then, cut out the markers. Flip a coin (heads=1, tails=2) to determine how many spaces to move. As you move, read/say each word aloud, using your good F sound.

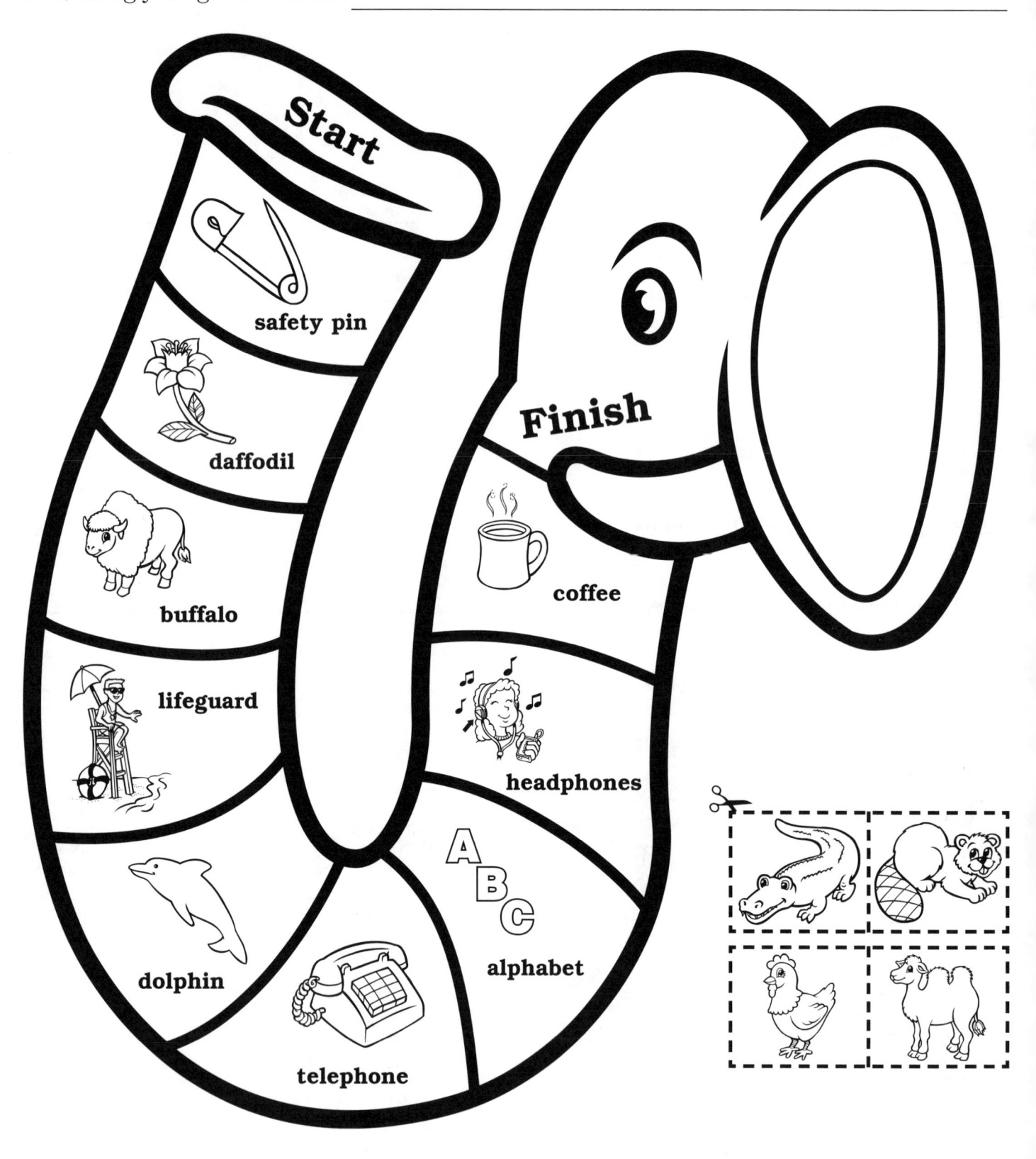

Start

safety pin

daffodil

buffalo

lifeguard

dolphin

telephone

alphabet

headphones

coffee

Finish

Homework Partner — Date — Speech-Language Pathologist

Medial F Words

216 #BK-291 Webber® Artic Fun Sheets 2 • ©2002 Super Duper® Publications • www.superduperinc.com • 1-800-277-8737

F Cube Roll

Directions: Assemble the cube as follows: glue onto construction paper for added durability. Cut along the dotted lines. Fold on solid lines and glue as indicated. To play: roll the cube. Read/say aloud the word you see using your best F sound.

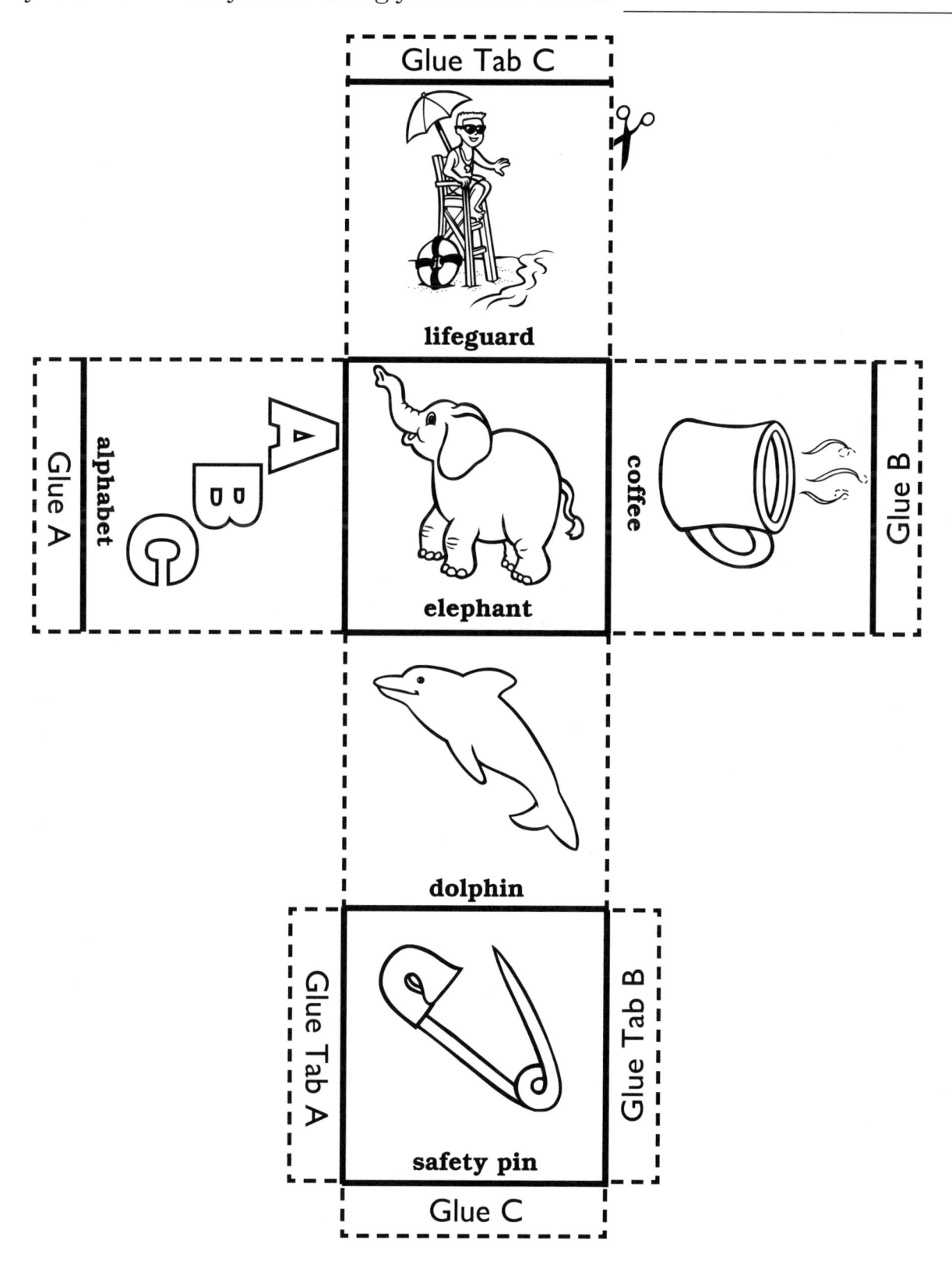

Glue Tab C

lifeguard

Glue A | alphabet | elephant | coffee | Glue B

dolphin

Glue Tab A | safety pin | Glue Tab B

Glue C

Homework Partner Date Speech-Language Pathologist Medial F Words

#BK-291 Webber® Artic Fun Sheets 2 • ©2002 Super Duper® Publications • www.superduperinc.com • 1-800-277-8737 217

Lifeguard Launch

Directions: Help Lifeguard Larry launch life preservers into the sea! Cut out the life preservers below. Read/say each picture-word aloud. Then, pretend to toss the preservers into the sea. Use your good F sound.

- buffalo
- lifeguard
- dolphin
- coffee
- alphabet
- telephone
- elephant
- headphones

Homework Partner   Date   Speech-Language Pathologist

Medial F Words

Syllable Secrets

Directions: Read/say aloud each picture–word below. Then, check as many boxes as there are syllables (coffee – check 2 boxes). When you finish, write the letters from the boxes you checked on the line below to reveal the secret message. Say each word using your good F sound. (Variation for younger students: clap out the syllables of the words as you say them. Count the number of claps you made and check off that number of boxes.)

Words | **Syllables**

1. coffee — 1:Y 2:O 3:P 4:L
2. elephant — 1:U 2:A 3:R 4:M
3. buffalo — 1:E 2:D 3:O 4:C
4. telephone — 1:I 2:N 3:G 4:D
5. dolphin — 1:A 2:G 3:E 4:F
6. lifeguard — 1:R 2:E 3:K 4:L
7. alphabet — 1:A 2:T 3:J 4:S
8. safety pin — 1:O 2:B 3:! 4:B

Secret Message: _____

Answers: You are doing a great job!

Homework Partner   Date   Speech-Language Pathologist

Medial F Words

X and O

Directions: Cut out each **X** and **O** below. Have each player/partner choose **X** or **O**. The first player reads/says a picture–word aloud and places an **X** or **O** on the square. Play continues in turn. The first person to get three in a row wins.

coffee	buffalo	lifeguard
dolphin	headphones	daffodil
elephant	telephone	alphabet

X X X X X

O O O O O

Homework Partner Date Speech-Language Pathologist

Medial F Words

3 Games in 1

Directions: Say aloud the picture–words below, using your good F sound. Then, play one of the following games:

- ☐ Lotto – Caller reads a word and student repeats the word and covers it with a token/chip.
- ☐ Tic–Tac–Toe – Each time you write an **X** or **O**, say the word you mark over.
- ☐ Memory – Cut out all the cards and place face down. Try to find matching pairs. Say aloud each word you find. Keep all matches.

telephone	safety pin	headphones
dolphin	coffee	daffodil
elephant	buffalo	lifeguard
coffee	lifeguard	safety pin
headphones	telephone	buffalo
dolphin	elephant	daffodil

Homework Partner   Date   Speech-Language Pathologist

Medial F Words

How Many?

Directions: Look at the pictures and count the number of items in each box. Write the number on the line. Then, read/say the phrase aloud using your good F sound (three daffodils).

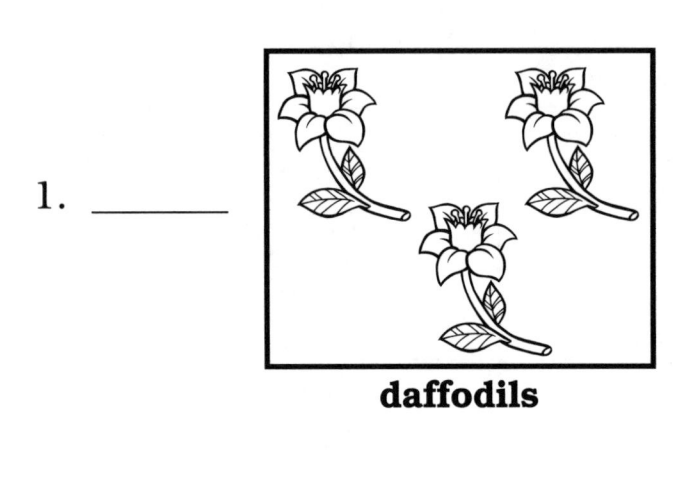

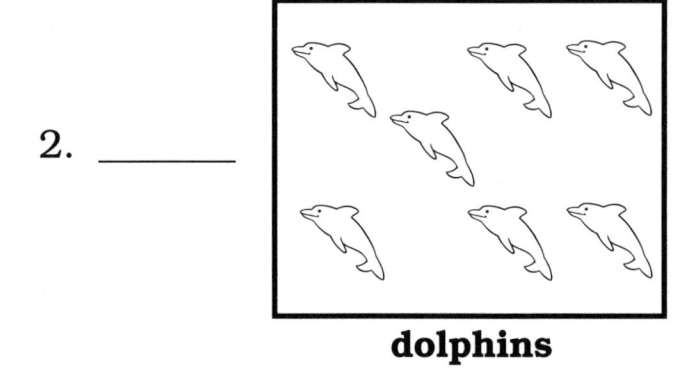

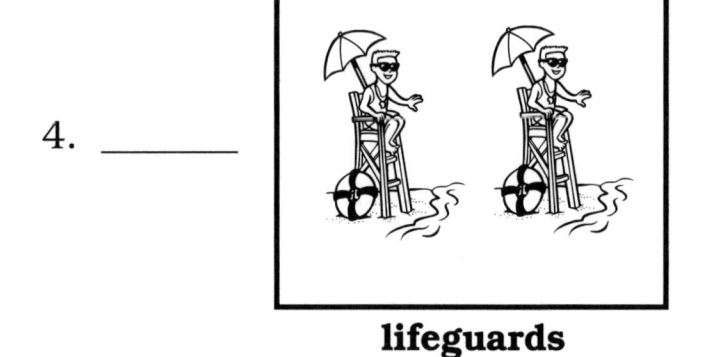

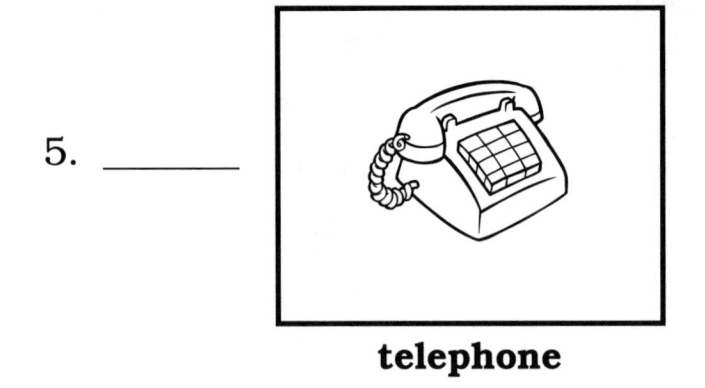

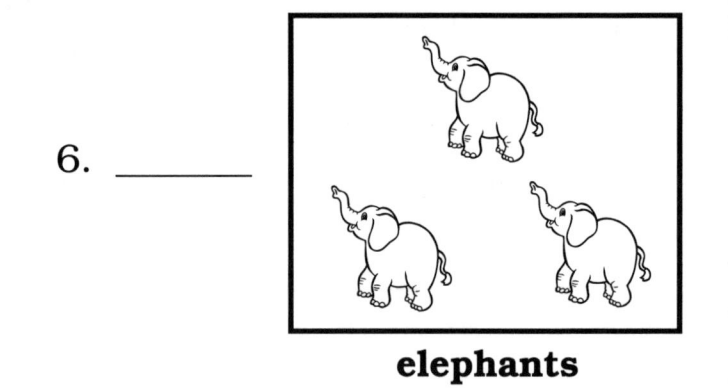

1. _____ **daffodils**

2. _____ **dolphins**

3. _____ **headphones**

4. _____ **lifeguards**

5. _____ **telephone**

6. _____ **elephants**

_____   _____   _____
Homework Partner   Date   Speech-Language Pathologist

Medial F Phrases

Mine or Yours?

Directions: Read/say each picture–word below. Cut out the pictures. At each turn, flip a coin. Heads means the student keeps the picture and says, "My _____" (My <u>elephant</u>). Tails means that the student gives the picture to his partner and says, "Your _____" (Your <u>elephant</u>). Player with the most pictures at the end wins. _____

elephant	telephone	coffee
headphones	daffodil	buffalo
alphabet	dolphin	lifeguard

Homework Partner   Date   Speech-Language Pathologist

Medial F Phrases

F Phrase It

Directions: Assemble the cube as follows: glue onto construction paper for added durability. Cut along the dotted lines. Fold on solid lines and glue as indicated. To play: roll both cubes. Read/say the word and picture together aloud to make up a phrase (pretty daffodil). Use your good F sound.

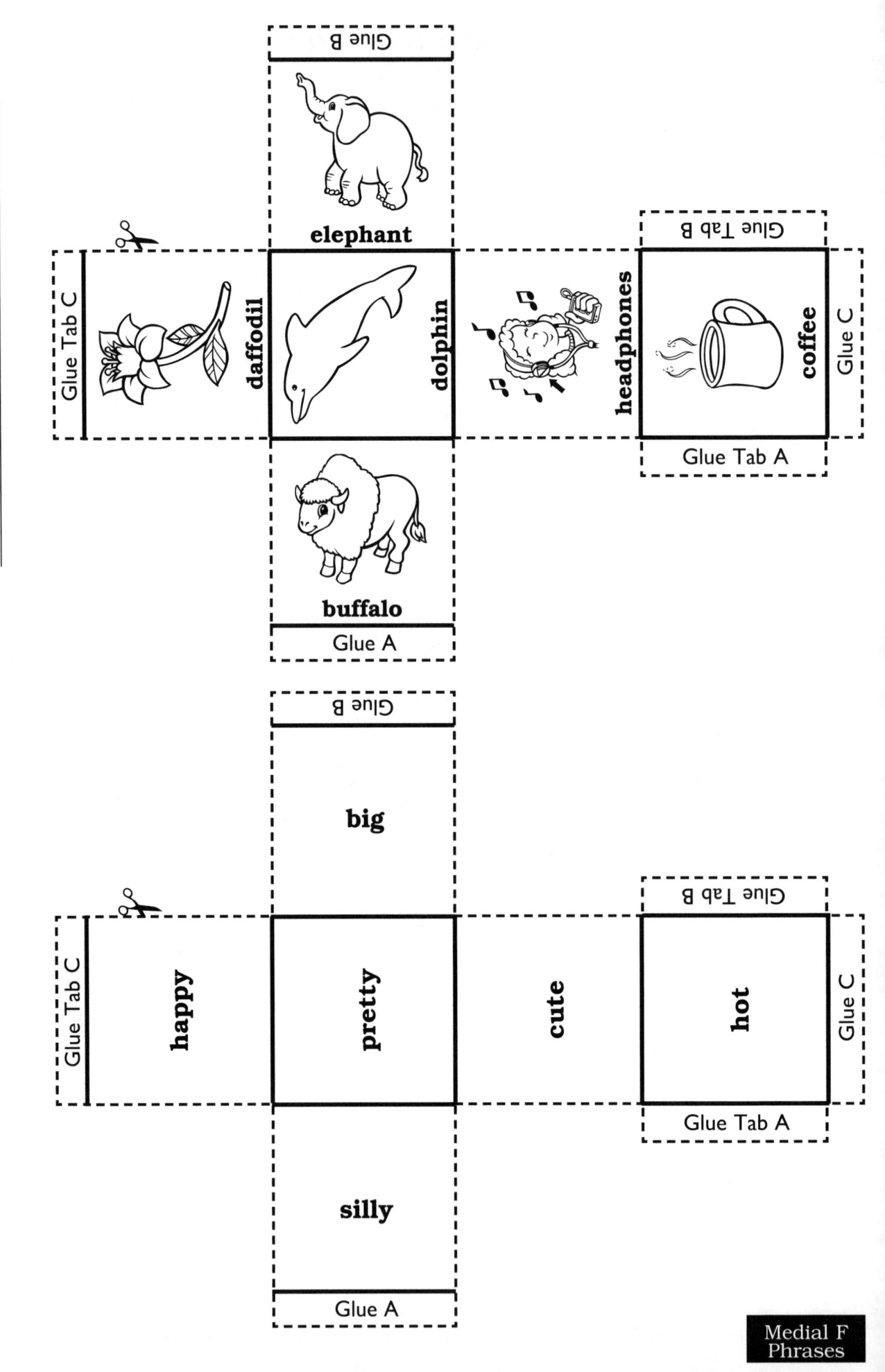

elephant

daffodil | dolphin | headphones | coffee

buffalo

Glue Tab C · Glue Tab B · Glue Tab A · Glue A · Glue B · Glue C

big

happy | pretty | cute | hot

silly

Medial F Phrases

224 #BK-291 Webber® Artic Fun Sheets 2 • ©2002 Super Duper® Publications • www.superduperinc.com • 1-800-277-8737

What Goes Where?

Directions: Practice saying aloud each picture–word. Then, read the word(s) in the middle. Find a picture that goes with the words in the middle. Then, draw a line from the picture–word(s) to each matching word. Read/say the picture–words again in a sentence, using your good F sound. (The buffalo has horns.) _____

buffalo

1. cup

headphones

2. chair

coffee

3. peanuts

4. ears

lifeguard

telephone

5. horns

6. diaper

safety pin

7. bee

elephant

8. answering machine

daffodil

Homework Partner   Date   Speech-Language Pathologist

Medial F Sentences

Line It Up!

Directions: Read/say the picture-word in column A. Then, choose a phrase from column B and column C. Read/say the sentence aloud, using your good F sound.

A	B	C
The elephant	dove into the ocean	and shared a cookie.
The dolphin	went to the movies	and ran out the door.
The daffodil	jumped over the table	and drank some water.
The telephone	had a sandwich	and saved a little girl.
The lifeguard	smiled at the sun	and ate popcorn.
The coffee	spilled out of the cup	and ran away with a spoon.

Homework Partner   Date   Speech-Language Pathologist

Medial F Sentences

Put Them in Order

Directions: Read/say the following sentences. Put the sentences in order from first to last. Write a **1** (first), **2** (second), and **3** (last) under the correct sentence. Read/say the sentences aloud in the correct sequential order, using your good F sound.

A. She picked a **daffodil** in the garden.   Her mother put the **daffodil** in a vase.   She gave the **daffodil** to her mother.

B. Kyle hung up the **telephone**.   The **telephone** rang.   Kyle talked on the **telephone**.

C. The **dolphin** got a treat.   The crowd cheered at the **dolphin's** trick.   The **dolphin** jumped through the hoop.

Homework Partner   Date   Speech-Language Pathologist

Medial F Sentences

Make It Fit!!

Directions: Circle the words that best finish the sentences below. Then, read/say the sentences aloud, using your best F sound.

1. I heard the _____ ring.   **spider**   **telephone**   **leash**

2. The _____ swims in the ocean.   **shirt**   **hot dog**   **dolphin**

3. The _____ is a pretty plant.   **daffodil**   **doctor**   **shovel**

4. I listen to music with my _____.   **dishes**   **headphones**   **shawl**

5. ABC's are also called the _____.   **bulldozer**   **shoe**   **alphabet**

6. The _____ watches you at the beach.   **lifeguard**   **ladder**   **sheep**

Homework Partner   Date   Speech-Language Pathologist

Medial F Sentences

228   #BK-291 Webber® Artic Fun Sheets 2 • ©2002 Super Duper® Publications • www.superduperinc.com • 1-800-277-8737

V Sound

Volcano Eruption!

Directions: Cut out the volcanoes and lava cards below. Each student gets a volcano. The first player reads/says the picture–word on a lava card, and places it on his/her volcano. Play continues in turn. Remember to use your good V sound.

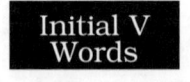

| vase | valentine | vest | violin |
| vacuum cleaner | vegetables | videotape | veil |

Homework Partner   Date   Speech-Language Pathologist

Initial V Words

Veggie Game

Directions: Cut out the vegetables. Then, cut along the dotted lines in the garden. Put the vegetables in the garden slots with only the very top of the vegetables showing through. One by one, "pick" each vegetable, reading/saying aloud the picture words. Use your good V sound

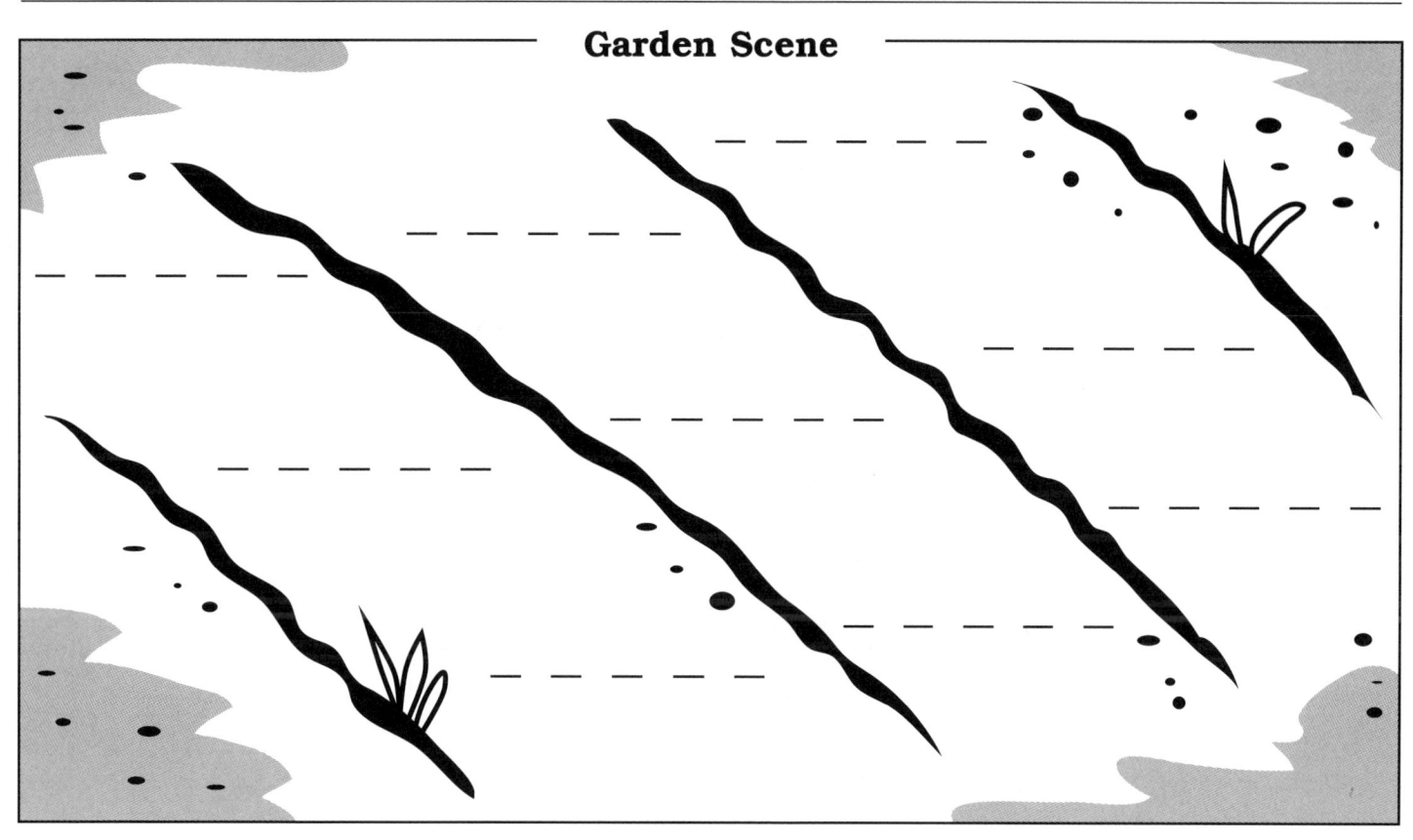

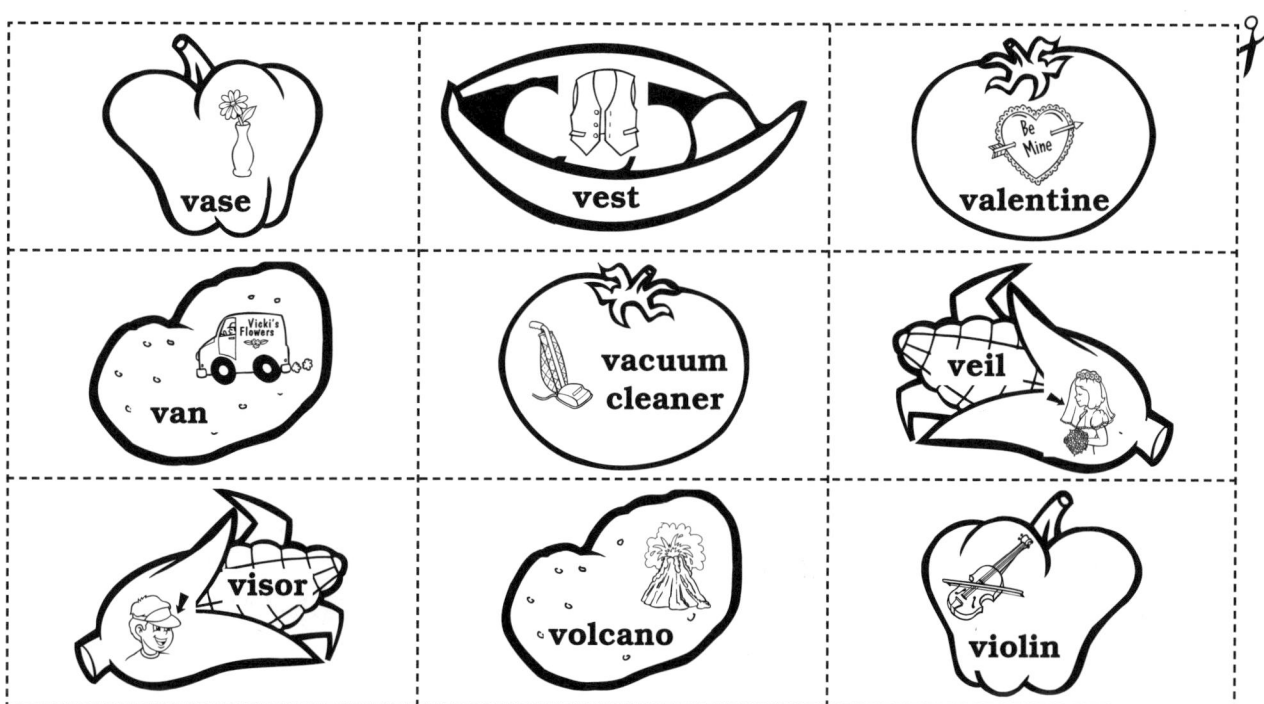

Garden Scene

vase	vest	valentine
van	vacuum cleaner	veil
visor	volcano	violin

Homework Partner   Date   Speech-Language Pathologist

Initial V Words

Paper Chain

Directions: Read/say aloud each picture–word below. Cut out the word strips. Turn them face down. Pick up a strip and read/say the word aloud. Then, staple/glue the strips to make a chain link. Remember to use your good V sound as you make your chain.

- volcano
- videotape
- veil
- vacuum cleaner
- vanilla ice cream
- vegetables
- vest
- vase
- van

Homework Partner   Date   Speech-Language Pathologist   Initial V Words

Listen Up!

Directions: Practice saying aloud each V picture–word. Answer the following questions using the pictures as clues. Read/say each word answer aloud. Then, follow the directions. Remember to use your good V sound.

vase

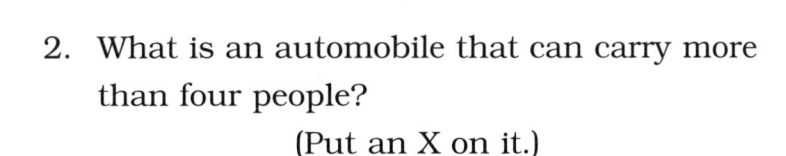

van

vanilla ice cream

vegetables

1. What is an instrument with strings?
   (Circle it.)

2. What is an automobile that can carry more than four people?
   (Put an X on it.)

3. What are good things for us to eat?
   (Draw a line through it.)

4. What do we use to clean our carpets?
   (Draw a line under it.)

5. What do we put in our VCR to watch?
   (Color it red.)

6. What shoots out hot fire?
   (Put an X over it.)

7. What do we put flowers in?
   (Draw a square around it.)

8. What is cold and goes in a cone?
   (Draw a circle on it.)

volcano

vacuum cleaner

videotape

violin

_____   _____   _____

Homework Partner   Date   Speech-Language Pathologist

Initial V Words

Name Me

Directions: Spell out each V picture on the lines below, using the Word Bank to help you. Read/say each word aloud, using your good V sound.

1. 
2. 
3. 
4. 
5. 
6. 
7. 
8.

Answers: 1. vest, 2. veil, 3. visor, 4. van, 5. violin, 6. vase, 7. videotape, 8. volcano

Word Bank

vase	volcano	van	veil
videotape	visor	vest	violin

Homework Partner   Date   Speech-Language Pathologist

Initial V Words

234   #BK-291 Webber® Artic Fun Sheets 2 • ©2002 Super Duper® Publications • www.superduperinc.com • 1-800-277-8737

Valentine Match Up!

Directions: Cut out the valentines below. Place each valentine on the picture–word above that goes best with the valentines. Read/say the words on each valentine aloud, using your best V sound.

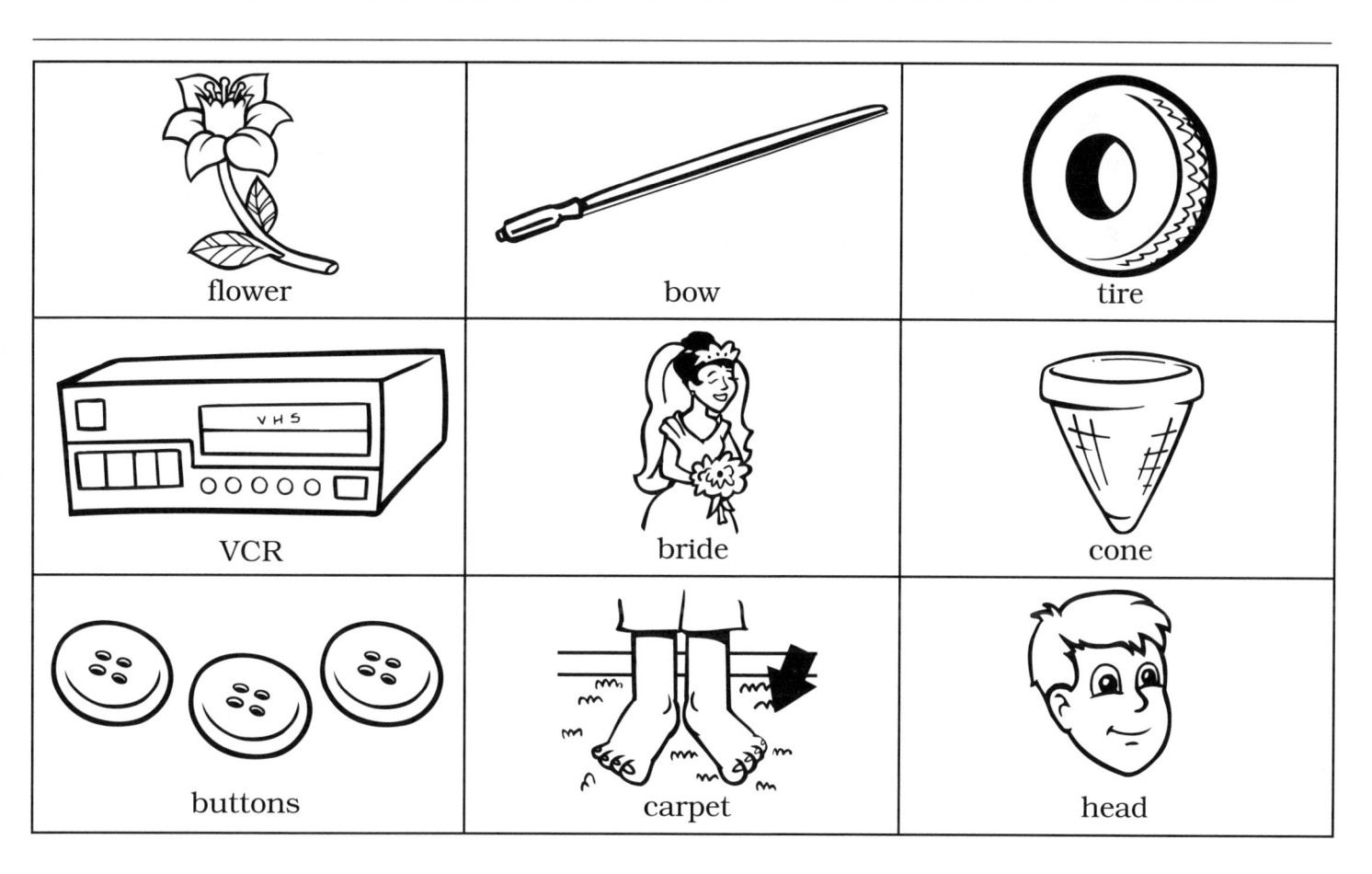

flower	bow	tire
VCR	bride	cone
buttons	carpet	head

vase	violin	van	vest

videotape	veil	vanilla ice cream	vacuum	visor

Homework Partner   Date   Speech-Language Pathologist   Initial V Words

#BK-291 Webber® Artic Fun Sheets 2 • ©2002 Super Duper® Publications • www.superduperinc.com • 1-800-277-8737

Phrase Racing

Directions: Cut out the vans. Give one to the student and one to a race partner. Begin at the starting line. Use a coin to determine the number of spaces to advance (heads=2, tails=1). Read/say aloud each phrase as you land on it. First one to the Finish wins! Play again. _____

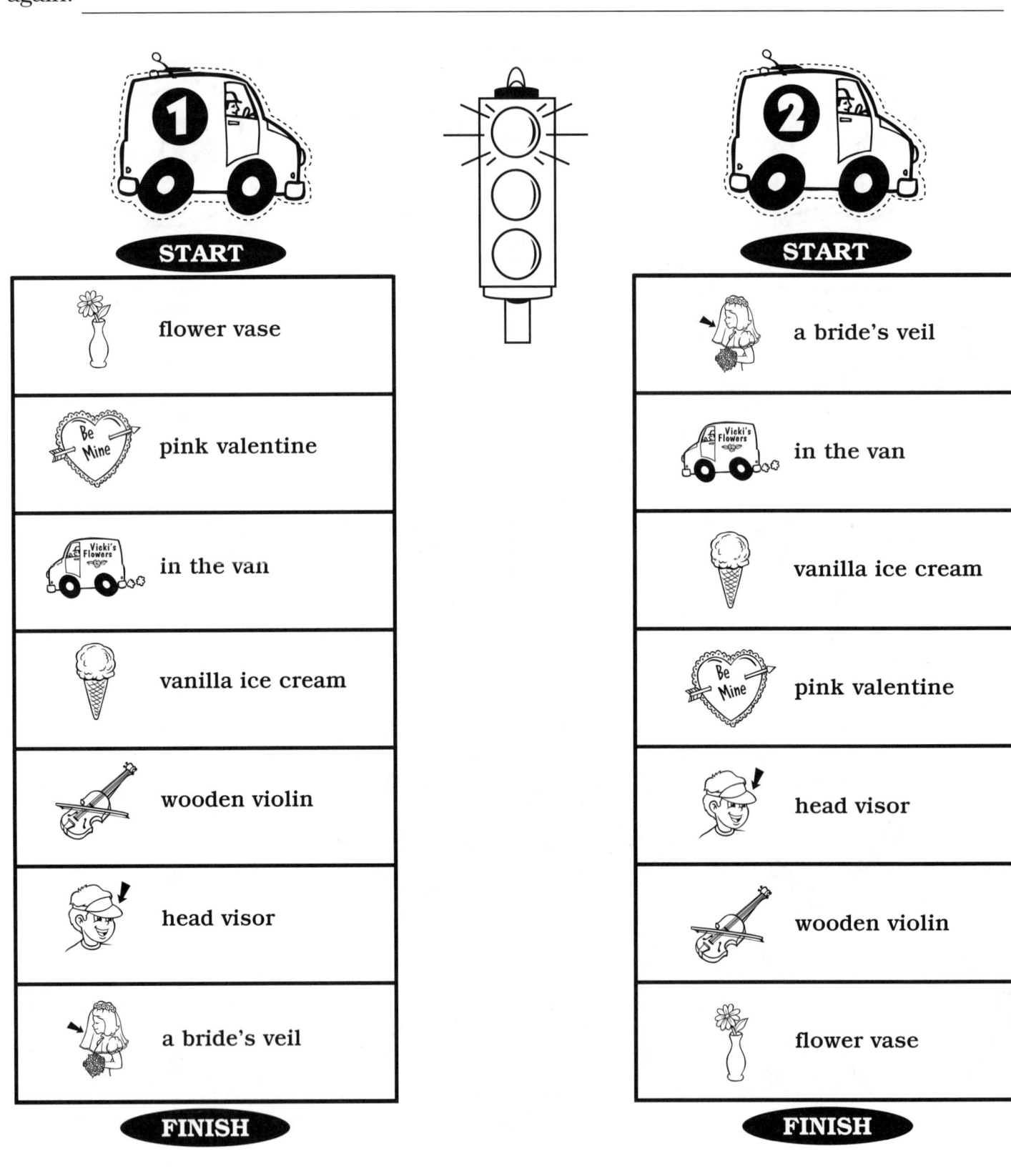

START 1

	flower vase
	pink valentine
	in the van
	vanilla ice cream
	wooden violin
	head visor
	a bride's veil

FINISH

START 2

	a bride's veil
	in the van
	vanilla ice cream
	pink valentine
	head visor
	wooden violin
	flower vase

FINISH

Homework Partner — Date — Speech-Language Pathologist

Initial V Phrases

236

V Phrase It

Directions: Assemble the cube as follows: glue onto construction paper for added durability. Cut along the dotted lines. Fold on solid lines and glue as indicated. To play: roll both cubes. Read/say the words and pictures together aloud to make up a phrase (funny van). Use your good V sound.

Cube 1 faces: vase, videotape, van, vegetables, valentine, volcano

Cube 2 faces: silly, yummy, broken, large, funny, happy

Initial V Phrases

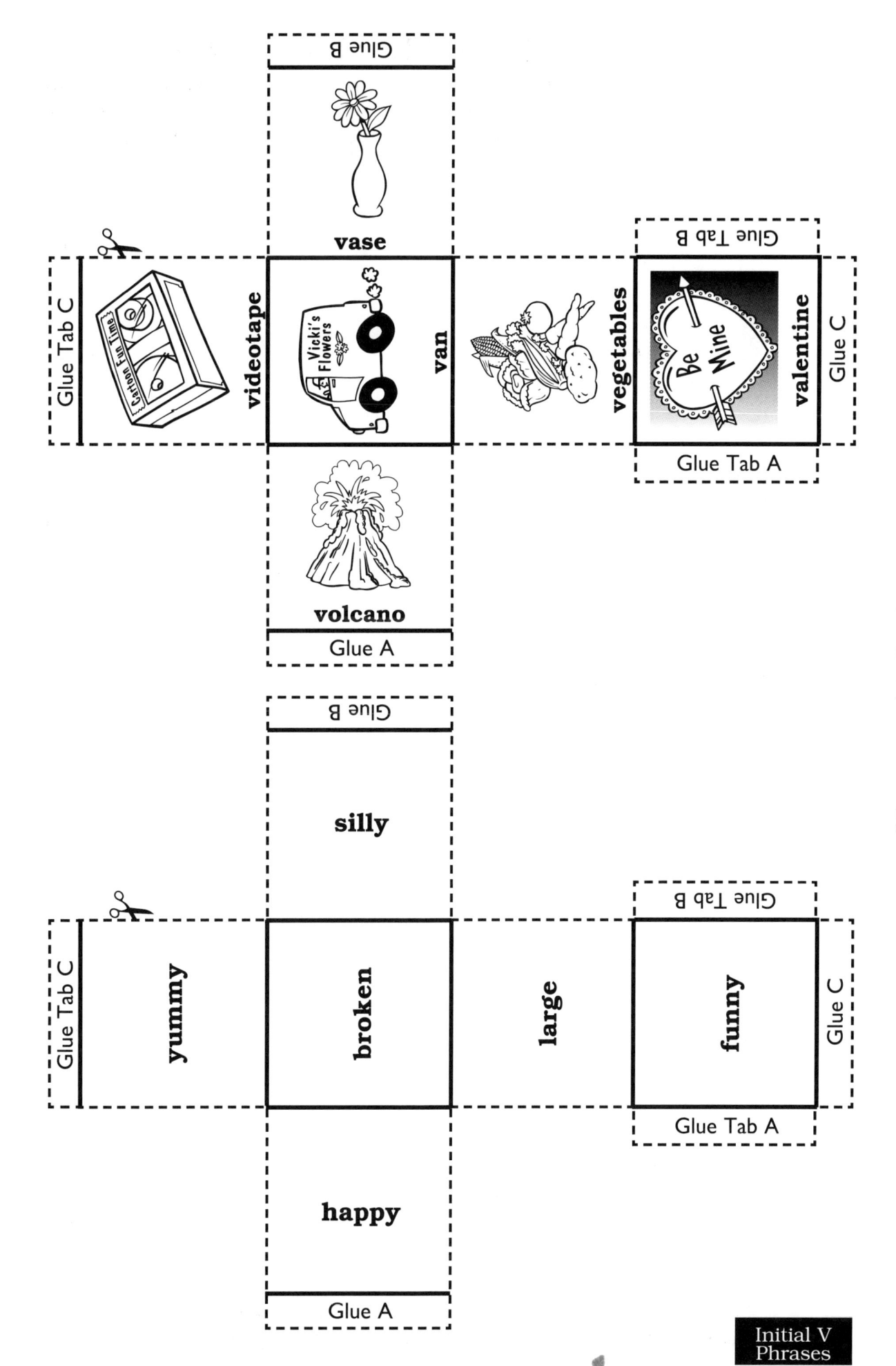

237

Go-Together Match-Ups

Directions: Read/say aloud the picture words on the left. Then find the words that "Go Together." Draw a line from the word–picture in column A to the word in column B that goes together best. Read/say each phrase aloud (vase and flower). Use your good V sound!

A	B
vase	card
vest	cone
valentine	shirt
vanilla ice cream	dirt
van	flower
vacuum cleaner	ride

Homework Partner   Date   Speech-Language Pathologist

Initial V Phrases

What's the Scoop?

Directions: Read/say aloud the picture–words in the picture below. Then, order different types of ice cream. Ask for a type of silly ice cream in a sentence beginning with, "I would like to order _____ ice cream." Say sentence aloud. Use your good V sound!

valentine   vegetables   volcano

vase   van   vest   violin   veil

Homework Partner   Date   Speech-Language Pathologist

Initial V Sentences

What's in a Picture?

Directions: Read/say aloud the picture–words in the Word Bank below. Then, look at the picture scene to answer the questions, using the words in the Word Bank. Follow the instructions, and remember to use your good V sound as you answer each sentence.

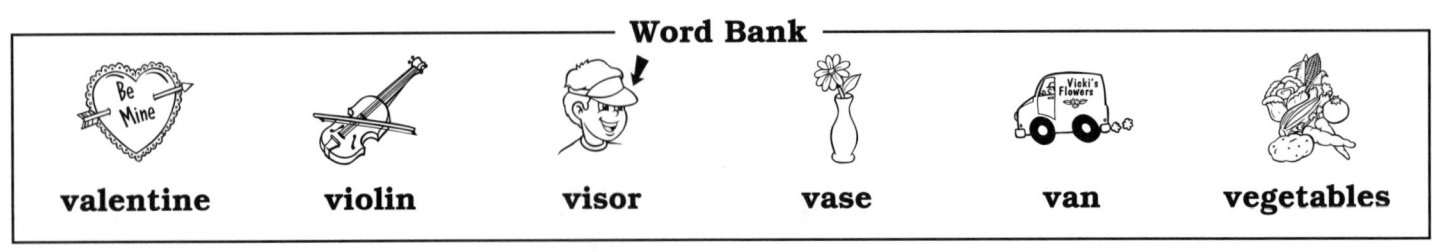

Word Bank

valentine   violin   visor   vase   van   vegetables

1. Color the flower yellow. The flower is in the _____.

2. Color the carrots orange. Carrots are _____.

3. Color the picture frame blue. The picture is a _____.

4. Color the boy's hair brown. The boy is wearing a _____ on his head.

5. Color the heart red. The heart is on the _____.

6. Color the window green. A flower _____ is going by the window.

Homework Partner   Date   Speech-Language Pathologist

Initial V Sentences

Search-a-Word

Directions: Read/say the picture–words aloud. Find and circle each word in the Word Search Box. Then, read/say the sentences. Use your good V sound. _____

van

vegetables

videotape

vanilla ice cream

```
R V J K T C R L V A L V A S M
T I X B U S V E R F L Y A A I
N O C G F T U I R A C I E N N
N L K C V Z Y V D J L R D I G
A I P E O N T E I E C E S A V
V N I C W O K F R E O T C J W
I L D T E O N T C R G T E O A
R C P F S V N I S P G Y A E P
W V F M P E A I U E X O I P K
S I J R W L V U O Y R A W H E
E T E Y L V D O V L F O E J R
Q D A I A G K X O L S P F W P
I D N V E G E T A B L E S P F
N A L L S E G G V R K F U E K
V V U O A I D R P P P V O A V
```

Answer Key on Page 280

veil

violin

vase

vest

1. Put the flowers in a _____.
2. The man wore a _____.
3. _____ are good for you.
4. The bride wore a _____.
5. He plays the _____.
6. Rewind the _____.
7. Ride in the _____.
8. I like to eat _____ on a cone.

Answers: 1. vase, 2. vest, 3. vegetables, 4. veil, 5. violin, 6. videotape, 7. van, 8. vanilla ice cream

Homework Partner   Date   Speech-Language Pathologist

Initial V Sentences

Beehive Game

Directions: Read/say aloud the picture–words below. Then, cut out the markers. Flip a coin (heads=1, tails=2) to determine how many spaces to move. As you move, read/say each word aloud, using your good V sound. First player to reach the beehive wins. _____

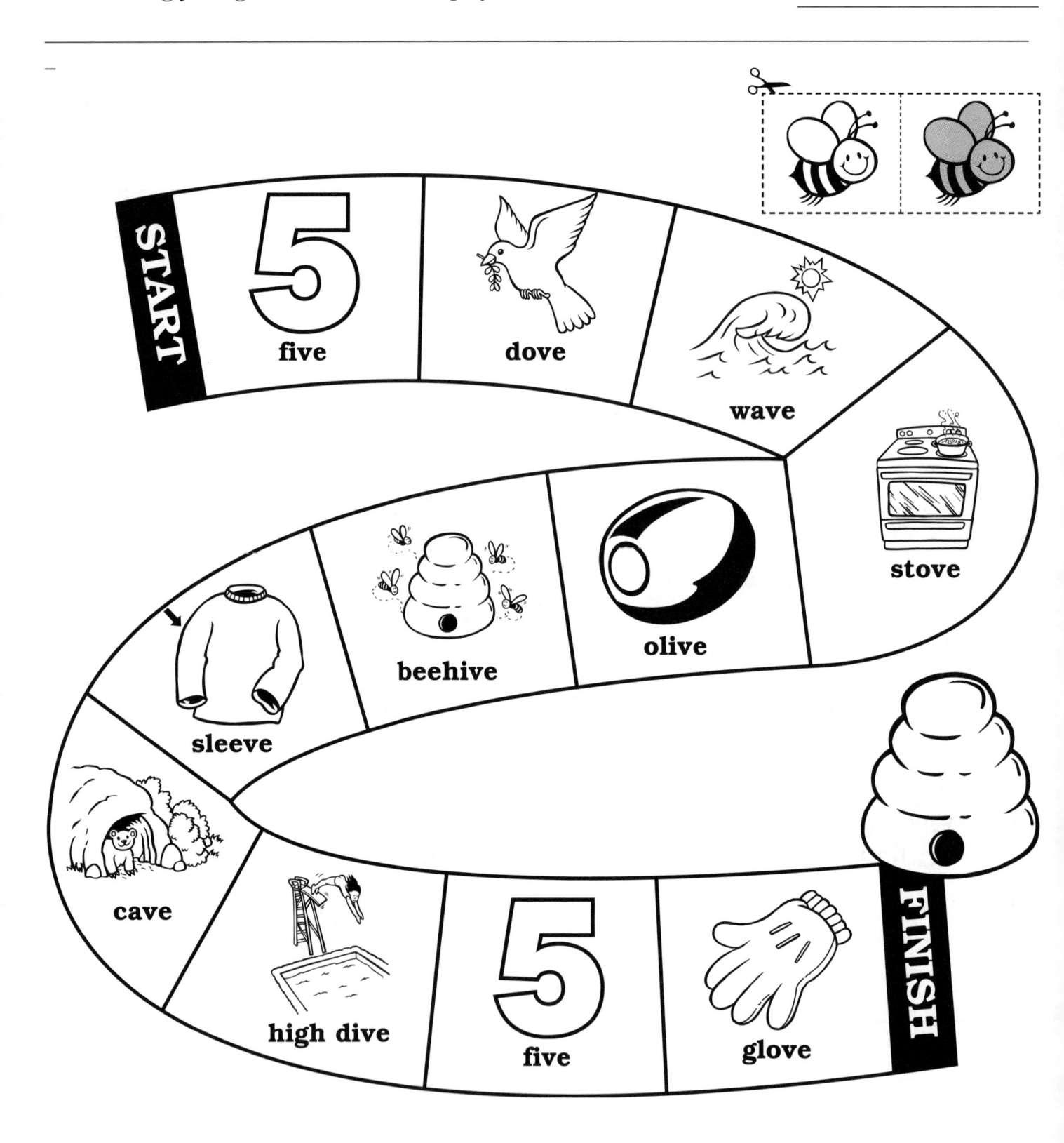

START — five — dove — wave — stove — olive — beehive — sleeve — cave — high dive — five — glove — FINISH

Homework Partner — Date — Speech-Language Pathologist

Final V Words

242 #BK-291 Webber® Artic Fun Sheets 2 • ©2002 Super Duper® Publications • www.superduperinc.com • 1-800-277-8737

Paper Chain

Directions: Read/say aloud each picture–word below. Cut out the word strips. Turn them face down. Pick up a strip and read/say the word aloud. Then, staple/glue the strips to make a chain link. Remember to use your good V sound as you make your chain.

- olive
- wave
- dove
- sleeve
- glove
- beehive
- stove
- cave
- high dive

Homework Partner   Date   Speech-Language Pathologist

Final V Words

Get a Clue

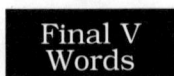

Directions: Read/say aloud the picture-words below. Then, read each clue and choose an answer from the Word Bank. Read/say your answer aloud using your best V sound.

1. A place a bear hibernates.

2. An appliance for cooking.

3. A food that is green.

4. An animal that is white.

5. Clothing for your hands.

6. Part of a shirt.

7. A board you jump from into a pool.

8. Surfers surf on me.

Answers: 1. cave, 2. stove, 3. olive, 4. dove, 5. glove, 6. sleeve, 7. high dive, 8. wave

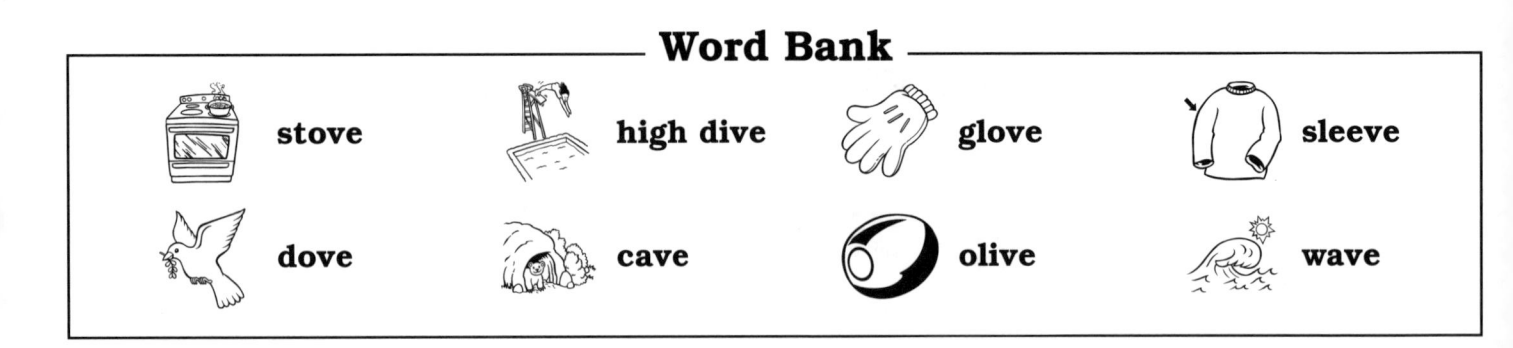

Word Bank

| stove | high dive | glove | sleeve |
| dove | cave | olive | wave |

Homework Partner Date Speech-Language Pathologist Final V Words

What's On Your Shirt?

Directions: Read/say aloud the picture-words below. Unscramble the words on each shirt using the picture-words in the Word Bank as clues. Write the unscrambled word on the lines provided. Read/say the words aloud, using your good V sound.

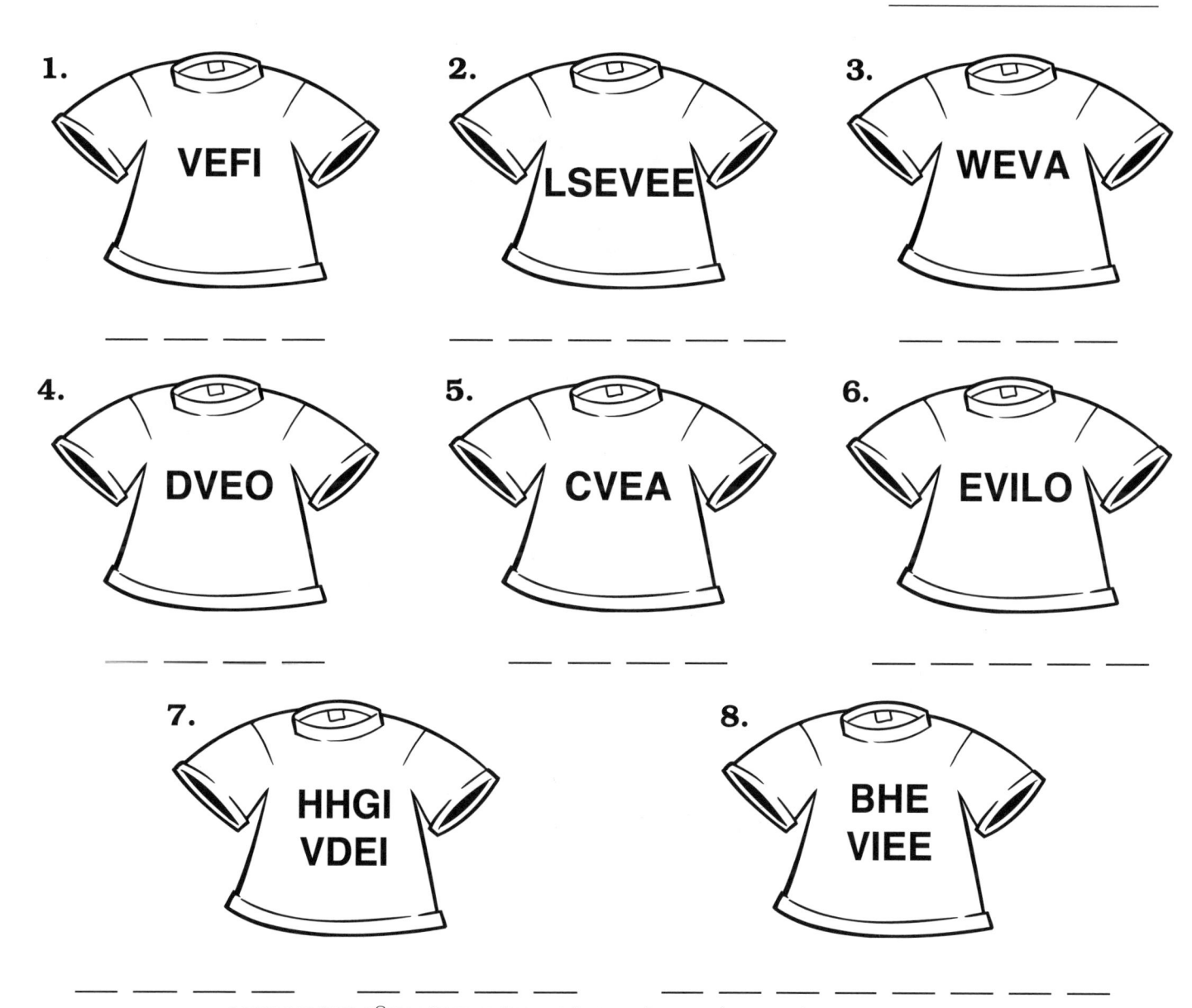

1. VEFI
2. LSEVEE
3. WEVA
4. DVEO
5. CVEA
6. EVILO
7. HHGI VDEI
8. BHE VIEE

Answers: 1. five, 2. sleeve, 3. wave, 4. dove, 5. cave, 6. olive, 7. high dive, 8. beehive

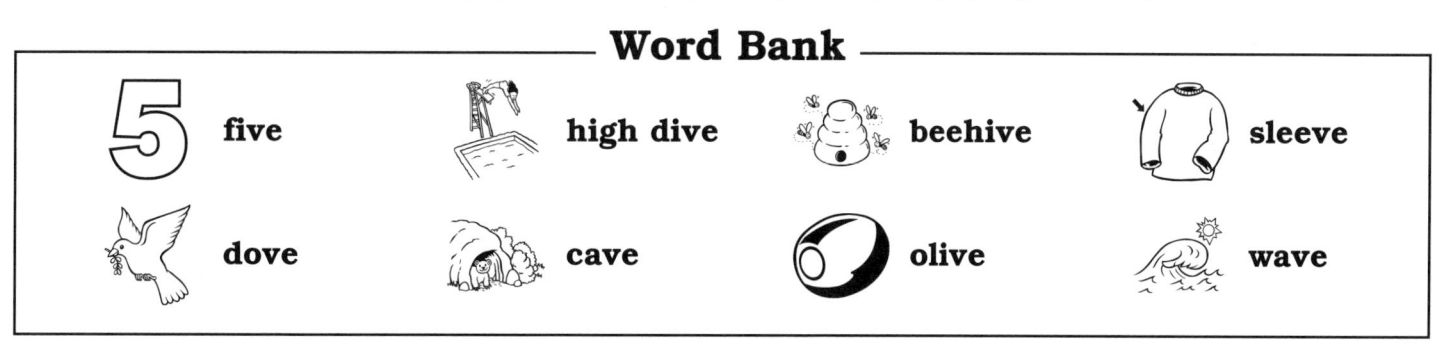

Word Bank

five — high dive — beehive — sleeve

dove — cave — olive — wave

Homework Partner   Date   Speech-Language Pathologist   Final V Words

Which Glove?

Directions: Read/say aloud the picture-words. Then, read the clues below and fill in the blanks. Use the words on the gloves for hints. Read/say each word answer aloud and color the correct finger on the gloves. Remember to use your good V sound.

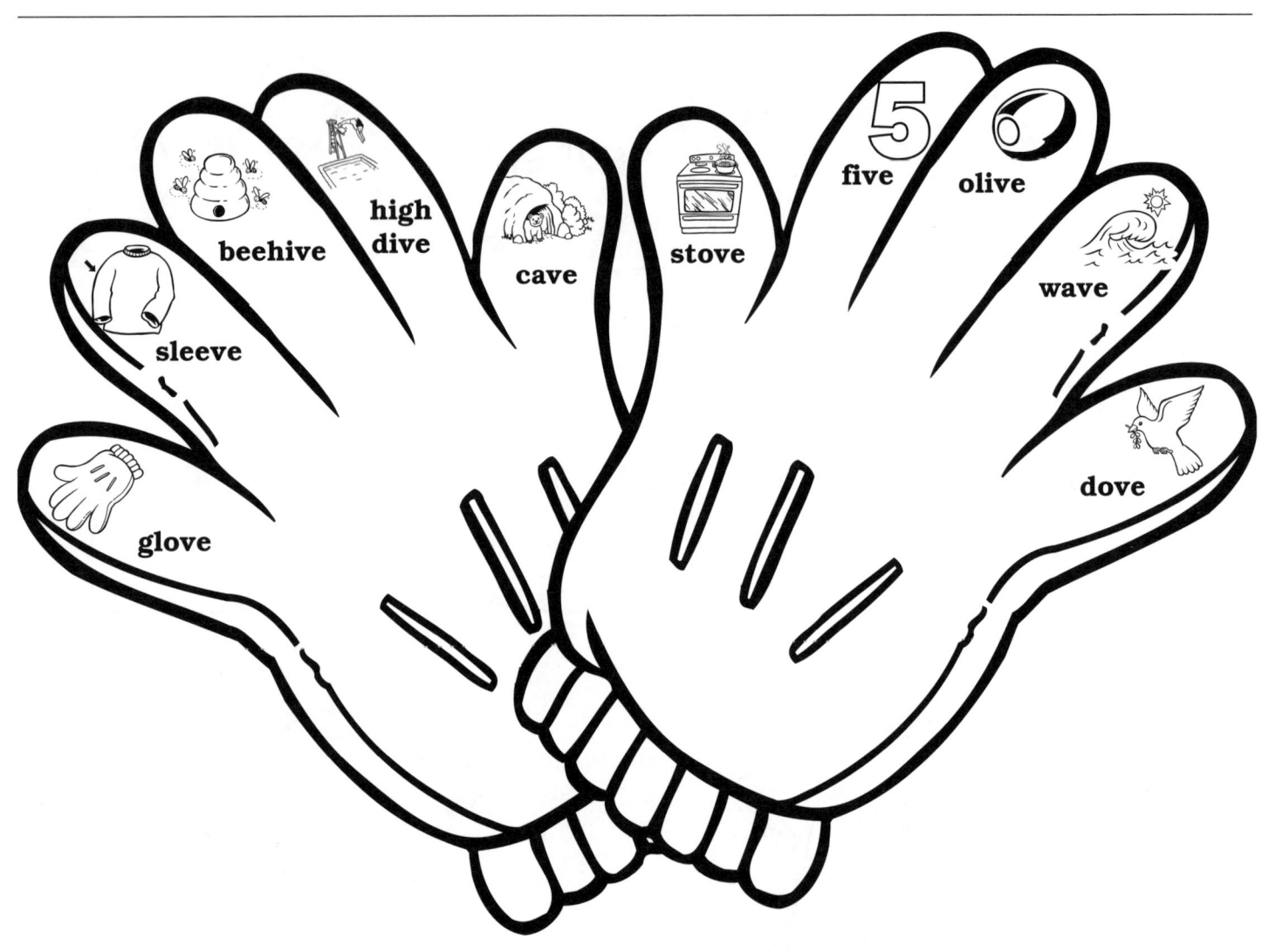

Gloves with labeled pictures: sleeve, beehive, high dive, cave, stove, five, olive, wave, dove, glove

1. A bear sleeps in a _____.
2. In my kitchen is a _____.
3. A bee works in a _____.
4. On my hand I wear a _____.
5. After 3 and 4 comes _____.

6. A surfer rides a _____.
7. My shirt has a _____.
8. I jump off the _____ _____.
9. A white bird is a _____.
10. You can eat an _____.

Answers: 1. cave, 2. stove, 3. beehive, 4. glove, 5. five, 6. wave, 7. sleeve, 8. high dive, 9. dove, 10. olive

Homework Partner   Date   Speech-Language Pathologist

Final V Words

Check it Out!

Directions: Read/say aloud the picture-words. Choose a word from the Word Bank and write it in the correct alphabetical space, or say the word aloud that goes in the correct space. Read/say the V word again, using your good V sound.

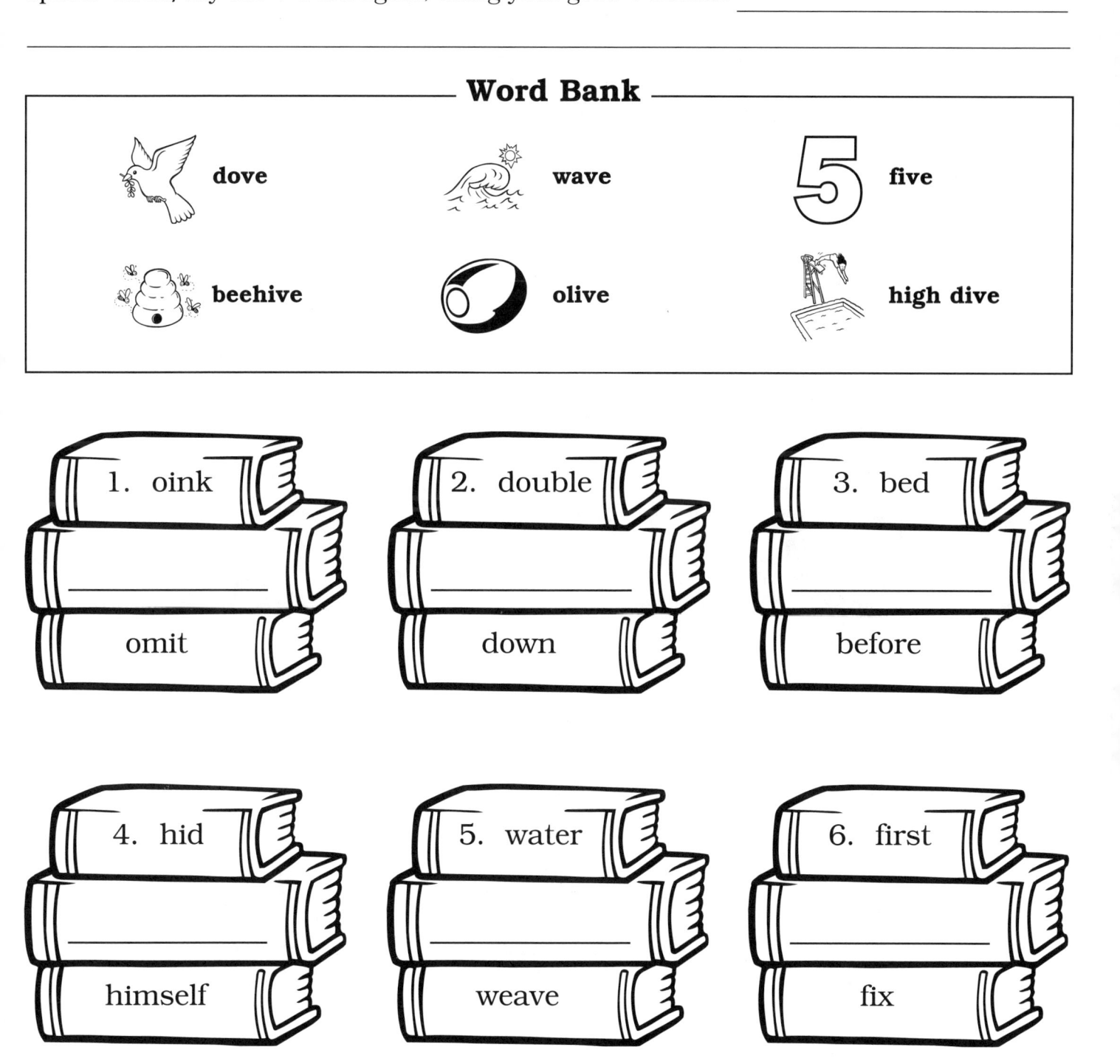

Word Bank

- dove
- wave
- five
- beehive
- olive
- high dive

1. oink / _____ / omit
2. double / _____ / down
3. bed / _____ / before
4. hid / _____ / himself
5. water / _____ / weave
6. first / _____ / fix

Answers: 1. olive, 2. dove, 3. beehive, 4. high dive, 5. wave, 6. five

Homework Partner Date Speech-Language Pathologist Final V Words

3 Games in 1

Directions: Say aloud the picture–words below, using your good V sound. Then, play one of the following games:

☐ Lotto – Caller reads a word and student repeats the word and covers it with a token/chip.
☐ Tic–Tac–Toe – Each time you write an **X** or **O**, say the word you mark over.
☐ Memory – Cut out all the cards and place face down. Try to find matching pairs. Say aloud each word you find. Keep all matches.

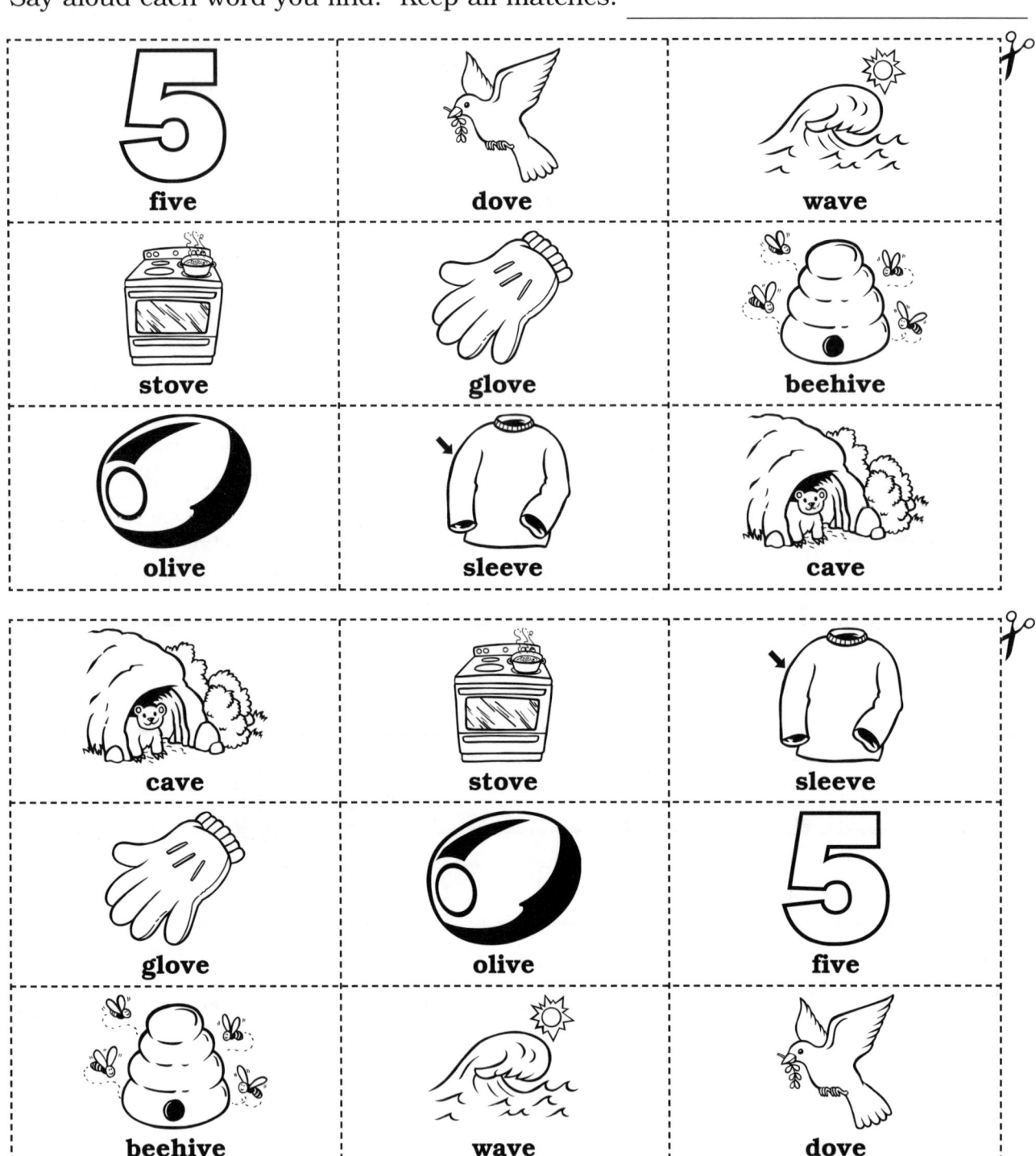

five	dove	wave
stove	glove	beehive
olive	sleeve	cave

cave	stove	sleeve
glove	olive	five
beehive	wave	dove

Homework Partner　　Date　　Speech-Language Pathologist　　Final V Words

248

What's Cooking?

Directions: Cut out the stoves below and place in a pile face down. Ask the student, "What's cooking?" The student draws a card and reads/says the silly phrase aloud, using his/her best V sound.

- baked wave
- cave casserole
- high dive cake
- five steaks
- dove pudding
- glove pie
- beehive surprise
- olive doughnut

Homework Partner   Date   Speech-Language Pathologist

Final V Phrases

Describe It!

Directions: Read/say aloud the picture–words on the right. Then, choose an adjective on the left that best describes the noun on the right (long sleeve). Read/say each phrase aloud. Use your good V sound.

1. _____ stove
   (hot/happy)

2. _____ dove
   (blue/white)

3. _____ wave
   (huge/dry)

4. _____ olive
   (green/yellow)

5. _____ sleeve
   (big/long)

6. _____ glove
   (warm/funny)

7. _____ beehive
   (bad/busy)

8. _____ cave
   (empty/silly)

Answers: 1. hot, 2. white, 3. huge, 4. green, 5. long, 6. warm, 7. busy, 8. empty

Homework Partner   Date   Speech-Language Pathologist

Final V Phrases

Answer It!

Directions: Read the questions below and choose the phrase that best answers the questions. Put an X beside the correct answer. Then, read/say your answers aloud using your good V sound.

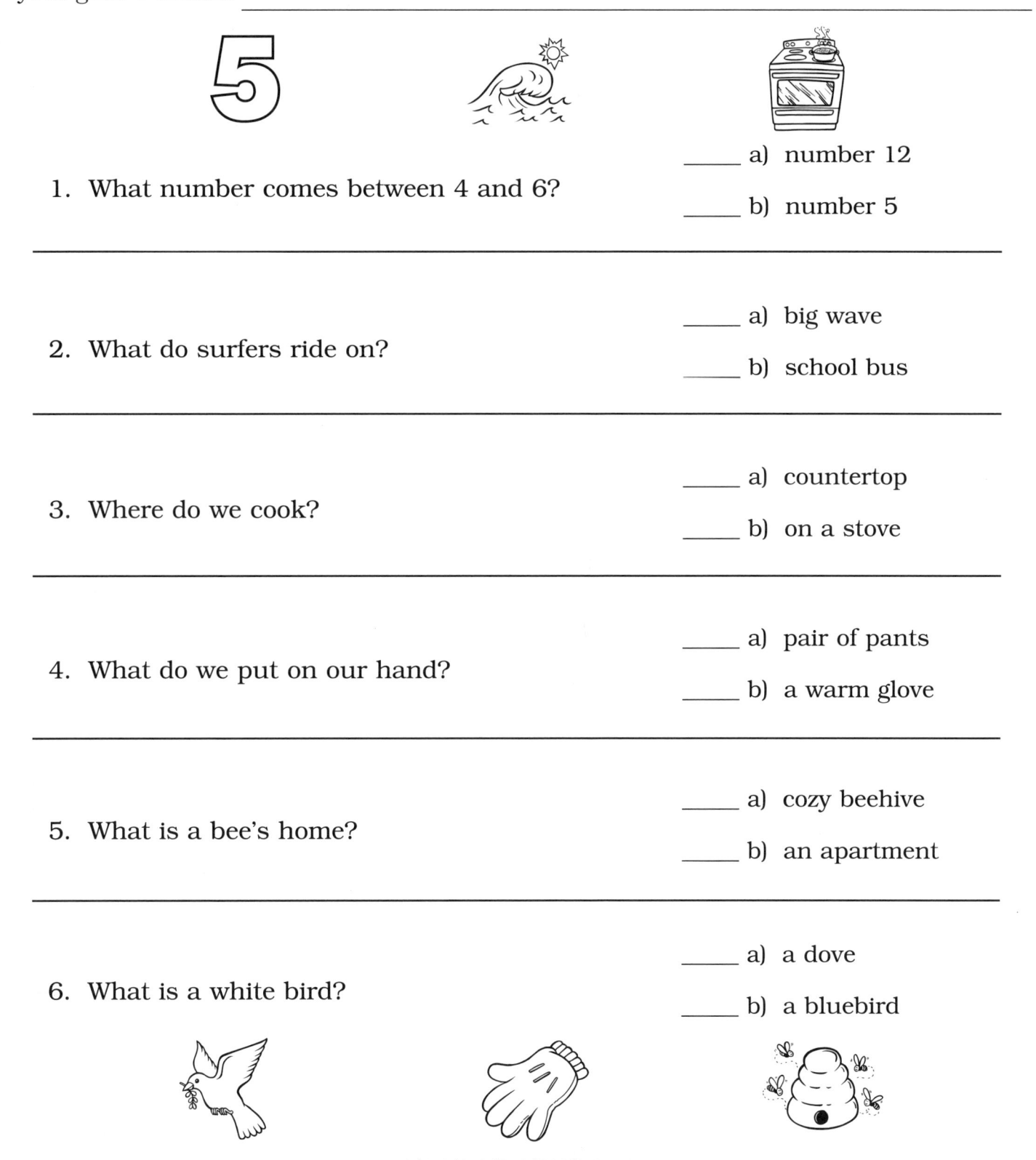

1. What number comes between 4 and 6?

   _____ a) number 12

   _____ b) number 5

2. What do surfers ride on?

   _____ a) big wave

   _____ b) school bus

3. Where do we cook?

   _____ a) countertop

   _____ b) on a stove

4. What do we put on our hand?

   _____ a) pair of pants

   _____ b) a warm glove

5. What is a bee's home?

   _____ a) cozy beehive

   _____ b) an apartment

6. What is a white bird?

   _____ a) a dove

   _____ b) a bluebird

Answers: 1. b, 2. a, 3. b, 4. b, 5. a, 6. a

Homework Partner   Date   Speech-Language Pathologist

Final V Phrases

Yes or No?

Directions: Read/say aloud the questions. Then, put an X in the correct boxes. Say your answers aloud in sentence form. (No, an olive grows on a tree.) Remember to use your best V sound.

	Yes	No
1. Does an olive grow on a bush?	☐	☐
2. Does a wave get you wet?	☐	☐
3. Is a dove a white bird?	☐	☐
4. Can a butterfly fly in a beehive?	☐	☐
5. Does a bear hibernate in a cave?	☐	☐
6. Can a glove fit your foot?	☐	☐
7. Can you cook on a stove?	☐	☐
8. Do you jump off a high dive?	☐	☐
9. Is five before three?	☐	☐
10. Can you put your head through a sleeve?	☐	☐

Homework Partner   Date   Speech-Language Pathologist

Final V Sentences

Dive In

Directions: Read/say aloud the picture–word on each diving board. Then, read each sentence below and choose a word from a diving board to complete it. Read/say the entire sentence aloud, using your best V sound.

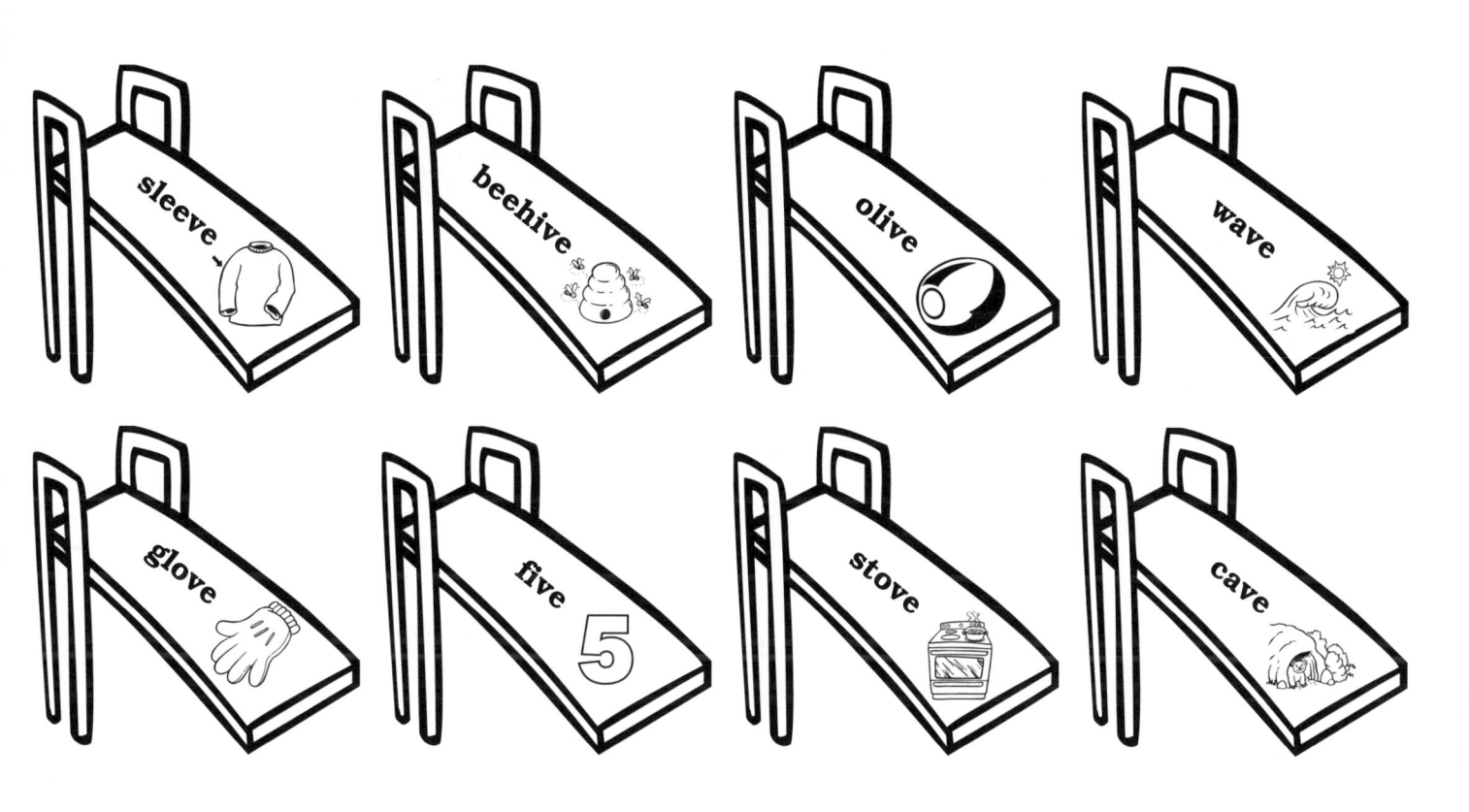

Diving boards: sleeve, beehive, olive, wave, glove, five, stove, cave

Sentences:
- He spilled ketchup on his ___.
- A huge ___ knocked me down.
- Don't burn your hand on the ___.
- A bear hibernates in a ___.
- I prefer a green ___ over a black one.
- The bees are busy working in the ___.
- He wore the ___ when he worked in yard.
- Amy has ___ cats and three kittens.

Homework Partner   Date   Speech-Language Pathologist   Final V Sentences

Create Your Own Picture

Directions: Write a sentence on the lines using the picture–words below. Then, draw a picture scene in the box to describe the sentence. Read/say the sentence aloud, using your good V sound.

1. cave

2. glove

3. wave

4. beehive

5. high dive

6. stove

Homework Partner   Date   Speech-Language Pathologist

Final V Sentences

Stuff the Envelope

Directions: Cut out the picture cards and the outside of the envelope below. Staple/glue the outside edges of the envelope to construction paper. Cut the flap of the envelope so that it opens/flips up. Place the pictures face down in a pile. Roll a die and draw a card, saying the word as many times as shown on the die. Then, stuff the card into the envelope. Keep playing until all of the cards are in the envelope. Remember to use your good V sound.

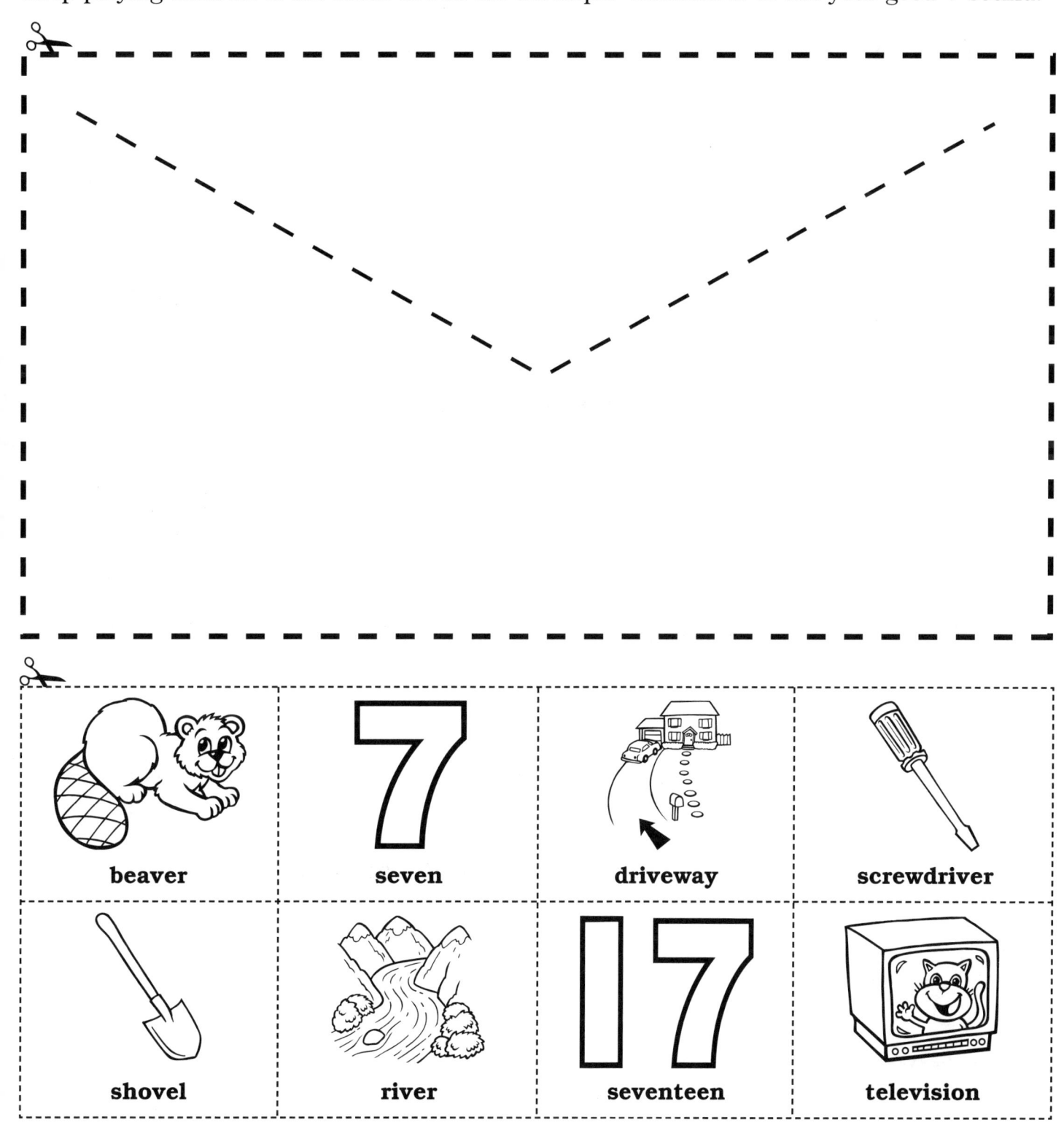

beaver	seven	driveway	screwdriver
shovel	river	seventeen	television

Homework Partner   Date   Speech-Language Pathologist

Medial V Words

Very Classy

Directions: Practice saying aloud each V picture–word. Then, follow the directions in the middle of the page. Say the words again as you follow the directions, using your good V sound.

seven	Color the tools red.	**shovel**
envelope	Circle the numbers.	**driveway**
screwdriver	Underline the things you find at home.	**seventeen**
river		**television**
beaver	Cross out the things you find in the water.	**skin diver**

Homework Partner   Date   Speech-Language Pathologist

Medial V Words

Spinner Action!

Directions: Read/say aloud the picture–words below. If you prefer, glue this page to construction paper for added durability. Cut out the arrow/dial. Use a brad to connect the dial to the circle. Spin the spinner. When you land on a picture, read/say the word aloud, using your best V sound.

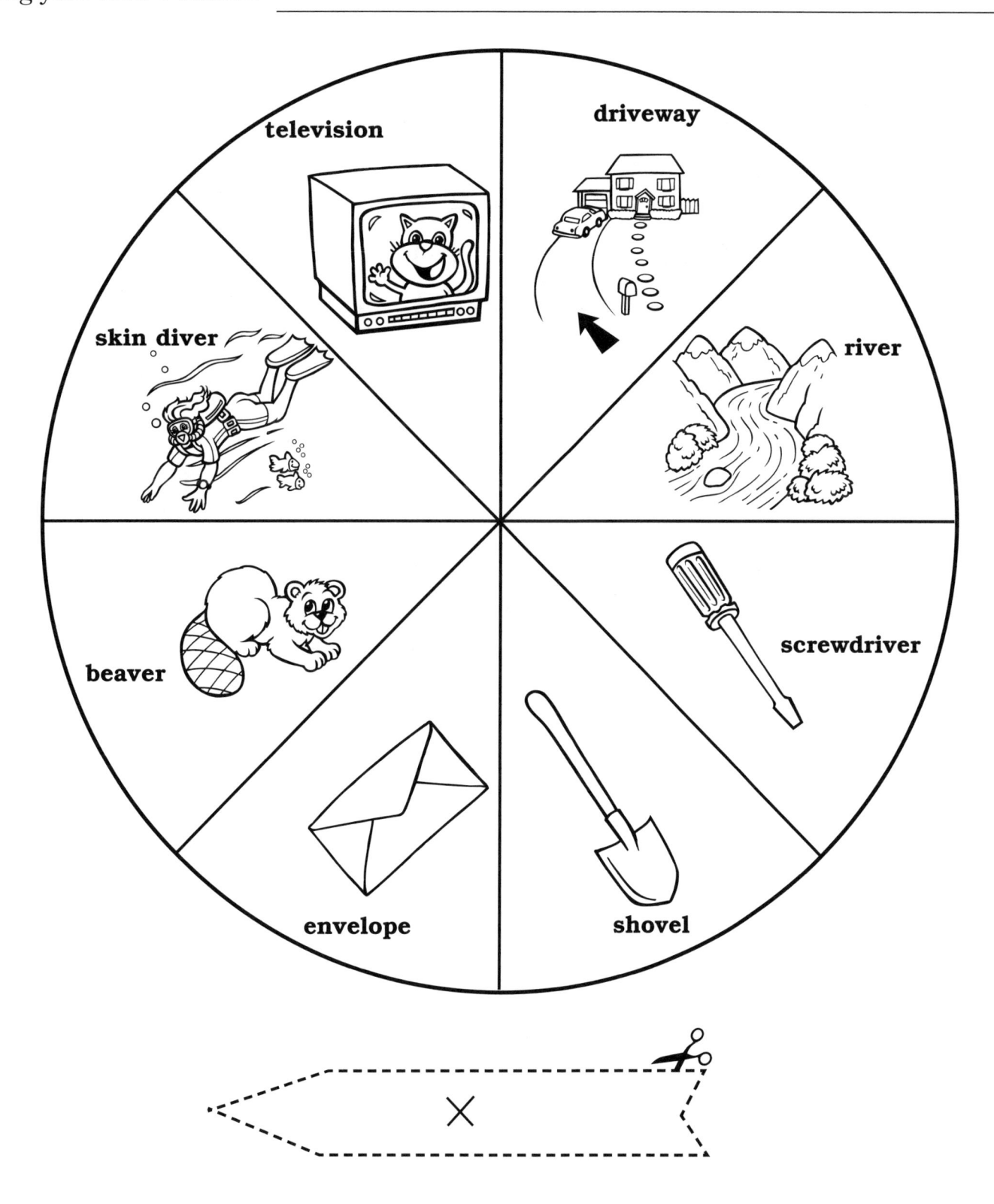

- television
- driveway
- river
- screwdriver
- shovel
- envelope
- beaver
- skin diver

Homework Partner Date Speech-Language Pathologist

Medial V Words

Search-a-Word

Directions: Read/say the picture–words aloud. Then, find and circle each word answer in the Word Search Box. Then, read/say the words again. Use your good V sound.

```
T L S B T A E E A S O C K W Z
N Q A K S R N T I F R A P C K
B W D E I V E X S E Q G R H U
K K N X E N W V V P X S S R W
X F G L S E D I I U E R P A Q
W C O C J X R I M R S M X F S
K P S B W D K X V I U R P V H
E Q B Z W C S W C E V I D Z W
N L B E S E I I H R R H R O I
E Z R B O T E L E V I S I O N
V C R N H A H B O P D R W W S
S S J E Q M R E V A E B E X M
V R R V E A B Z C B K B W O C
J R H E N E A I K B J U A Y O
V D H S E V K B H H Z V Y J X
```

Answer Key on Page 280

- beaver 
- river 
- skin diver 
- driveway 
- screwdriver 
- television 
- envelope 
- seven

Homework Partner Date Speech-Language Pathologist

Medial V Words

Memory Game

Directions: Read/say aloud each picture–word below. Cut out the pictures. Place all cards face down. Try to match the cards. Say each card as you pick it up, using your good V sound.

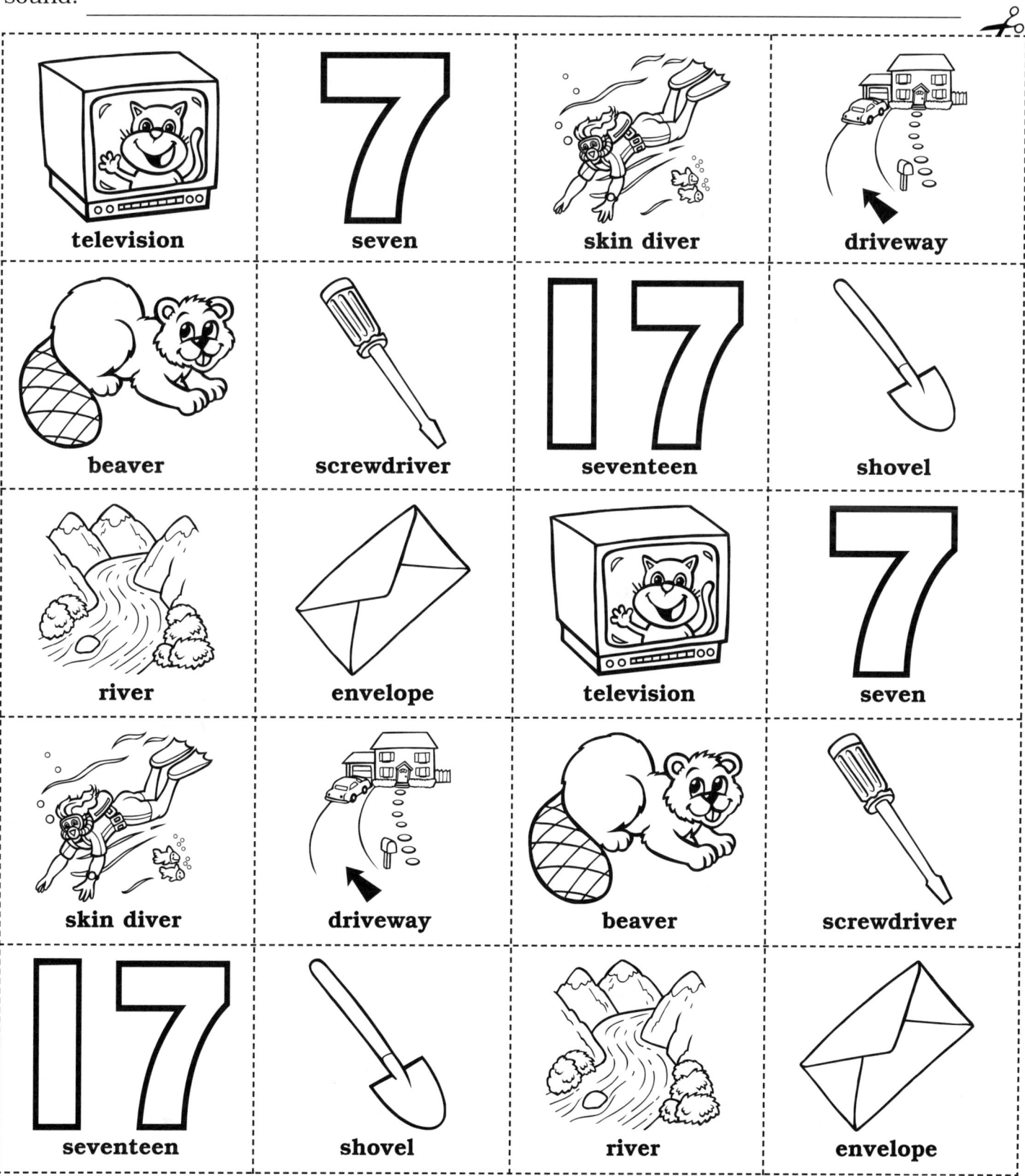

television	seven	skin diver	driveway
beaver	screwdriver	seventeen	shovel
river	envelope	television	seven
skin diver	driveway	beaver	screwdriver
seventeen	shovel	river	envelope

Homework Partner Date Speech-Language Pathologist

Medial V Words

Read the Book

Directions: Each word below has a missing letter in it. Fix each word by writing in the missing letter. Use the pictures as clues. Read/say aloud each word, using your good V sound.

1. bea____er

2. sev____n

3. ____iver

4. e____velope

5. ____hovel

6. tele____ision

Answers: 1. v, 2. e, 3. r, 4. n, 5. s, 6. v

Homework Partner   Date   Speech-Language Pathologist   Medial V Words

Associate It

Directions: Read/say the words in the Word Bank. Then, find the envelope that goes with that word (driveway/car). Read/say aloud your V words as you put them in the envelopes.

Word Bank

- skin diver
- envelope
- driveway
- television
- shovel
- beaver

A. car — d _ _ _ _ _ _ _ _

B. letter — _ _ v _ _ _ _ _

C. logs — _ _ a _ _ _ _

D. dirt — _ h _ _ _ _

E. ocean — _ _ _ n _ _ _ _ _

F. shows — _ _ _ _ _ _ _ _ i _ _

Answers: A. driveway, B. envelope, C. beaver, D. shovel, E. skin diver, F. television

Homework Partner | Date | Speech-Language Pathologist | Medial V Words

X and O

Directions: Cut out each **X** and **O** below. Have each player/partner choose an **X** or **O**. The first player reads/says a phrase aloud and places an **X** or **O** on the square. Play continues in turn. The first person to get three in a row wins.

concrete driveway	high river	broken screwdriver
seven years old	on a television	envelope stamp
baby beaver	snow shovel	seventeen candles

X X X X X

O O O O O

Homework Partner | Date | Speech-Language Pathologist

Medial V Phrases

Number Phrase

Directions: Cut out the cards below. Keep A cards and B cards in separate piles and place face down. Draw one card from each pile and say the number phrase aloud (one skin diver). Use your good V sound.

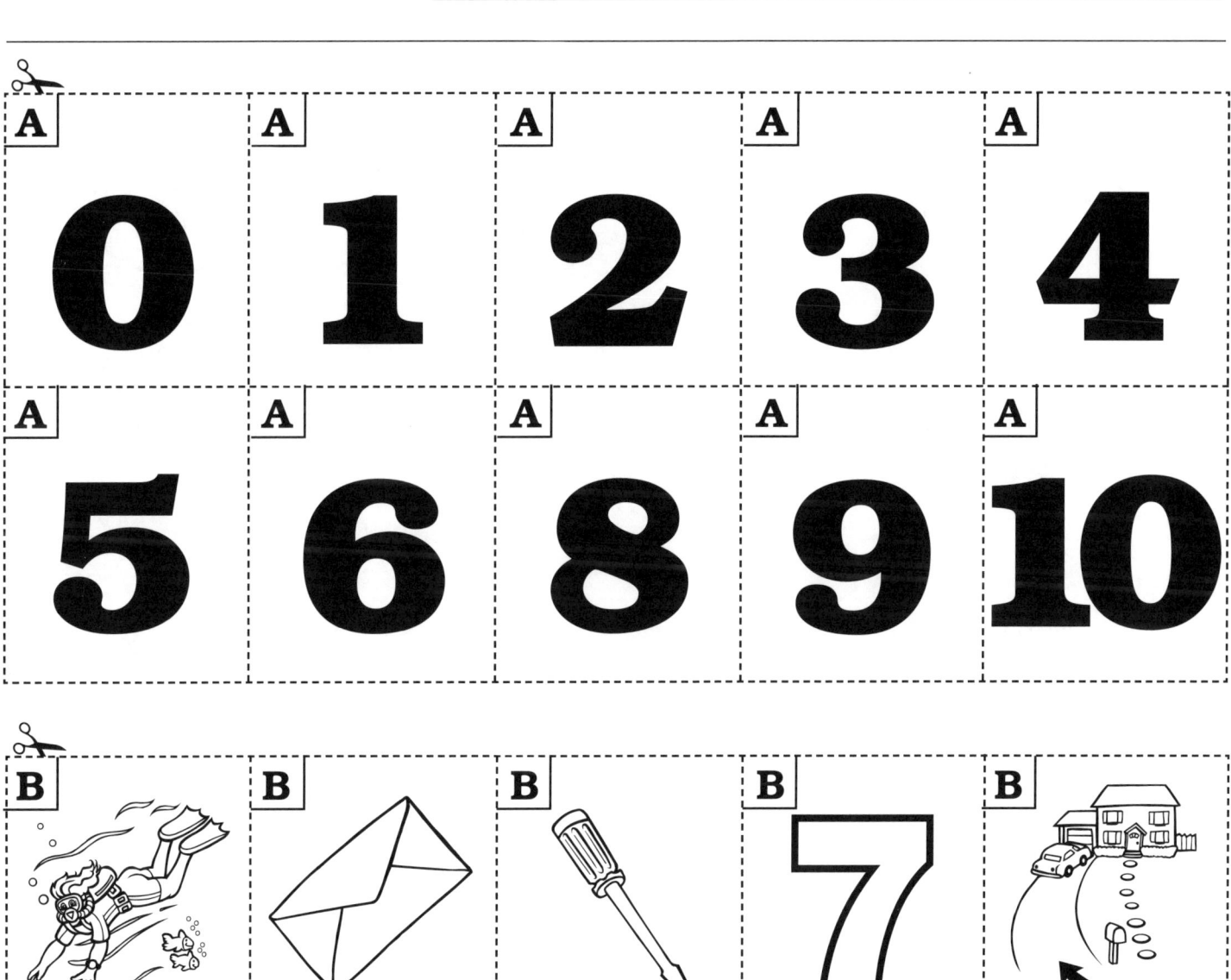

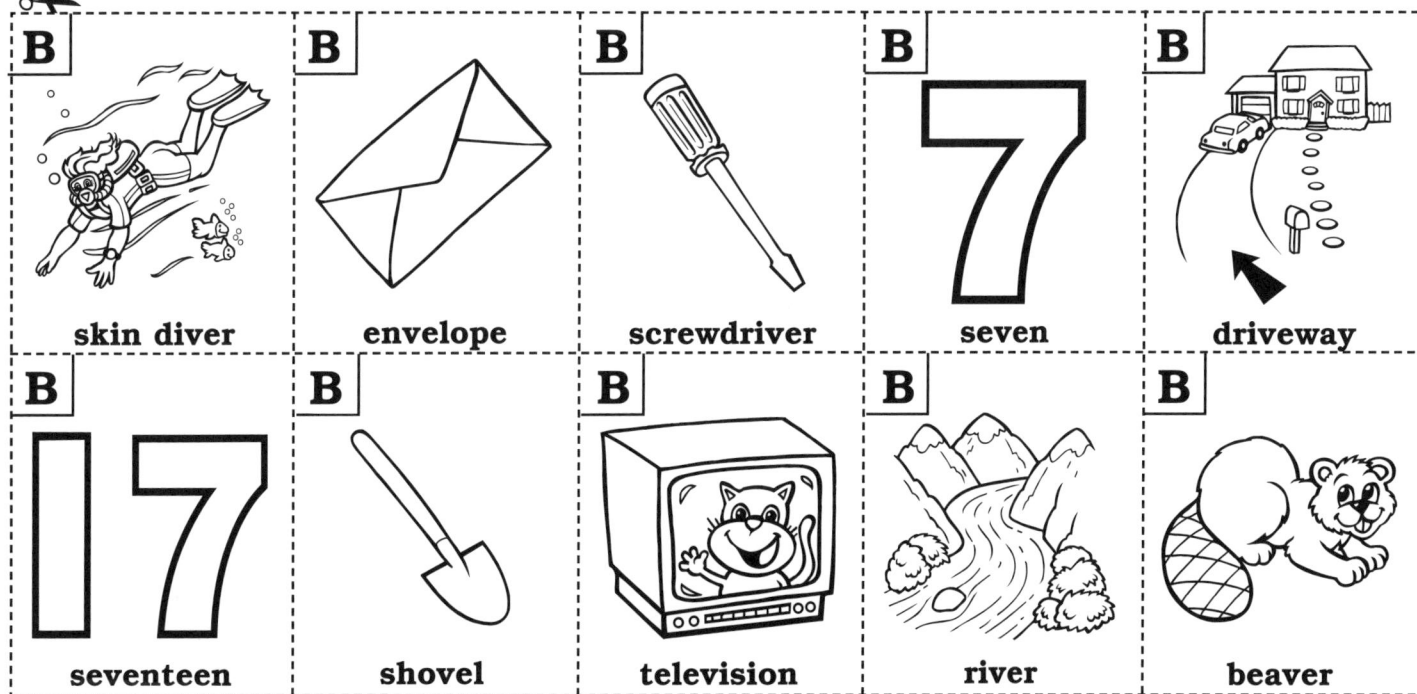

A	A	A	A	A
0	1	2	3	4
5	6	8	9	10

B	B	B	B	B
skin diver	envelope	screwdriver	seven	driveway
seventeen	shovel	television	river	beaver

Homework Partner   Date   Speech-Language Pathologist

Medial V Phrases

Roll Them Up!

Directions: Roll a die two times. The first roll gives you a word from column A and the second roll gives you a word from column B. Put the words together to make a phrase (small shovel). Read/say the phrase aloud. Remember to use your good V sound. Roll again and again!

A	B
1. cold	1. **television**
2. small	2. **beaver**
3. hot	3. **river**
4. long	4. **envelope**
5. big	5. **shovel**
6. broken	6. **driveway**

Homework Partner   Date   Speech-Language Pathologist

Medial V Phrases

Match the Beavers

Directions: Cut out the tails below. Match and glue/tape each tail to the right of a beaver to complete the sentence. Read/say the sentence aloud, using your good V sound.

Turn on the ____.

Float down the ____.

The ____ is in my toolbox.

Mail the ____.

Park the car in the ____.

That teenager is ____ years old.

____ the snow.

You are ____ years old in the first grade.

---

seventeen

driveway

screwdriver

shovel

envelope

television

river

seven

Homework Partner   Date   Speech-Language Pathologist

Medial V Sentences

Scrambled Sentences

Directions: Try to unscramble each sentence. Write it on the line below the egg. Then read/say the sentence aloud using your best V sound.

1. am I today years seven old

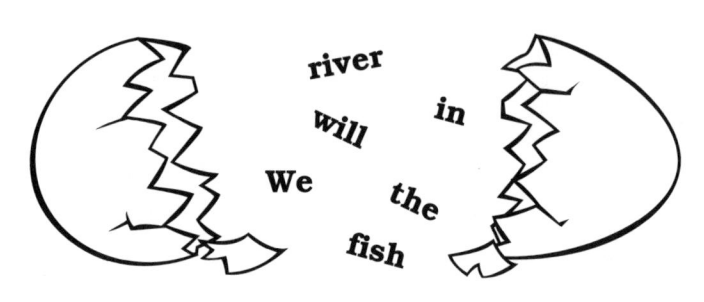

2. river in will We the fish

3. to Don't envelope forget mail the

4. water The skin diver into jumped the

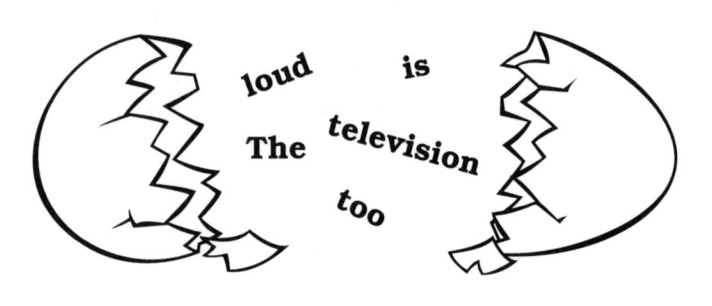

5. loud is The television too

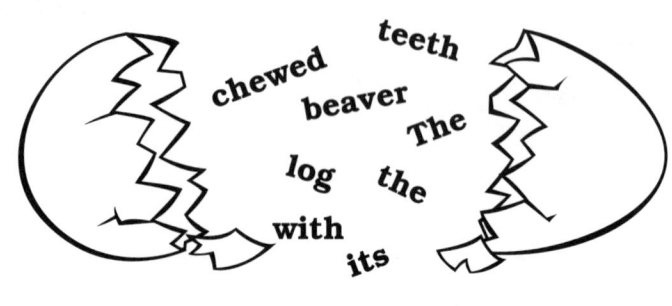

6. teeth chewed beaver The log the with its

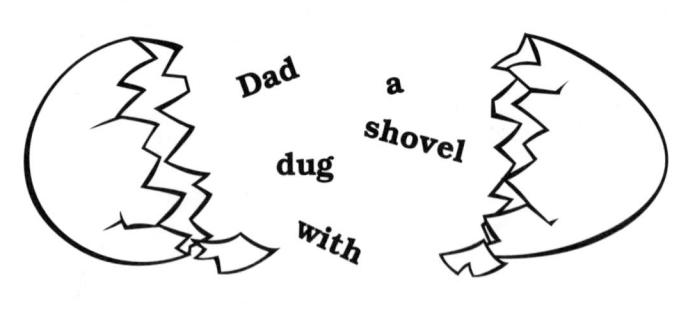

7. Dad a shovel dug with

8. truck parked The driveway in the is

Answer Key on Page 279

Homework Partner   Date   Speech-Language Pathologist

Medial V Sentences

Where Does the Sentence End?

Directions: The following story does not have any punctuation or capitalization. Read the story and determine where to put periods, question marks, exclamation marks and capital letters. Then, read/say each sentence in the story aloud, using your good V sound.

bobby the beaver was bored his mother told him to shovel the garden he wanted to watch television instead bobby walked to the river he saw a skin diver there he went to the mailbox and found an envelope addressed to him he was so excited to see what was inside he opened it up and inside was seven 7 dollars it was a good day

Homework Partner   Date   Speech-Language Pathologist

Medial V Sentences

Story Loop

Directions: Read/say aloud each picture–word. Make up a story using all of the pictures in the circle. You can start anywhere in the circle and go in either direction, but you must always end where you started to complete the loop. Say your story aloud, using your good V sound.

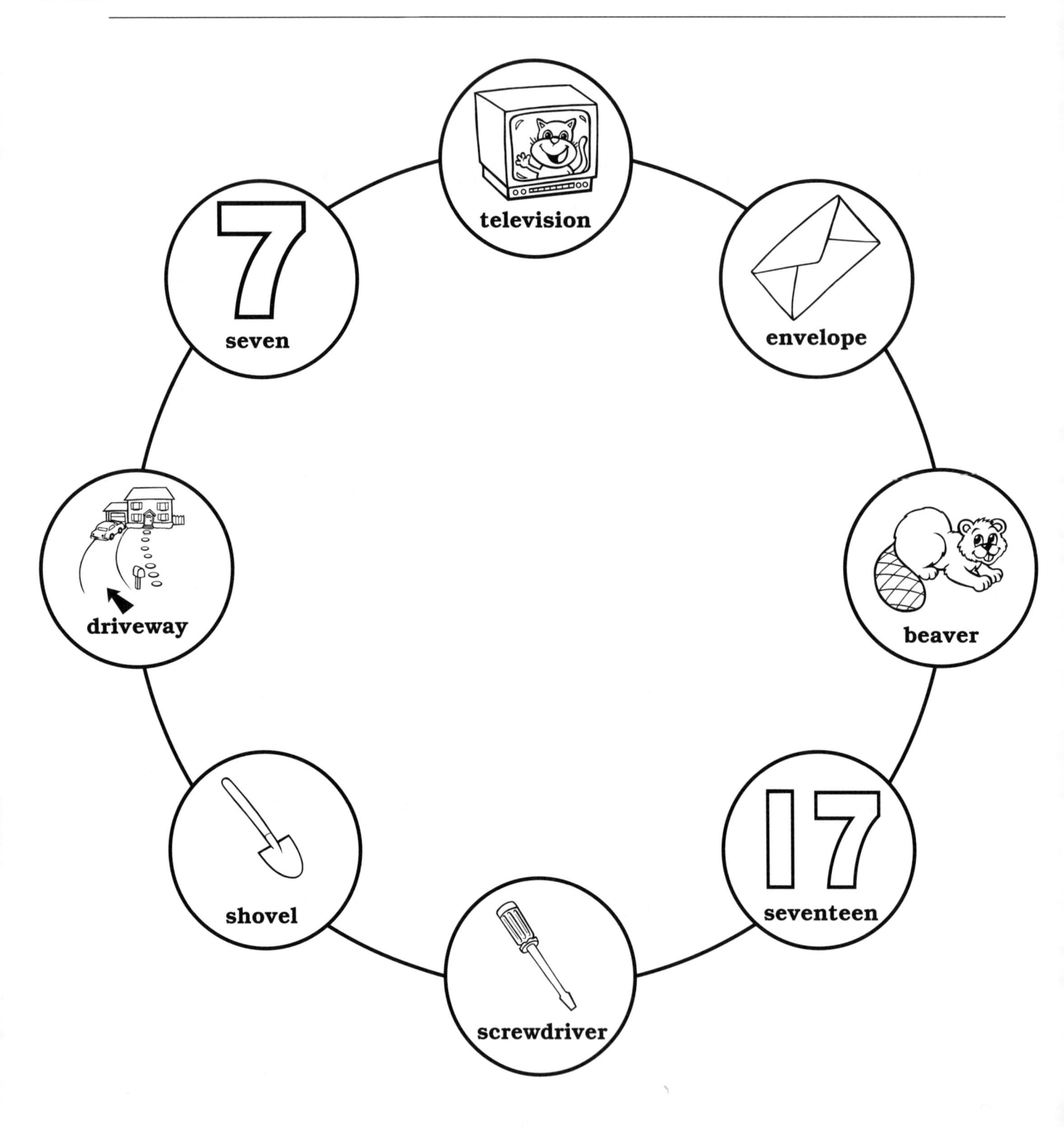

- television
- envelope
- beaver
- seventeen
- screwdriver
- shovel
- driveway
- seven

Homework Partner Date Speech-Language Pathologist

Medial V Sentences

Awards

SH Super Star!

This certifies that

_____
Name

is an SH speech Super Star!

_____   _____
SLP   Date

Hip Hip Hooray!

_____ makes an Excellent CH sound!

Name

_____   _____
SLP   Date

You Did It!

This Certifies that

_____
Name

makes a great TH sound!

_____
SLP

_____
Date

My K is Awesome!

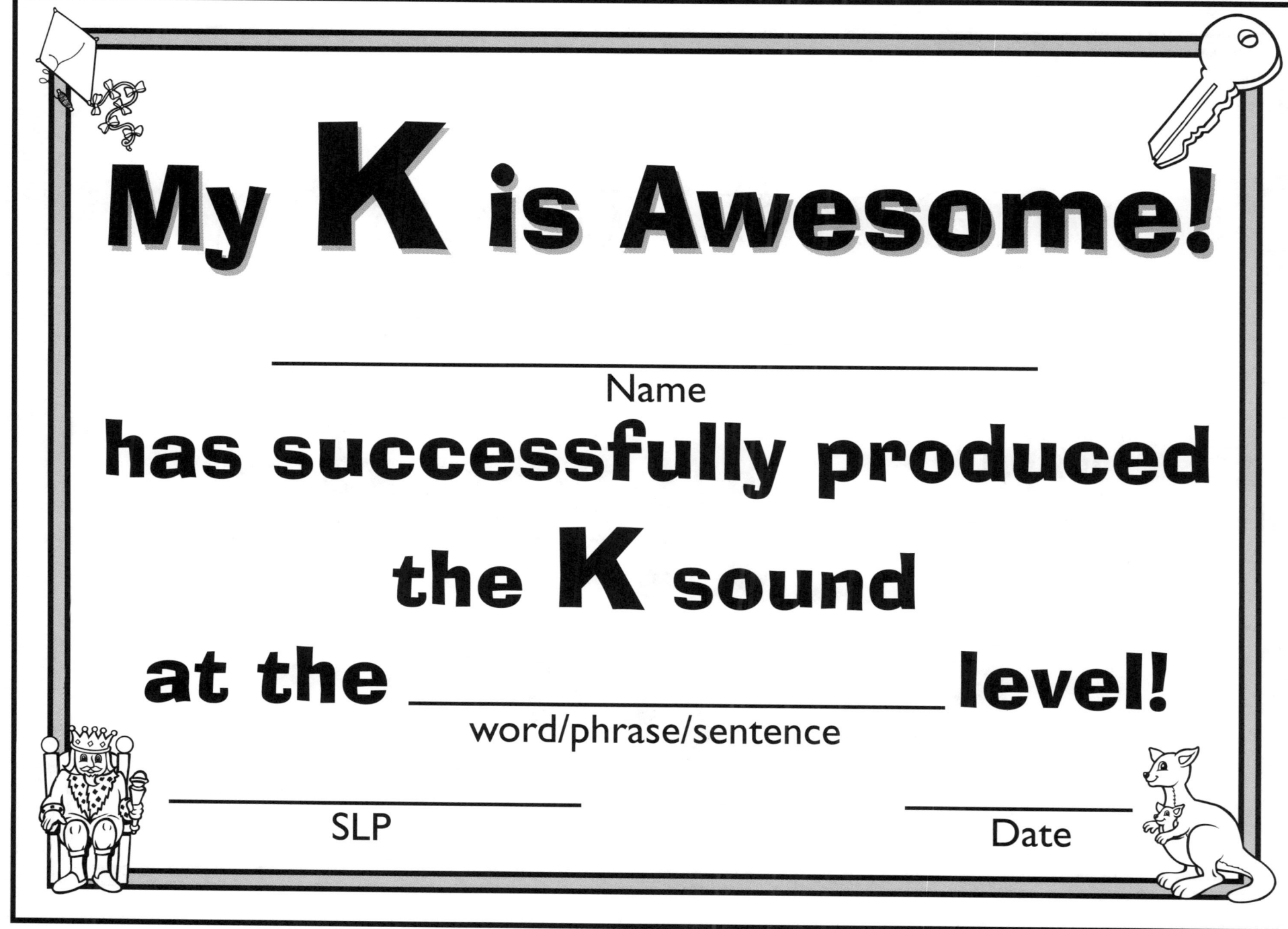

_____
Name

has successfully produced the K sound

at the _____ level!
word/phrase/sentence

_____ SLP

_____ Date

Great Speech!

_____'s

G sound is great!

Name _____

SLP _____   Date _____

Fabulous F Sound!

_____ has successfully produced the F sound
Name

at the _____ level!
word/phrase/sentence

_____   _____
SLP   Date

Very Good Job!

_____ Name

has successfully produced **V** in Speech Class!

_____ Date

_____ SLP

Be Mine

276 #BK-291 Webber® Artic Fun Sheets 2 • ©2002 Super Duper® Publications • www.superduperinc.com • 1-800-277-8737

Blank Cube

Directions: Assemble the cube as follows: glue onto construction paper for added durability. Cut along the dotted lines. Fold on solid lines and glue as indicated. To play: roll the cube. Read/say aloud the word you see using your best _____ sound. _____

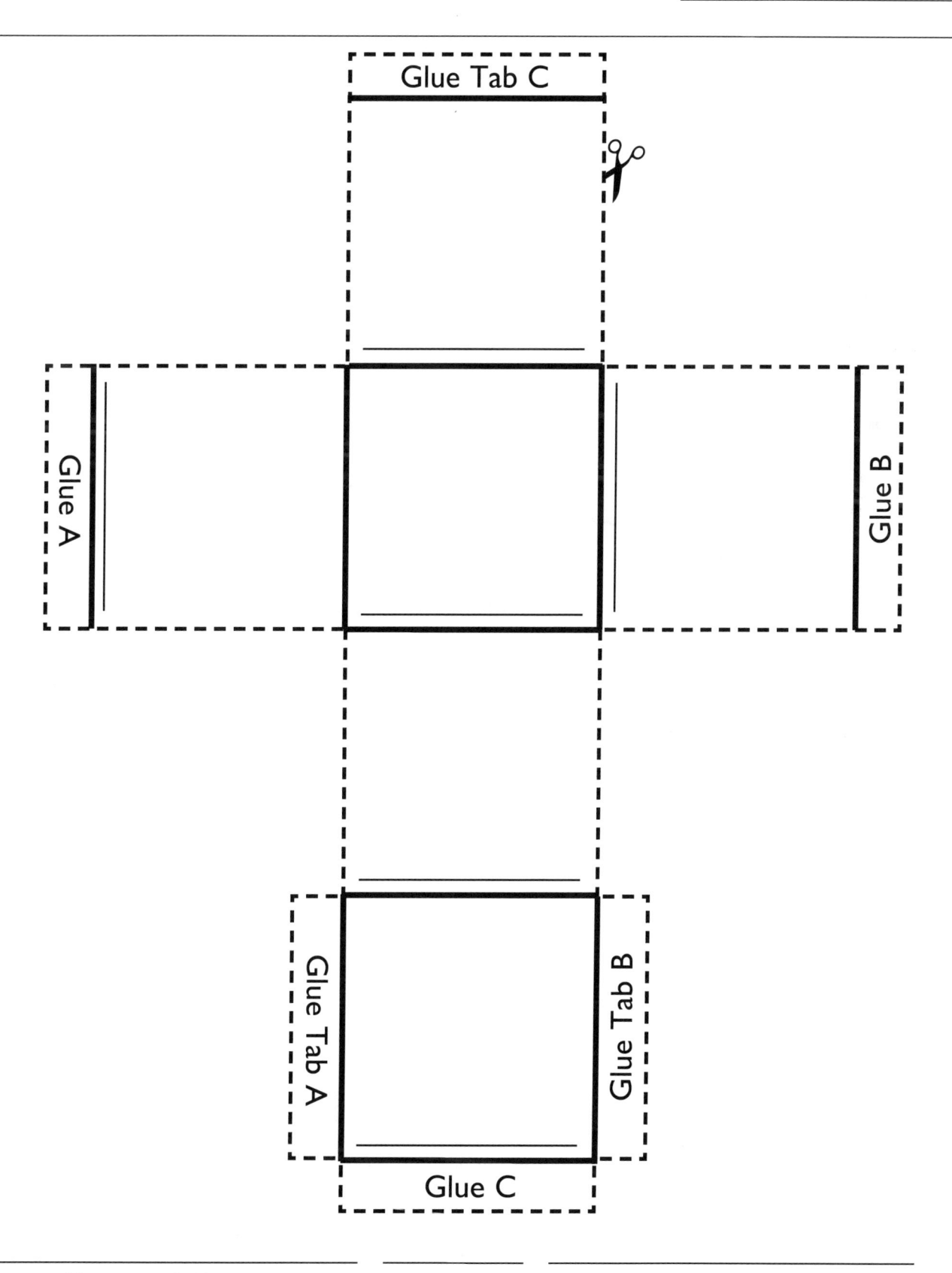

Glue Tab C

Glue A

Glue B

Glue Tab A

Glue Tab B

Glue C

_____ _____ _____
Homework Partner   Date   Speech-Language Pathologist

Blank Board Game

Directions: Read/say aloud the picture–words below. Then, cut out the markers. Flip a coin (heads=1, tails=2) to determine how many spaces to move. As you move, read/say each word aloud, using your good ____ sound. First player to reach the finish wins. _____

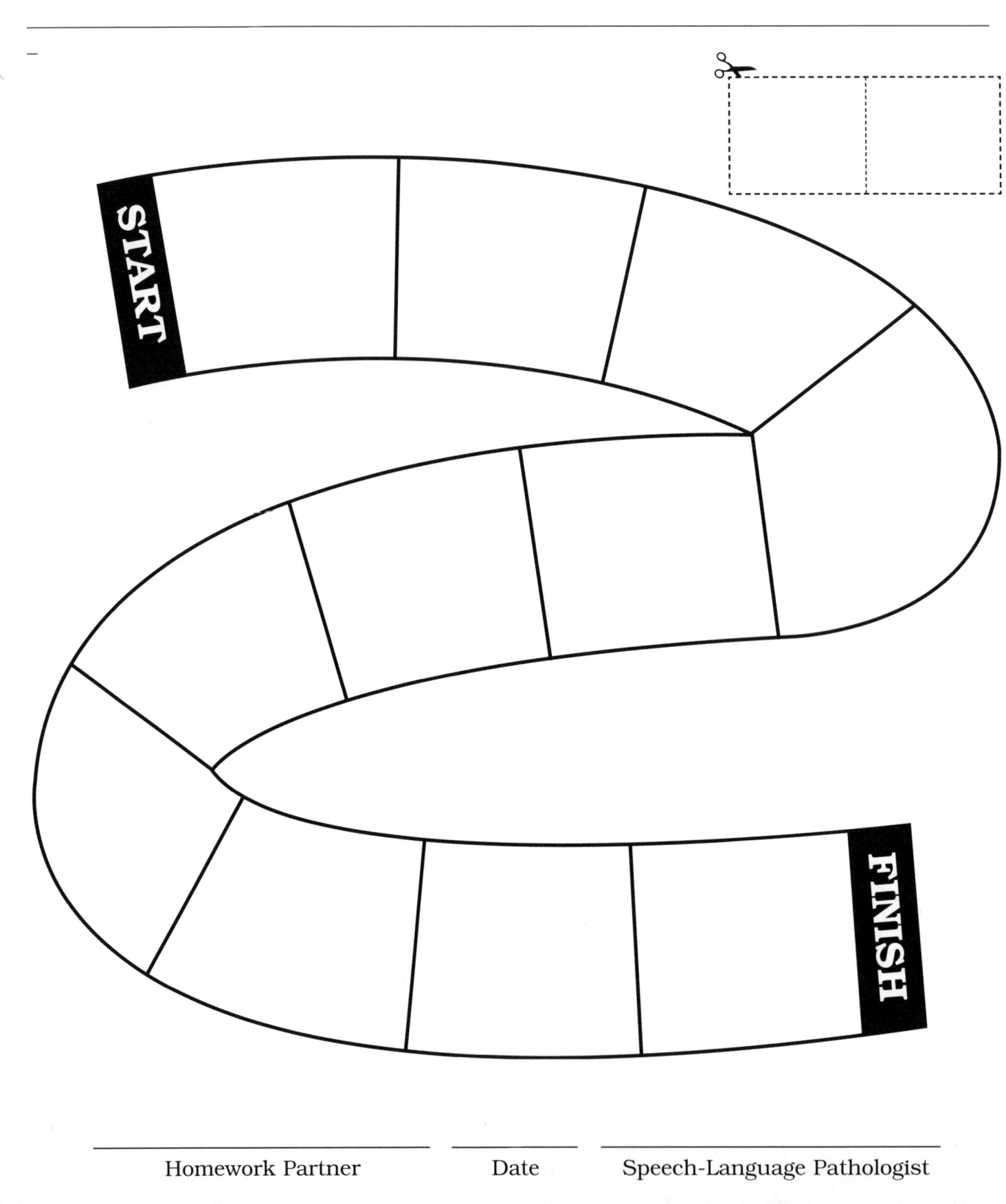

_____

START

FINISH

_____   _____   _____
Homework Partner   Date   Speech-Language Pathologist

Activity Answers

Pg 17 1. squash 2. toothbrush 3. cash 4. brush 5. fish 6. radish 7. leash 8. bush
secret word: starfish

Pg 26 1. Paula got cash for her birthday. 2. The ball rolled under the bush. 3. The rabbit ate a radish for breakfast. 4. Remember to bring your brush. 5. The dog's leash is hanging in the closet. 6. Dad bought a paintbrush at the store. 7. I left my toothbrush in the bathroom. 8. A squash grows on a vine.

Pg 44 1. children 2. chicken 3. chain 4. cherries 5. chimney 6. chin 7. chow mein
secret word: charm

Pg 100 **Across**: 1. slow 3. dentist 7. teeth 8. material   **Down**: 2. water 4. tooth 5. Superman 6. door

Pg 190 **Across**: 3. wagon 6. alligator 7. tiger 8. luggage   **Down**: 1. igloo 2. spaghetti 4. eagle 5. seagull

Pg 202 1. Water put out the fire. 2. The man caught a fish. 3. We went to the football game. 4. She got lost in the forest. 5. I will water the fern. 6. Three plus two equals five. 7. I ate salad with a fork. 8. I used a fan to get cool.

Pg 266 1. I am seven years old today. 2. We will fish in the river. 3. Don't forget to mail the envelope. 4. The skin diver jumped into the water. 5. The television is too loud. 6. The beaver chewed the log with its teeth. 7. Dad dug with a shovel. 8. The truck is parked in the driveway.

Page 124

```
K L E B T C A T A C K C K W G
N A A U S R B T I A M A P N K
H W N E E A N X S N Q G I H U
K K N G R I W S V D X K M R W
X F G Y A E J X L Y A W P A Q
W C C C J R C U M N S M X F L
K X Z B W E O X D I U R C O W
C E B Z Q U B O P V D W L Z U
N L Y V C O W G I R L H K O I
O Z N B O B Q U O C A R R O T
V N R I M A H B O A D W J W M
W S J J B M P J Y M K R S O K
S R R I Z A B Z C E K B O H I
J R H E N E A I K L J U X Y T
C A R R H N K B S H Z V M J E
```

Page 171

1. dog → cat
d o t
c o t
c a t

2. pig → ton
p i n
t i n
t o n

3. leg → red
b e g
b e d
r e d

4. bug → hat
b a g
b a t
h a t

5. wig → pen
w i n
p i n
p e n

6. log → bit
b o g
b i g
b i t

Activity Answers

Page 174

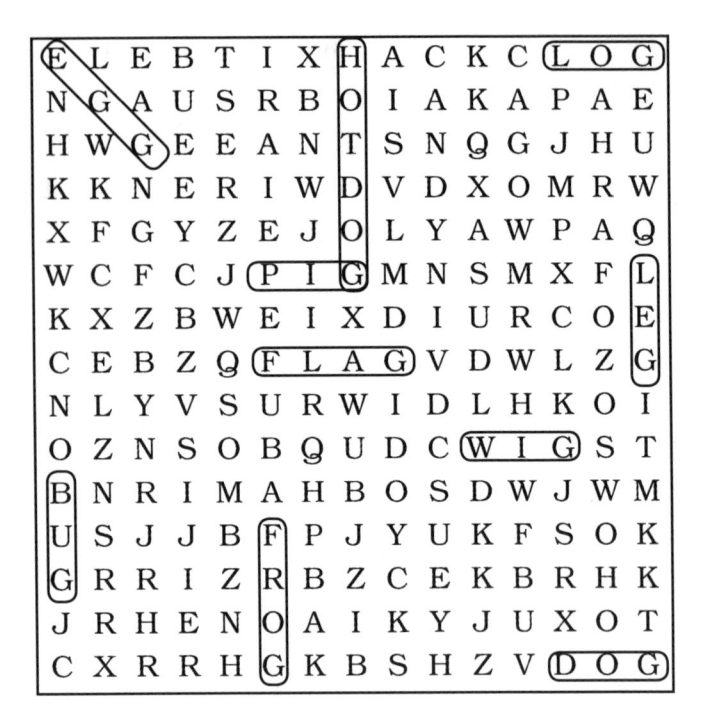

Page 211

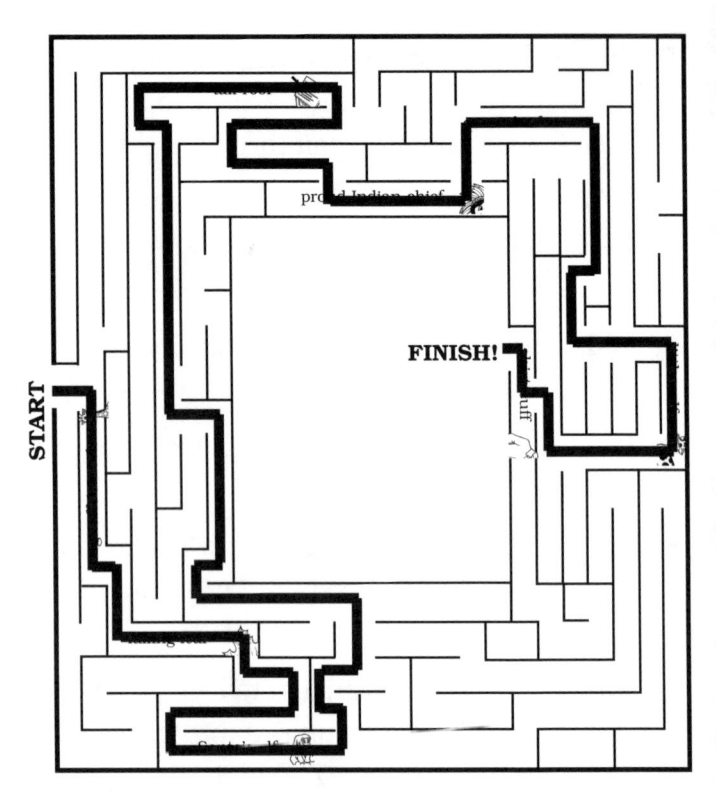

Page 241

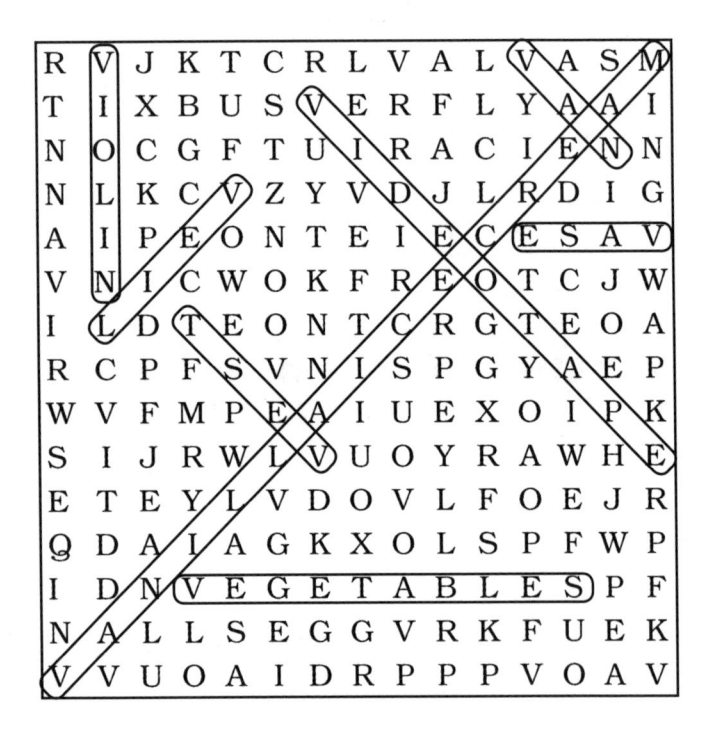

Page 258

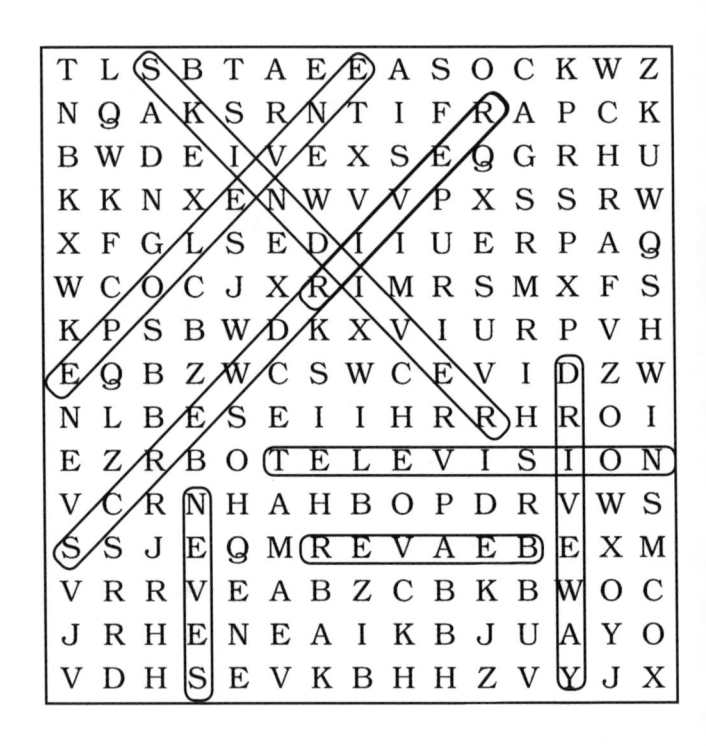